Fighting is normal. But often it is *how* we fight that needs help. In the heat of a fight it might be hard to realize, but there are unfair issues being brought up—old wounds resurface, old memories are reconsidered, the possibilities of the future are tossed around like the certainties of the past, motives change in mid-stream, and personal attacks replace those emotions and problems that are too hot too handle.

Learn how to change unfair conflict into open negotiation with the advice of this helpful family healing guide.

WHEN FAMILIES FIGHT

How to Handle Conflict with Those You Love

Dr. Jeffrey Rubin
Dr. Carol Rubin

BALLANTINE BOOKS · NEW YORK

Library of Congress Catalog Card Number: 88-28396

ISBN 0-345-36572-0

This edition published by arrangement with William Morrow and Company, Inc.

Manufactured in the United States of America

First Ballantine Books Edition: March 1990

DEDICATED WITH LOVE

to Frances & Zoltan Rubin,
Ades & Fred Mynatt Milligan,
who taught us the meaning
of family.

And to Sally, Noah, & David Rubin,
who gave us a family
of our own.

Contents

Foreword

Families fight. They fight a lot, a little, constructively, destructively, fairly, unfairly. Sometimes the fights are about what the people involved think they are about, and sometimes they are about something else entirely. Sometimes they end in tears and misunderstandings, sometimes in refreshed views, relief, and smiles, or in new insights into the way the family works as a group. Sometimes, too, they can result in very real and damaging sadness, in imbalances in that group we are as a family, in the loss of self-esteem or respect for someone else—even in physical harm.

Family conflict—the family fight—worries a lot of people. We know that from our friends, our own families, and from the people with whom we work professionally. As psychologists (one of us a therapist, the other an expert on negotiation), we have seen a lot of families whose fighting scared them enough to seek outside help; but as parents and friends of other families, we also see a lot of the "normal" conflict and fighting within families that can be resolved without the intervention of a professional. But no matter what the individual case, people tend to *worry* about their conflict. It is the perception of that worry and concern on the part of family members that led us to write this book.

For whom is this book intended? In its broadest implications (and as every author would like to think), the "wisdom" shared here is for everybody. More narrowly, this book is intended for families of more than likely two parents (or parent and step parent) and one or more children. This is not to be construed as excluding the single parent. Much, if not all, that we say here is relevant to anyone and everyone in more than the given situations in the book. We are, after all, talking about the role of conflict in our lives—and our lives are not lacking in conflict. But the primary examples are of traditional nuclear families: Mom, Dad, kid(s).

Our point of view? Through all of our experience with family conflicts and fights—the angry, hurtful, unfair, and sometimes physical fights; the ''petty,'' fairly quickly resolved skirmishes within family groups; the long-smoldering and unresolved issues that provide endless rounds of conflict—we have concluded two things. First, family fighting is normal. *Normal.* That cannot be stressed enough. Second, learning how to understand and use the results of *fair* fighting can be a positive way to create useful and interesting changes in the growth of the family and its members.

If this sounds Pollyannaish, let us disavow that right now, because there is a very dark and damaging side of family conflict. Fighting unfairly—and this includes the use of force—can be an ugly weapon in the family arsenal, a very destructive one that can tear families apart and do immense damage to individual members. We will address both the light and dark side of the family fight in this book.

The most important and, we hope, valuable things this book will do are allow us to look at the family fight as a normal way of doing business within that group that is so important to each of its members, and to help us understand how we can turn that way of doing business into a profitable one for each and every family member.

JEFF RUBIN
CAROL RUBIN
Sanbornville, New Hampshire

Acknowledgments

A great many people lent us a willing ear and sharp eye along the way. Special thanks go to Bill Ury and Bruce Patton, of the Program on Negotiation, for their helpful comments on an earlier draft of the manuscript. Roger Fisher, also of the Program on Negotiation, kindly allowed us to present our ideas to a group of Harvard Law School students, who in turn helped us sharpen our assumptions and clarify our thinking. Dean Pruitt, who collaborated on an earlier book on social conflict, stimulated many of the ideas on conflict escalation and settlement. Larry Wrightsman, Louise Kidder, and Ann Harris were each extremely supportive in the early days of the project, when the idea was first conceived and shaped into a workable plan. Our editor, Liza Dawson, was most helpful in shepherding the project through to completion. Jean Intoppa and Linda Underwood provided secretarial assistance at every point along the way; Bill Breslin offered an editorial hand whenever one was necessary; Andra Hollis and Bill Breslin proofread from morn to night.

Without Barney Karpfinger's vision and insight, support, and wisdom, all offered over cold beer and pretzels in pubs throughout the great city of New York, this book would never have seen the light of day. He was far more than literary agent *extraordinare*. Barney was friend, confessor, psychotherapist, as well as editor.

It was Richard McDonough, our literate and quirky friend, who transformed the rough manuscript into more readable prose. And it was Leslie Arnold, his charming spouse, who provided us with the critical editorial commentary that helped move us ever closer to a product that we could all begin to like.

Finally, to staff and colleagues of the Program on Negotiation at Harvard Law School, special thanks for providing a learning environment in which ideas of all sorts could be exchanged freely, sharpened, and transformed into the pages of this book.

Part One:

HOW AND WHY WE FIGHT

1
The Good Fight

Ever since the second person inhabited the earth, there has been conflict. Take the traditional Creation story as a starting point, and imagine the scenario after the first bite of the first apple, and the introduction of shame:

"For goodness' sake, Adam, will you cover up? Get something on now, before somebody comes by and sees you like that!"

"Listen, Eve, I don't know what you're carrying on about. Those fig leaves seem to suggest more than they hide, my dear. So don't you talk. What kind of woman are you, anyhow? Talking to animals . . ."

"It wasn't my idea to come to Paradise. Anyhow, I thought it was your snake."

And on and on. The human story.

Whenever two human beings are in the same place for any extended period of time, and for anything more than the most superficial reasons, differences of opinion will arise. Sometimes these differences result in conflict. "No, the apple." "Yes, the pear." "Cover up, you hussy!" "You're such a slob." "I am not, you fat . . ." Two people, conflict, escalation, a fight. We all do it, we all fight. Life is even built on conflict. That snap of conflict between the lightning and the drought-dry savanna

3

of prehistory brought us fire, brought us light against the uncertainties of darkness. And so with human conflict in love, in work, on the playing field; with words, gestures, attitudes, and, unfortunately, sometimes with fists. Heat, light, assurance against the darkness. The good fight.

Most often and most intensely, we fight at home. Home is where the heart is—where there is the most at stake, where we have the most to gain and to lose from the conflicts we call fights. It is through conflict that we gain the sense of who we are, define our outer edges, articulate our *selves*. The baby's cry conflicts with the parents' need for sleep. The warm breast milk or formula, comfort in the arms of a yielding parent who has conceded the point, ending the conflict, communicates love and acceptance while filling the nutritional and physical demands of the dependent infant; and the parent gets to return to sleep. The child who fights for its rights against the occasional unreasonableness of siblings or parents creates a bit of history of the *self*, whether the child yields or is yielded to. Each conflict, each fight, results in a small accretion of what he or she will ultimately become. Fighting is thus normal.

Normal. That is the first and foremost thing to remember about fighting. Everybody does it. It is an essential part of growing, as much as touching and affection, learning to delay pleasure as well as enjoy impulse. It is so normal that there is not much we can do about it. We really have no choice, for there is always going to be a conflict of wishes as long as there is more than one human being in the universe. But we can do something about how we think about conflicts and how we conduct our fights.

Since we have all grown up in a family of one sort or another, we each think ourselves experts on the subject of family fights. The problem is that some of what we think we know is wrong; and knowing the wrong about something so important to growth and identity, to ourselves and to our children, can be harmful. It can be harmful because of guilt over fighting; because of traditional ways of behaving toward each other in conflicts, repeating patterns from the past that not only can be harmful in the short term, but can lead to longer-term alienation. In light of that, it might be useful to look at some of the major erroneous attitudes and beliefs that get in the way of our learning to fight the good and fair fight.

1. Fighting is bad. Not only is it nonsense to perceive fighting as intrinsically bad, but it is also folly to ignore the potential for growth and change that can be a by-product. It is through fights within a healthy give-and-take atmosphere that family members get to test themselves, their boundaries, their peers, their children, their parents, to ultimately emerge with a sense of who they are. (Of course, this does not include battering and abusing, using one's psychological sophistication or physical strength to damage weaker, less capable family members. That kind of behavior is harmful and just plain wrong.)

Jim and Anne, two happily and long-married people, began fighting over "nothing at all." The focus was the time Jim would arrive home on a particular day. He said he would come home at six o'clock rather than at the usual five-thirty. Anne took the oral message, but paused significantly before doing so. No slouch in nonverbal communication, Jim knew that the pause was pregnant: Anne did not approve. He jumped on her hesitation and began to argue. "What am I, a wind-up toy? Wind him up and he leaves at eight-thirty, returns at five-thirty, eats, undresses, goes to bed, peck on cheek, nighty-night? Are you kidding me?" To which Anne began to complain about Jim ignoring her feelings. The issue broadened quickly to the concept of punctuality in the Western world, my industry versus your slothfulness, and finally escalated to the point where wrongs and slights of ten years ago were coming back like last night's garlic sausage. Then an interesting thing happened. Anne giggled a bit and asked Jim if he really wanted to keep fighting. "Well, actually, yes," was his surprised answer. Her amusement and his visceral response allowed them to gain insight into the fight they were having: When they were getting along too well for too long, there seemed to be nothing better than a good fight to keep them on their toes.

After a little time for reflection, it became clear to Jim and Anne that they did not really enjoy feeling too close for too long; it made them feel uncomfortable. A nice little fight once in a while worked very well to keep some necessary distance between them. Having fought, survived, and self-consciously begun to understand why such fighting seemed necessary, while also discovering that they could fight without spinning out of control, Jim and Anne could now be closer to each other than before.

There is nothing intrinsically wrong with fighting as long as it is fair, as long as it's not simply a fight for the sake of inflicting damage in the process. The fair fight allows hidden feelings to surface without crippling, permitting the heretofore submerged feelings to be explored in what should be a safe environment, the family. Fighting can produce camaraderie and cooperation where none existed before, and when there is a measure of self-conscious awareness—"We're fighting again, aren't we? Maybe it isn't so bad. Maybe we'll learn something if we don't lose control."—fighting can not only be survived but can even result in growth.

The other side of the coin is when a family stifles its feelings constantly—where anger, disagreement, or conflict of any kind are not part of the family menu of behavior. Nonconflict can be seen as a "solution" in such families, but may result in truly repressed and confused emotions. When fights do erupt in those families, the escalation can be dramatic, and the results severe and traumatic.

Fighting is not inherently bad, but we need to learn when it is useful, healthy, and growth-oriented, as well as when it is destructive and leads only to more fighting and hurt.

2. Families that fight regularly are sick and need help. It might be argued that the Jameses, as in Henry, William, and Alice, were a very sick family, for it is said that a night at their dinner table was like a night at the jousting matches of a medieval court. If you did not have a good seat, eye, and a firm grip on the pommel, you were likely as not to wind up metaphorically knocked out of your chair. There they sat, often to the discomfort of their guests, honing their intellects and wits. Yet they left us a remarkable body of fiction, philosophy, and poetry. Perhaps, then, it is reasonable to say that a family that fights regularly but fairly, reducing the risk of serious damage, is healthy and life-affirming rather than sick.

While we are not all Jameses, most of us are resilient, resourceful, and inventive. When we can tolerate the intensity of our differences, we can fight creatively and survive, enriched by our exchanges. (It is also very important to know when damage is being consistently done. That recognition should result in seeking help.)

3. Family fights can be prevented. No way. No matter how many strawberries kids get as an after-dinner treat, there are never quite enough. No matter how many bicycles, hugs, or new sneakers, someone is always going to feel shortchanged. Rivalries are inevitable; they are a part of life.

Not only are family fights unpreventable, *they should not be prevented.* It is important, of course, that we learn where, when, and how to intervene, so that what could simply be a producer of heat and hurt can become a producer of light and growth. Sometimes, however, a fight has its own small agreed-upon reason that all the analysis, thought, and best impulses will not retard—and should not retard. Sometimes it is no more than a boredom/anxiety discharger, sort of like the cat's tail wagging away at the ball of yarn on the floor.

Margaret and Daniel were traveling with their parents on a long car trip. As the family was nearing its destination, the weekend rush hour arrived, adding another good chunk of time to the trip and deferring pleasurable expectations just a little bit too long at this late point in the journey. As nine-year-old Margaret and seven-year-old Daniel got verbally antsy in the backseat, the parents paraded out a game that had worked in quelling backseat riots in the past. Each person would take a turn thinking of some real or imaginary animal or person, and in the manner of Twenty Questions, the others would ask a series of yes/no questions that would, with luck and skill, lead to its identification. For a while, the game worked splendidly. The kids enjoyed the chance to match wits with each other and their parents. Just as Dad's not terribly imaginative choice of George Washington was identified, Daniel said, "Boy, have I got a great one now!" To which Margaret announced, "No way! It's my turn.

You'll just have to wait.'' So it was big sister versus younger brother, and no matter what Mom and Dad said, the squabble over rights seemed unstoppable for several stop-and-go miles. Finally, Dad lost his cool and started yelling. ''What's wrong with you guys? You're always fighting about one thing or another, and you're always arguing about who goes first, who gets the most, who gets the best of this or that. Why can't you try to be a little more generous and cooperative with each other? Wouldn't it be nice if one of you could just offer to let the other go first? Wouldn't that be a welcome change from all this wrangling?''

The kids' response to this parental harangue came as a complete surprise. Both Margaret and Daniel said that they would be happy to let the other go first this time. How nice—except that they next became mired in a fight about who would be the more generous! Finally, Daniel, who often seemed to be the more conciliatory of the two, agreed to be the one in this new topsy-turvy world to go first. ''I'll do it,'' he said, ''but I sure don't want to!''

The two kids in this story clearly wanted to fight with each other, and were going to do so no matter how clever the parental intervention. Margaret and Daniel had their own little game of fighting over the guessing game, and that agenda was not to be stopped.

4. All family disputes can be settled by agreement. ''Never let the sun set on your anger'' is an old bromide offered as a guiding philosophy for family fights. ''Make sure that you have settled your argument, kissed, and made up before going to bed for the night.'' Hmmm. This is the militaristic approach to family conflict, for in serious disagreements there can often only be agreement if one or more members capitulate on a position that is elemental to their feelings, when forced to by an opponent of great strength, will, and stamina. That is no agreement at all. More important, perhaps, than the superficiality of an agreement reached under the ''no anger beyond bedtime'' dictum is the loss of a family's ability to tolerate differences.

Doreen has decided at her ripe age of eighteen to smoke. She likes it, she says. Nobody in the family can understand why. Nobody wants her to smoke in the house, and she has agreed not to. She's thoughtful, in general, and is particularly aware of the hardships that smokers impose on nonsmokers, so smoking outside of the house is fine with her. But it is not fine with Dad.

He is crestfallen that his eye's favorite has so little concern for her health, etc., etc. The others in the family feel bad that Doreen is doing something that is clearly not good for her health, but they recognize that Doreen is Doreen, and that she has the right to be dumb as well as smart—at least, they all agree, she is the latter more often than the former. But at 10:00 P.M., when she arrives home from dinner with friends, Dad is there to settle things, to put it all in perspective, to bring the light of rationality to Doreen.

He reasons with her. Statistics are paraded out. She knows them. Well, then, why don't you decide to stop? Dad asks. Because I like to smoke, she says. It really is painful to him, Dad argues, to see a smart girl like her making that kind of decision. Where did we go wrong? No big deal, she says, disingenuously, not the end of my life or yours. How callous of you, says Dad. Your mother and I are very disappointed. It looks cheap. Cheap. Nasty habit. Cheap, vulgar, nasty.

It is 11:30 P.M. and we are very close to character assassination. Dad is relentless. Doreen is very strong. If agreement comes it will be at the cost of something vital—not to minimize the harm smoking could do to Doreen's lungs—but, if all goes as one might expect, these will not be fatally damaged because she will stop, in all likelihood, as soon as she has proven that she is Doreen, and Dad is Dad.

The degree of coercion required to bring about family "harmony" can be very costly. Families, and individuals within a family, draw strength from the ability to tolerate differences, from learning that people can live together and enjoy one another, despite profound differences of values and outlook. Children who grow up with the understanding that, although Mom and Dad disagree, they have a stable relationship characterized by respect for one another, have a head start in learning to deal with the vast array of people and styles that they will encounter in the world beyond the doorstep. A child who grows up in an atmosphere that tolerates differences will have an easier time carving out and establishing a true inner identity than will one who grows up feeling that who a person is or can be is determined by nonnegotiable "shoulds" and "musts." Families that learn to live with differences are stronger as a result.

By resorting to what amounts to psychological force or brainwashing, it may be possible to bring a family conflict to a screeching halt, but the real concerns remain unaddressed, and such tactics may serve to actually prolong differences while undermining familial relationships.

5. All family fights, once settled, are settled. Some people are surprised to find that a disagreement "settled" years ago suddenly crops up in a new and just as sticky form as before. Gee, we think, I thought we were through that one, once and for all. Life is not like that. Life is always in the throes of becoming, just like us. We grow, age, and change. Our opinions, clothes, hairstyles, and taste in music are all subject to change. We are not the same person at seven as at fourteen or the same person at thirty as at fifty. Given this, it is very difficult to nail everything and everybody down so that they are where we expect them to be when we turn our attention to them again.

So, what's the answer? Flexibility; learning to live in the face of eternal ambiguity; tolerance for change within ourselves and others; realizing that there are no single answers; looking toward the very process of fighting for enrichment rather than just to the settlement and burial of each dispute. These should be our goals, while we always, of course, remain aware of our obligation to be fair, loving, and accepting of the others engaged in the battle for identity.

6. Parents and kids are sworn enemies. More nonsense. The needs of parents largely coincide with those of their children. Finding areas of commonality in particular instances is often a difficult trick, but when located, family attention can be focused on the areas that bind rather than divide. Clearly, it is in the interest of kids to help clean up the house so that the family is ready to take a trip. Motivating kids, choosing the right tasks for the right ages, maintaining interest, turning a chore into an opportunity and a facilitator of goal achievement (even if it is a quid pro quo)—these are the keys.

⟡ Finding the key of common interest, applying it, making it work, requires effort, thought, and patience. What may be a burning issue for a parent may not be for a kid. A parent has to decide whether there will be negotiation to achieve the desired end, whether the effort and time required will be worth the result, or whether the better part of valor is to move on without what can seem an endless and not particularly useful confrontation. Of course, there is always the option of "Do it or . . ." which, in context, can be one of the few reasonable solutions to a set of circumstances.

While these six misunderstandings of conflict are the most common, they are not the only ones that we will encounter. Each of us has probably grown up with our own brand of specious knowledge, our own misapplications of Psychology 101 to family dynamics, our own generalizations from our own particulars, which may be no more than blocks to settling fights, learning from them, using them to stimulate change and growth. The obligation of each of us, then, is not only to be aware of these roadblocks, but also to examine our other attitudes toward conflict, particularly family fights. It is in these fights, where there is so much emotional baggage to carry, that our very identities—our always-evolving identities—as spouses, parents, children, are at stake. How we deal with family fights helps to define us. We need to learn to fight fairly and to foster that in our children; to fairly resolve strong differences among ourselves while respecting each other's rights. If as in the Hippocratic oath, we resolve to "do no harm," we will be a long way toward creating a good and healthy environment for our continued growth.

2

The Anatomy of a Fight

It started out as not much of a fight at all. Joe, sixteen, had borrowed Dad's car for the night. Joe was supposed to fill up the tank, but did not. The next morning, Dad was late for work because he had to wait in line for gasoline in the middle of rush-hour traffic. Dad let Joe know that night what inconvenience his forgetfulness had caused. Joe apologized, but in that moderate and offhand adolescent way—while looking over his shoulder at the Celtics-Knicks game on TV.

That was when things started to heat up. Miffed at what he saw as Joe's lack of real concern, Dad remarked again on Joe's inconsiderate and irresponsible behavior. Joe's response, grunted between bites of pizza and slurps of Coke, was found wanting. Now, a *real* apology was demanded. Since it was not quickly forthcoming, Dad started to bring out the records of previous behavior that reinforced the image of an irresponsible and inconsiderate kid. Clothes strewn about, lawns left uncut, eating the last of everything without letting somebody know the supplies needed to be replenished. The list continued.

After a few minutes of this, Joe decided that he had had enough. He exploded. "Who the hell are you to tell me what to do? I don't see you doing much around here. When was the last time *you* did the dishes? For that matter, when was the last time you gave anybody a smile? As far as you're concerned, I don't do anything right. All you do is complain about me and everyone else in the family. You don't really care how *other* people in the family feel, do you?"

"And you don't care about anyone but yourself, mister," came the response. "You can forget about using the car again, too."

Here comes Mom! "He's had exams, lot of pressure, we all make mistakes," she says to her husband. "Gee, give him a break, honey."

"Why don't you butt out, okay? I had an important meeting, and I missed it because of this self-centered, arrogant S.O.B. who can't think about anybody but himself. Why don't you stay out of this? You always spoil him and defend him, which is why he is so undisciplined, anyway!"

"I will not have you speaking to me in that tone of voice," says Mom, her voice ascending the scale and increasing in decibels. "When you think you can be civil again, let me know!" With that, she leaves the room, followed by Joe's kid sister, and shortly by Joe. There sits Dad, alone, wondering what happened. Why did I become so angry? he thinks. What went wrong?

The scenario is a familiar one that takes place in millions of households daily. The actors change, the subject that gets the action going differs, but the distinctive markers of an escalating fight remain the same. By distinguishing these markings, we can do a better job of keeping fights under control.

Escalating family fights have a number of distinct features consistent from one situation and family to the next:

Proliferation of Issues A simple exchange between Joe and his father over the matter of remembering to buy gasoline widened to include a variety of other issues stored in the memory bank. Typically, the list could be endless, and often appears to be. A fight over a single issue widens to become a whole alphabet soup of concerns.

As missiles launched by each side begin to hit home, the protagonists need to protect themselves by increasing the evidence against the other. More ammunition is fed into the fray, and as each starts to feel mistakenly accused and misunderstood by the other, the desire to prevail is increased, and thus the further escalation.

Elephantine Memory Our memories of various outrages committed by the opposing party miraculously sharpen. Past incidents that have been half-buried become vivid and heavy with emotion in the intensity of angry accusations. Moreover, our sharpening memory often seems to focus on particular historical events that assume special meaning in the family's idiosyncratic collective "racial" past.

In one family, competence and total control over oneself and one's possessions are highly valued. As a result, many quarrels begin because of accusations and blaming that arise when something belonging to the family is lost, broken, or mishandled. Most such incidents are viewed as involving acts of negligence rather than as accidents. Almost all incidents return to the Day of the Camera, that fabled day when the husband left his wife's expensive camera on the hood of the car only to find it gone before it could be retrieved. When he says to his wife, "I can't believe you locked the keys in the car!" she can handily retort with the Day of the Camera, now fifteen years old!

Crystal Ball Gazing We reach not only into the past but also into the future for the weapon against our adversaries, telling them not only what they were and are, but what they will *always* be.

Jim usually handles the financial transactions in his marriage to Ann. One day Ann used the family checkbook to pay a few bills and forgot to record the amounts paid. When a couple of Jim's checks bounced a few weeks later, he became furious with Ann. As things heated up, Jim turned to his wife and screamed, "You really blew it this time! You really let me down! How many times has it been that you've screwed up? . . . From now on, I'm going to have to manage things on my own. I just can't count on you." In effect, Jim is closing the book on Ann. She will never learn, she will never change. Period.

Getting Personal As fights heat up, the warriors move from attacking issues to attacking each other.

What was initially a quarrel between Joe and his father over Joe's failure to buy gasoline (a particular act of behavior) soon moved into the realm of attack on each other's personality. In another family, the old "I know you love him/her more than me," may be trotted out. Thence, it is not any longer a fight about issues *out there*, or abstracted, but one about personal traits, of who you are. We could see that in operation in the international sphere when a Korean passenger plane was shot down by the Soviet Union several years ago. The possible act of overflight and the act of commission by Russian military became rather quickly secondary to President Reagan's characterization of the Soviet Union as an "evil empire."

When an angry exchange shifts from focusing on the problem to be solved to blame and criticism of the other's personal qualities, differences not only cannot be resolved but are heightened.

Moving from Gray to Black and White As family fights heat up, what were once multiple options tend to be reduced to yes/no.

In regard to shared access to a family car, barring the growing sense of anger that accompanied their fight, Joe and his father could have addressed the basic issue in any number of ways. A series of gentle reminders might have been developed, thereby assuring that the user returned with at least a half-full tank of gas. A schedule of availability might have been worked out, together with a list of responsibilities of the users, thus making car assignments on a more predictable basis. If the problem between Joe and his father had really been nothing more than the use of the car, the two might have worked things out. But the car was simply the focus for feelings that mushroomed, and what soon emerged was a tussle between Godzilla and Son of Titan over the Steel Bullet, aka family car. The issue had become, Either you win or I do in this contest of wills (Either you get to use the car or you don't). Gone was any possibility of finding a solution to the "car problem" that could allow both sides to feel good and get something of what each party wanted.

Proliferating People In many, but not all, family fights, what starts out as a simple exchange between two unhappy, aggrieved family members is replaced by a widening circle of combatants. Bystanders choose sides, get sucked into the fight, and before long there is a free-for-all. That's what happened when Mom and Sis got involved with the argument between Joe and his father.

There is another version of proliferating people wherein a fight between two family members is really an excuse to vent angry feelings that have been building up among *other* family members. Such feelings may explode on the scene not because members have chosen sides but because an occasion exists for them to vent those feelings, even though these feelings may be irrelevant to the issue on the table.

Shifting Motives Most fights start out with the combatants hardly aware that they are in a fight at all. Each just wants to accomplish something, to reach a mental goal. The other person represents an unfortunate impediment, either by being in the way or through lack of compliance and cooperation.

Frank was rushing to get his hay into the barn before the rain when his tractor broke down for the third time in recent days. His wife, Joanne, was taking care of the kids while she put up the last of the green beans, folded the laundry, and started dinner. From under the tractor, Frank shouted, "Honey, would you bring me that big wrench from the toolshed?" "I can't right now," Joanne answered. "I'm cleaning the chicken for dinner." "I need it now," Frank hollered. "Come on!" "I can't, I said. Just wait a minute and I'll—" At that, Frank let out with, "I need it now, I said. I *can't* wait a minute. How come you're never around when I need you?" That one final question was enough to have this couple off on a major brouhaha, for the elementary questions of mutual consideration and relative importance of their respective needs were under the microscope.

In such situations, the focus tends to shift from doing as well as possible, accomplishing the goal with as little fuss as necessary, to focusing on minimizing losses. Each side seems to reason as follows: "It's now clear that we are adversaries, so it's not a question of getting what I want or not. You're in a position to prevent me from reaching my goal, so now the question is, 'How much will I have to lose?' ''

With Joanne and Frank, the question was not how to get the tractor repaired as quickly as possible while she kept the rest of the house going. The issue became the fundamental balance of the relationship—mutual respect, and an underlying struggle for power. In short, this had become an exchange in which one side could do well only at the expense of the other.

In the final throes of a heated exchange, well beyond the point at which we left Joanne and Frank, lies the situation in which each is so heavily invested in intransigence that each becomes determined to inflict as much damage as possible upon the other. If I am going down the drain, the reasoning goes, I am going to be sure that you go with me. It is in this last stage of escalating exchanges that face-saving concerns come tumbling into the foreground. Angry fighters are determined to avoid the appearance of humiliation at the hands of their adversary, and each wishes to preserve elements of ''face'' that remain undamaged during the exchange. The United States and the Soviet Union fretted over face-saving issues off the coast of Cuba during the 1962 missile crisis. Labor and management negotiators are forever worrying about such considerations in anticipation of any possible agreement with the other side. Family members are no different, similarly carrying their fragile egos into the fray, looking for ways to look strong but come out as little damaged as possible.

Eight-year-old Veronica and her sister, five-year-old Heather, were playing a game of Chutes and Ladders. Veronica expected that her superior skill and greater age would result in her victory, but little sister pulled ahead and was on the verge of winning, at which point Veronica cunningly observed, ''Oh, well, of course you're winning, because it's a baby game, anyway, and babies win baby games.'' Heather's response: ''It's *not* a baby game; I'm just winning!'' Veronica held her line: ''Babies win baby games.'' Frustrated and angry, Heather stood up and deliberately turned over the gameboard. Veronica had succeeded. She didn't win the game, but by getting her sister to act the "baby," she didn't lose, either, thus saving face.

In the early stages of a fight, people typically resort to a series of moves that appear "nice" in some way, to influence the other party. Perhaps a family member offers a promise of reward if only the other side will agree to something the promiser wants. Perhaps one side tries to win over the other by the powers of persuasion. As a fight heats up, however, these relatively pleasant and positive forms of influence are replaced by nastier, more threatening counterparts. Promises fade into threats. Offers to reward compliance become threats to punish for noncompliance. Persuasion is replaced by coercion, and "if/then" statements ("If you do this, then I'll do that," or, "Unless you . . . then I will") are replaced by plans to move ahead no matter what the other person does.

Margo and Bill were very unhappy with the latest report card brought home by Sarah, their happy-go-lucky fifteen-year-old. Margo decided to discuss the report card with her daughter and offer some suggestions that might result in a change in performance. The discussion went something like this:

> "Gee, Sarah, Dad and I were wondering about this report card. You're bright, and we know you can do better than this. We're willing to offer you two dollars for every improved grade on your next report card."
> "I don't know, Mom, I have a lot of commitments—gymnastics two afternoons a week, swim team three nights, baby-sitting two afternoons—and I do have to have some time with my friends, don't I?"
> "Now, look, Sarah, your attitude is really a little irresponsible. Don't you care . . . ?" etc.
> "I don't understand why you and Dad are so hung up on marks, anyway. The report card is just a piece of paper. I'm learning what's *important*. . . ."
> "Sarah, we're telling you, not asking you. We expect an improvement, *or else!*"
> "What do you mean, 'or else'?"
> "Sit down and listen. If you don't, you can forget

about that party. You'll be upstairs doing that home-work you hate so much.''

"Don't tell me what to do. I'm fifteen years old and . . ." Sarah leaves, slamming the door behind her, and we hear her mother shout after her, "You're grounded for the next three weeks!"

The shift from nice to nasty occurs subtly and in incremental stages with psychological "plausibility." By first trying to get Sarah to do what *Mom* wants, Margo sees herself as a nice sort of person. Her husband would agree. If Sarah fails to capitulate, of course, then Margo is justified in shifting to the stick. "You didn't do it the nice way, now let's try it with the gloves off" is the message. This allows the user of the nasty tactic to present himself or herself as resorting to such tactics only as a last resort in relation to the intransigent.

As confrontations move along such pathways, reversals become much more difficult. Why? What is it that makes fires so much easier to stoke than to dampen? What is it in the throes of the family fight that makes the passions hard to cool down once they have gotten beyond a certain point? It is because of the next mechanism, it seems.

Through the Glass Darkly Just as a glass of water can be viewed as half full or half empty, most of the things that family members do to and with one another can be construed in different ways. Typically, the way in which we interpret what others do is not so much about what they do as our *perception* of what they do.

If we like somebody, we use our perceptual bias in their favor.

"Oh, Mom forgot that she'd promised to take me shopping today after work! Well, I'm disappointed, but I realize that she had a real busy day at the office, and I know that she loves me a lot, anyhow."

"It was really nice of Dad to take us to the park today. He really tries hard to do the right thing by us. What a nice guy!"

"Wow, wasn't Joe grumpy when he came into the

kitchen today! Something must be bothering him; I'll have to sit down and talk with him to see if there's anything I can help with.''

In times of turbulence, or when our biases are not in favor of the person in question, our responses might be quite different:

''What an inconsiderate and selfish mother. Going out for a drink with her friends from work, after she promised she'd take me shopping! She is so self-obsessed I can't believe it!! I wonder if she really loves me?''
''Dad's a pretty slippery character. First he yells, and then he tries to bribe us by hauling us off to a park. Mom probably put him up to it.''
''Who does that Joe think he is, anyway? First he comes tearing into the house, and then he acts like he's the only person alive. What a pain. He's got to get punished!''

All of us play this half-empty/half-full game all of the time. But when we use it to judge others, and not ourselves, it can become a serious and intense driver of the family fight.

Why Do I Hate You? Let Me Count the Ways It's one thing to see the glass half empty or half full, but quite another to create a testing situation that only serves to confirm one's expectations. When a glass you expect to be half full turns out to be just that, it may be because of your superior scientific skills—or maybe it's because you had stacked things so that you would have the presumed result.
''Why do you always manage to stand in my way?''
''How long have you been feeling so angry?''
''Why are you so defensive?''
Each of these seemingly innocuous questions is guaranteed to provide ''data'' that confirm the hypothesis. When questions are asked that presume guilt over innocence, the answers will be distorted in ways that tend to confirm the loaded question. The best known such question is the mythical one asked of a husband by his wife's

lawyer in a divorce proceeding: "Just when was it that you stopped beating your wife, sir?"

One can readily see the difference between the two following ways of asking the same question of a person you believe to be shy: "Why are you so shy?" vs. "In what situations do you wish you could be more outgoing?"

We know what answers to expect in each instance, just as we know that pollsters can get the results they want from a poll by slanting the questions; but each of us, as real or potential protagonists in family fights, must similarly be aware of our uncanny ability to "frame" our adversaries in the very same way. If you have ever been on the receiving end of this kind of "guilty as charged" tactic, you know how difficult it is to respond without becoming an accessory to your own framing.

The genius of asking someone why he/she is so defensive, for instance, lies in the interpretation that can be reasonably placed on *any* response. To answer "because . . ." is to confirm the hypothesis; to deny the charge is to be defensive! Similarly, to respond to a question about how long you have been feeling so angry is to provide the rope for your own lynching. Denying any anger at all is to invite the follow-up comment, "It's okay to express your angry feelings, you know. We love you."

These questions put you in a no-win or double-bind position. But in the long tradition of the best defense being a strong offense, consider this response to the "How long have you been so angry" question: "For as long as you have been asking foolish, double-bind questions. Why don't you stop being a fool, and see how quickly I can smile again?"

Heads I Win, Tails You Lose As family fights heat up, we increasingly distort the explanation of our own behavior vis-à-vis that of our adversary. Whereas we construe the other person's conciliatory gestures to reflect manipulative intent, we regard our own, similar moves as the result of an open-ended and well-intentioned nature. We view our own angry actions and their destructive results as the natural result of provocation, while viewing the other person's similar action as the result of a flawed personality. We can see this operating in many areas of our life. "He/she was *lucky* to win; *I* won because of hard work and lots of talent."

This tendency to distort in self-serving ways is very human. We all do it a lot of the time. But when there is family strife, it conspires to escalate the conflict and create havoc. The only thing we can do is be aware that there is this tendency among us who walk upright, that it is silly because it only leads to escalation and a cycle of self-deceit, not peace and self-knowledge.

The Art of the Self-Fulfilling Prophecy Sandra and Jim were married for three years when Mike was born. Unfortunately, Sandra thought the marriage was a disaster, so when Mike was one year old, the parents divorced. Sandra viewed her ex-husband as irresponsible, lazy, a liar, and basically a bum who let her down. While she loved Mike dearly, she harbored fears that he might grow to be a copy of his father.

At five, when Mike was caught in lies (typical of a child that age) on a few occasions, Sandra thought, He's just like his father. When reports from fifth grade about undone homework came back home, her sense of Mike being a clone of his father was simply reinforced. Even when Mike's room was not as tidy as she would have hoped, Sandra could only think that her fear was founded, that Mike was to be his father's double.

In each of these instances, and in many others over the years, there were lots of alternative explanations for Mike's behavior. Kids don't always tell the truth, they feel that there are better ways to spend their time than cleaning up rooms, they love to test authority. Those realities could have been taken into account by Mike's mom. Unfortunately, a pattern had developed over the years as a result of Sandra's bad experience with Mike's father, and was communicated directly and indirectly: "I know you're untrustworthy, sneaky, and that you're going to let me down." As a result, Mike didn't always tell the truth about failures, or talk about problems, for fear that his mother would scream, scold, and punish.

The more Mike hid things from Sandra, the more accusatory she became. By the time he was eleven, Mike's relationship with his mother was a standoff. Mike was fearful and secretive, and he had problems meeting his obligations. Sandra felt furious that her long-standing fears were being realized. Every squabble and difference erupted in tears, accusations, and anger. Mike felt rebellious, lonely, and sad; Sandra felt betrayed. This is the self-fulfilling prophecy in action. One person expects certain negative behavior from another. The expectation is communicated in some way, and the predicted behavior is produced.

Confirmation of our predictions about another serves only to intensify the dire nature of our expectations, which, in turn, makes more likely the relationship's deterioration. The deterioration of the relationship intensifies the occurrence of behavior that confirms our fears. And so it goes.

The Tar-Baby Effect This is another version of the self-fulfilling prophecy, but only one party is aware of expectations. The name comes from Joel Harris's *Uncle Remus Stories*, in which the author describes an ingenious trap that a fox devises to catch a rabbit. The trap is simply the likeness of a rabbit, fashioned of tar and left by the side of the road, where the real rabbit is known to pass regularly. The rabbit approaches this tar-baby rabbit one day, greets it, and on receiving no response, gets annoyed. As the tar baby continues not to respond, the rabbit gets angrier and angrier until it finally hauls off and takes a punch, which only gets him stuck into this tar image of a rabbit, thus making him easy prey for the wolf. It works the same way with people.

You go to a party, notice somebody sitting quietly and alone on the other side of the room, and hypothesize that the person is stuck up. To heck with him or her, you decide, and go on to introduce yourself to more animated people. All evening, the person sits there, quietly, alone, so at the end of the evening you are sure of your hypothesis. In fact, the person was shy, not stuck up at all, but you never found that out. The person sitting there never knew anything about your expectations, and your prophecy was fulfilled. In the absence of knowledge of what we think, feel, or expect, the other person can do nothing to change our views.

Getting Trapped In the midst of fighting, the warring sides often make statements that commit them to positions from which subsequent retreat will seem difficult or impossible. Once people feel too heavily invested in a fight to quit, they are trapped.

That was operating in the confrontation between Joe and his father about the use of the automobile. Their exchange heated up quickly and continued escalating until the father reached a position so extreme that it would seem difficult for him to back down. He had decided that Joe was irresponsible, and it might be as difficult for him to congratulate Joe for subsequently earning straight A's in school as to loan Joe the car. Dad was in danger of overinvesting himself in showing Joe that he meant business, that he was a man of his word, thus making it nearly impossible to back down. Positions in a fight can become so pregnant with psychological meaning for the combatants that the fight itself takes on its own meaning, and the issues become lost.

So, too, with Sandra. She had held her fear/belief for so long that even the availability of contradictory evidence would serve, paradoxically, only to remind Sandra how invested she was in her hypothesis, and how certain she was that her hypothesis was correct. The longer we suffer for things, the more convinced we become that our suffering is worthwhile. The more we have committed ourselves to regarding the world and people in it in particular ways, the more convinced we become, contradictory evidence notwithstanding, that we are correct.

Fighting Over X When Y Is the Issue On lots of occasions, family fights ignite because of issues quite unrelated to those involved in the fight itself.

Eleven-year-old Eddie and his mother, Lucy, had always been very close. Suddenly and inexplicably, quarrels began to break out between the two of them. For example, Eddie asked his mother if he could take karate lessons, something he had wanted to do for a while. Lucy was not enthusiastic, but said that she was willing to go to the gym with him and check it out; they did, and Eddie was signed up for lessons. Three hours later, when Lucy heard Eddie yelling at his younger sister, she called out to him, ''There you go again with that yelling and fresh talk. Karate is off until your behavior improves.'' Eddie reacted with his own anguished, ''But you promised me! You can't do this, you worm! I always knew you didn't love me; you care about her, not me.'' Lucy came back with, ''Surely you don't expect me to do anything special for you after that outburst, young man, swearing and cursing like a brat! Everything is off until I see some improvement . . . starting right now. Go to your room, immediately.'' ''I don't have to,'' retorted the defiant Eddie. ''Anyway, what are you going to do about it, you ugly turkey?''

Just then, Dad arrived home to see the standoff, and before he could get his coat off, Jennie entered the fray. She hollered at her brother, flailing about and knocking over a glass of milk, and then a chair, as a prelude to kicking Eddie, to whom she yelled, ''That's the least you deserve for yelling at Mom!''

Dad sent Jennie to her room, and Mom told Dad that Eddie and she were in a terrible fight, that Eddie is an impossible child, and that he is now grounded for a week. The yelling between Jennie and Eddie recommenced, and soon everyone was involved at a feverish pitch. Dad punished the kids, and the whole family was extremely unhappy over the episode.

What turned a fight between Eddie and his mother into a multicornered squabble was the entrance of Jennie in such a dramatic fashion. She was disturbed by the fight between Eddie and her mother, and she was willing to take the heat in order to divert everyone's attention from the intense quarrel, thereby protecting her mother.

Underlying this dramatic fracas were issues about the development of the family that had nothing to do with the fight proper. Eddie was looking for a way to separate from his mother. It is natural for a boy to move away from Mom and closer to Dad. The karate was probably a part of that, and certainly the intensity of the fight and insults flung were another aspect of that. Mom was threatened in some ways by her ''little boy'' growing up and wanting to separate, so her somewhat overreactive intervention in the hardly unusual rift between younger sister and older brother may have been a way of holding on and exerting some measure of control that she saw herself losing to karate lessons. Jennie reacted to the severity of the conflict in her own way, which changed the focus so that nobody could think about what might be in operation. Dad wanted to return at least some superficial sense of order—and thus some sense of his own mastery—to a household that he had just entered. What this describes, of course, is a chaos that does not allow for addressing real issues, but dealing only with the surfaces that they sometimes present.

Underlying needs that are potentially in conflict may have been lying around unaddressed for days, months, even years. Feelings of resentment may also have been building up, unnoticed, untouched. Then some precipitating event occurs that sets off a chain reaction, bringing them all together and creating chaos.

Awareness of the fight's contours, of its surfaces, is essential, but sometimes awareness of what lies beneath those surfaces can also prove to be very useful.

3

Notes from the Underground: The Subtext of the Family Fight

We go to the refrigerator to conduct a search. We are not exactly sure what it is we are looking for, but as we say about art, we'll know what we like when we see it. Our eyes scan the shelves almost aimlessly; we may not even quite remember the sequence of thoughts or events that brought us to that temple of food, but there we stand, looking for something. "What are you looking for?" someone in the house says. "We just had dinner. You're hungry?" "Yes," we answer, "I'm starved."

Earlier, we had sat reading, preparing for a Monday meeting, a Tuesday class, a Thursday examination, whatever are the important upcoming events in our lives. We became anxious. If the meeting doesn't go well, if the exam is failed, if . . . This occurs on an unconscious level. That little hollow feeling comes creeping in, a little tummy activity takes place; we shut down the anxiety over the upcoming event and fix on food as a way of making that stomach feel good, full, comforted. There we stand at the refrigerator, looking for the solution to the questions that matter most.

The snack is the surface. The anxiety over the future is the subtext. The anxiety has driven the stomach to say "fill me." The hidden agenda or subtext has caused our action, but we often see the surface response—I'm hungry—as the whole story. It is natural. We lead our lives that way, the surfaces becoming for some of us the sum and substance of our lives. But there is still the unconscious to deal with, that collection of wishes, needs, compulsions, fears, and memories that lie beneath the surface of our lives, and although not consciously explored, the driving force for much of our behavior. That certainly includes the conflicts called family fights.

It is important to look at the text below the surface, the stuff of human feeling, the imperatives of our lives. Knowledge is good in and of itself, of course, so we can justify the journey below the surface that way. It is even more important to know what is going on in our lives in a more than superficial way, for such knowledge helps us to understand, and therefore modify, our own behavior. It also allows us to seek out and understand what may be the forces fueling the behavior of other family members. But first, some caveats.

Looking beneath the surface is no panacea. Considering the kinds of feelings and needs that drive us along in family fights provides no assurance that we will be able to change things radically as a result. Self-insight and something less than a dollar will often only get you a cup of coffee, and even then, only if you're lucky. Knowing and changing are different things, and in the heat of a fight it is sometimes better to find the first aid that will cool the situation down than to look for root causes. Nevertheless, we do learn from such exploration, andthis can have an impact on our ways of seeing and behaving in the face of conflict. That knowledge should be used positively, of course, never as a psychologizing weapon against one's spouse or children, stripping identity away, reducing the subject to a package of categories and labels. It must be used fairly.

Real looking and open examination, that is what we argue for. And it works. Think back on Joe and Dad, his mom and sister, a story of a fight about a car. Remember the escalation, the moves and countermoves, the proliferation of issues, the angry and accusatory words. Then peel back the surface of that family fight and find not who gets the use of the automobile but people struggling with issues of trust, control, autonomy, separation, emotional openness, and self-esteem. A lot of jargon, perhaps, but we will see in our exploration that these are just words for very human feelings. As Dr. Freud might say, "Now we begin, yes?"

Robert is eleven, and lives with his father and mother and his sister, Judy. Judy didn't go to school today because she has a heavy cold she probably got from somebody else in the fourth grade. She got bored with her toys and decided to have a go at some of Robert's. Today, when he came back from school, Robert found his sister using his electric trains. He no sooner spied her with his favorite toy than he started to scream bloody murder. Judy does not seem particularly fazed by the loudness or ferocity of Robert's attack, however; she has heard it before. Robert is not a good sharer, that's all there is to it, so if you want to use something of his, you have to take the risk of detection and a lot of screaming, Judy figures. And she sure does like electric trains.

(This is not to be confused with normal "That's mine" behavior. The child defines itself through possessions early on, so we hear a lot of "my toy, my car, my everything." In its most visible and sometimes maddening state, this syndrome has pretty well dissipated by age four or five. We never lose it, of course, and can observe the extent to which we continue to define ourselves by our possessions.)

Robert's mom stayed home from work today to be with Judy, so when she hears Robert's whoops of displeasure she figures she better get upstairs and see that nobody gets hurt. Robert is two years older than Judy, and is really getting strong and—she doesn't know why—a little aggressive with his strength. Mom says, "Now what's this, Robert? What a fuss over nothing! Let Judy play with the trains. No harm done, for goodness' sake. She won't eat them." During this, Robert keeps whooping along and Judy resists his attempts to take all of the trains from her.

"Let you sister play with them. Come on, be a good boy. My goodness." No change. "Robert, let her have them and I will take you to McDonald's for dinner—fries, shake, burgers." No response from Robert, just a renewed struggle for his trains. "Soon as Daddy gets home, okay?" Robert is now extricating the last train from between Judy's defiant clenched fists and at the same time aiming good, hard knee lifts at her right thigh, which appears to be taking on a distinct black-and-blue hue. "Robert, suppose we go to that movie on Saturday. Oh, Robert, don't you ever listen? You've got to learn to . . ." In midsentence Mom goes back downstairs to finish the casserole she started at noon and had been meaning to get back to all day. Five minutes later, there is quiet, but an uneasy one. Judy is softly sobbing over her bruised nine-year-old thighs, and Robert is in his room securing his trains against any further assaults from *them*.

We could say that Robert is just a poor sharer and be done with it. We do that all the time, and we solve the problem by *making* him share, or talking about how he will outgrow it, "just you wait, Judy." Neither of these "solutions" is what we should be looking to. The *surface* problem is that Robert cannot share; the *real* problem is that Robert cannot trust people to do what they say they will do. As a result, Robert starts fights in situations like the one here.

Trust is basic and central to human relations. We need to be able to count on others to do what they say. When our experience shows us that we can't rely on others, our reaction to another's "I love you" becomes, "I bet he doesn't mean it"; "You can count on me" inspires "I wouldn't bet on it," in response. Trust cuts through every single instance of interpersonal relations. Without it, life is a can of impossibilities, let alone worms; one becomes estranged, alone, defiant, defensive.

Psychiatry tells us that trust begins in the infant's dependency on his mother for protection, comfort, food, the very milk of life. I will not be dropped, my cries will be responded to, no harm will come to me, I will be fed, assumes the totally dependent infant. If the experience is generally good, trust develops. Trust is learned as the toddler takes its first steps and swims its first strokes— wherever and whenever a dependent child is able to count on another human being for support. Our continuing experiences within the family inform our views of trust. The more tightly interwoven the family, the more frequent the occasions where trust becomes a central issue. Our experience in trusting during our formative years goes a very long way in defining our ability to trust—and to be trustworthy—in later life.

Robert, in the hypothetical situation above, has not had great experiences in trusting. Mom's attempts to get him to share by making one promise after another were not successful because Robert knows from experience that Mom is not well enough organized to follow through on her promises. She has repeatedly made promises and forgotten—indeed, not just repeatedly but consistently. And if he can't trust Mom to come through on even the little things, much less the big ones, how in the name of reason can he rely on his sister not destroying his favorite trains? Dad is no prize package, either. He gets home late, is usually tired, doesn't like to go out for burgers and fries, and quite honestly, from Robert's viewpoint, Dad is not really there when the crunch is on. So know well that what is Robert's is Robert's. But don't be too certain that Robert will always recognize the other side of the line, that hers is hers. If you can't trust, and if others don't put a lot of emphasis on keeping their word, then what the heck: "What's mine is mine and what's yours is mine" is not too far away.

When children do not live with consistency, with word-keeping (within reason), they lose their anchor. The family is that anchor, that place of solidity, from which sorties can be made into the world until one gains enough confidence and familiarity with it to separate. If the anchor is not there, where will one find it? The answer too often is nowhere, and the results are isolation, suspicion, fear of what others say as not being what they mean. Without trust, we walk around with a perpetual chip on our shoulder, itching for the inevitable fight that comes from not being able to depend on others. Without trust, it is hard for us to care or to be cared for; it thus makes love difficult.

When we see certain kinds of behavior in ourselves and others in times of conflict, we may examine it and see that perhaps trust is an underlying issue. Trust was certainly one of the issues in the Joe/Dad/automobile fracas. Dad had decided he could not trust Joe because Joe had not fulfilled obligations in the past. Dad may have been premature in his judgment, and may have been less than analytical in thinking about what may have been a reason for Joe not being trustworthy in that respect. Perhaps inconsistency in his being called to task or a lack of reciprocity had left Joe feeling he didn't have to measure up, but no matter what the extent of trust as an issue, it was there. To know that gives Dad an opportunity to think about some of the basic ways in which he and his son relate to each other, and to help both of them to change it for the better so that they may create new bonds, reestablish old ones, and get the relationship civilized so that disagreements can be just that, and not grounds for mutual alienation.

"What do you mean, get my hair cut? It's just getting there. You're nuts!"

"Do I come into your room and tell you how to decorate it? Come on, give me a break!"

"And don't come out of there until you've put on the new jeans; those things look like they're painted on!"

If you haven't heard those lines before, you were never the child of any parent born on this planet or the parent of any child of a certain age. The struggle over dress, cosmetics, hair, and tidiness is an eternal one, and one in the absence of which television situation comedies would have died in the borning. There is an inherent humor in these situations, because as parents we can recognize on one level that we are trying to impose a value system on somebody who couldn't care less, for whom those values have no immediate meaning, except perhaps as things to be rebelled against. There are other versions of the struggle, too, between siblings.

"*You* put it back, 'cause *you* took it out.
"I said put it back.
"Put it back *now*.
"I SAID PUT IT BACK NOW!
"You're not going anywhere until you . . ."

"Give it to me, I need it. Give it to me now."
"But it's mine, and I don't want to, because you always break my stuff, and anyhow, I don't want to."

"But I want it," he says, as his face grows redder and he is thinking about putting a little muscle behind his request. It goes on for a long time.

In these "I want you to . . ." situations there can be great and harmful explosions of passion. On the basis of observing the surface, which appears to be fairly reasonable, as in, "I only asked that she clean up her room/ that he not litter the house with all his clothes; after all, it is my house," the ferocity can seem inexplicable. *Only, just, after all.* Innocuous words. In fact, from the child's point of view, what can be at stake is identity, and the loss of same, through the forced adoption of customs and mores defined by parents; or the loss of a sense of an independent, autonomous self in the face of the efforts of a sibling who uses his or her will to try to force one to give over what one does not wish to. The real issue, then, is one of control.

Control is something that each of us needs to feel. We need to think, This is under control. I am making this happen. Control is a desirable thing, of course, unless it gets out of hand. It is reasonable that we should want to have some measure of control over our lives and those that intersect ours, for the world is a complicated and scary place to children as well as to adults. We try to take some of the scare and unpredictability out by exercising control over our own behavior and by trying to exert some control over the external environment. Another way we try to take control, and the one that gets us involved in conflicts, is through attempting to control *other people*. That isn't to say that we try to control simply to make another a slave to our needs; it is more that we need to feel competent and assured in a relatively unpredictable environment. We need to feel that we can get done what we need to get done, to get some of the things that we want.

We can see what an important need there is for control when we observe behavior in situations where there is little control possible. Old prison movies often had a scene where the calendar is scratched on the wall and the days ticked off until freedom is at hand. The very act of

crossing off the days on the prison wall (or the desk calendar until vacation time) gives us a sense of control over
reality, although we do not have any *real* control at all.
Without that feeling of control, our lives can begin to
feel torn at the edges and ready to unravel.

Dad needed to have the car for the morning meeting.
Joe needed the car for the night before. Dad needed to
count on his ability to control Joe's behavior through one
or another method (he suggested that a just plain built-in
sense of responsibility was lacking in Joe, you will recall) to get what he needed. The child needs to be able
to stand up on its own, after a time, to take its own steps
without Mom and Dad hovering, in order to feel independent, whole, competent. And the infant needs to
know that its cries in the night will bring a concerned
parent.

Without a sufficient degree of control over our lives,
we do not feel whole; we feel at risk, threatened, fearful.
If we do not have at least some minimal control over the
lives of others in the family, we will become stuck in our
growth and find ourselves fighting for the control we lack.
Unfortunately, such fights often take on forms of sniping
driven by a sense of fear and inadequacy, which only
makes us anxious, which drives our sense of lack of control, which makes us redouble our efforts to gain control,
which . . . As you can see, control has the potential to
escalate into an issue with all capital letters, which can
become a new problem in itself.

When the emphasis on control becomes obvious to
family members, it may lead to the interpretation of every
move as an effort to exert control. Here we have an example of "psychologizing": "You're so controlling. Gee,
you never give anybody the benefit of a doubt. Everything has to be your way. Can't I lead my own life? I'm
not you, you know"; these can be the responses even
when the efforts are legitimate ones aimed at changing
destructive social behavior. Then, too, the response can
mirror an underlying fear, the reverse side of the need to
control, the fear of anyone having a measure of control
over the complainant's life. But the important thing to
remember is that we have the need to control, and to a
certain extent, we have a desire to be controlled, as in
having limits set on our behavior.

Sometimes control arguments can be the result of everybody feeling as if they are *out of control*, as in the husband and wife who go at it feverishly over major issues, such as the decision to buy a new house, or even minor ones, such as which movie we go to. Neither feels particularly in control; in fact, the reverse is true—both feel out of control and indecisive. But making a decision will relieve the anxiety for each, so the fight for the power to make the decision is not really about the decision but about the need to take control over lives and life issues that make those involved anxious.

When we examine the way that we fight, when we explore the content of those fights, we should be aware of the control mechanism. We should make efforts to judge if control is an issue in a particular situation, whether it is reasonable or not, whether it is control as in ''Don't touch the red-hot coals,'' or ''Don't wear your hair that way.'' While each of us needs assurance that we are in charge, at the very least, of ourselves, and that acceding to the wishes of others in normal social intercourse does not indicate a lack of self-control and individuality, we must be aware of where the lines are drawn, where positive behavior begins, where negative and harmful control issues lurk.

Janet is from a very strong, old family. She has had the benefit of good schools, good bones, and a respect for hard work. For the last several years, she has been living in New York City. She is home talking with her parents in the house that has known six generations of Todds. At twenty-six, she has decided to marry, and has just told her mother and father that her husband-to-be is Pakistani. The parents smile. They continue to listen, waiting for the word *doctor*. It is not forthcoming.

''Well, children do have a difficult time, of course, in such marriages, what with concerns about color and all. But I would imagine that would not be a factor here. Professional people aren't that way. And the children can be so beautiful . . .'' They continue to wait for the volunteered profession, but finally relent.

''What does Mr. Karaswamy do, Janet?'' her father asks. The answer that he deals cheap electronics from a

loft on the Lower East Side catches even the Todds at a
momentary loss for words.

Before Janet's visit to her parents' house is over she
knows this: that she will not have her parents as guests
at her wedding, that she will not be welcome to visit
again, but that the children from the marriage will have
the necessary funds for college when, and if, they desire
it.

Or let us consider a somewhat less radical situation.

George is ten years old. Mrs. Jones has just asked him
if he would like a cookie. He wants it, but he is with his
older sister, Helen, who is sure that George does not
want it. Her body language communicates this to him.
So George smiles a wan smile and declines. He spends
a lot of time with Helen because their mother works and
there is no dad. Helen is baby-sitter, companion, mother-
substitute. Five years older than George, she seems to
like the responsibility and the power of her role. Anyhow, George figures he ought to please Helen because he
doesn't seem to have any other choices beyond open re-
bellion, which he is disinclined toward.

Later . . . George is fifteen. A friend comes by his
house and asks him if he would like to go out and have
a Coke. George would like to, but then he declines. "For
crying out loud," his friend says, "don't you ever want
to do anything?" George gets angry and says some pretty
strong words to his friend, including that everything they
do together is boring, and who the heck wants to go
downtown and sit in that joint and just hang out doing
nothing but drinking stupid Cokes. His friend suggests
that George stuff it, and leaves. After a couple of minutes, George stops feeling angry at his friend. When
Helen returns from the movies, he picks a fight with her,
saying, "Where have you been; what have you been up
to; you're so stupid"—a lot of unrelated questions and
accusations. Helen doesn't know what he's talking about,
and so belittles him, ignores him. George feels bad about
yelling, but he also feels quite angry at Helen. George
doesn't know which end is up. And if he did, he wouldn't
be sure if it was his.

* * *

We can say with some certainty that Janet's parents have a problem, a blind spot, probably related more to class than to color, and we could extrapolate that the fight is precipitated by their bias, with its results so dramatic and final—and probably foreseen on Janet's part—as "the issue." As for George, isn't he a bit of a wimp? He isn't very social, he's a faultfinder, he's inhibited, he is a nag when his sister comes home. Maybe he depends too much on her for companionship, maybe that's the problem.

In each instance, what is most likely at the center of the fights is that both George and Janet, some thirteen years apart in age, have a problem of autonomy and individuation.

Individuation and autonomy Where do I begin and where do I end? Who am I? Who am I not? These are the questions related to autonomy and individuation. Individuation and autonomy are about having such clearly defined borders that one feels comfortable and safe. Without boundaries, edges to the self, we are amorphous, unsure of who we are; and without that self-knowledge, how can we even begin to know others, to cooperate with others as equals in the world?

Identity, that definition of the self, is dependent upon the drawing of borders, upon learning to know where you stop and another begins. Where there are problems with definitions of who we are, there will be reasons to fight, for in such battles one can be said to be literally fighting for life.

Consider Janet. She had clearly walked outside the unspoken yet powerful parameters set down by her parents long ago. The transgression of the rules was dealt with gravely. Janet was to be banished as long as she had this husband. The children would not suffer for the mother's "error," but would receive the benefit of what the family had traditionally valued highly, education.

Janet's act can be seen either innocently—a powerful love inadvertently conflicting with family rules—or it can be seen as a complicated but workable solution to finally drawing a line between parents and self; by doing so, she has extricated herself from what was psychologically a too close and demanding family relationship.

We *can* view George as a wimp, but he is just confused, not knowing where he begins and where Helen ends. His anger, his picking a fight with her, are signs that George wants to be George. At the moment, he does not seem to have the strength to break away and draw his own lines. Until he does, he will fight out of frustration, out of fear of not knowing the boundaries, out of fear of drowning in someone else's definitions of who he is. Not knowing who he is, he will withdraw from others.

Returning yet again to Joe and Dad and the car, we can see that beyond the fighting and screaming about inconsiderate behavior there is a subtext that says, "Hey, I define a part of myself in terms of how my superiors at business see me. You made me look bad, that makes me feel anxious and unsure of whether I'm good or not. Don't do it again!" On the other side is Joe, saying, "To hell with the rules, I'm going to use my own judgment, and what the heck, it's one of the chances I have to define myself as Joe, and sometimes Joe screws up . . . just like you." Joe is Joe, Dad is Dad. To some extent, they fought to say that, to define their selves for themselves and for each other.

We can sometimes go overboard in our concern for the development of autonomy by overindulging our children when they act in particularly obnoxious ways, fearing that our pointing this behavior out to them, or punishing it, will result in their arrested development. In that extreme scenario, you may wind up with a narcissistic child who thinks that any behavior in the pursuit of freedom is no sin; but with that said, it is clear there is more risk at the other extreme, where we almost naturally smother a child with our "caring." That is the point here, to avoid that extreme "caring" that smothers identity. If one does not know who one is, one cannot connect with others. Know thyself, Socrates said, implying that all knowledge comes from self-knowledge. What he forgot to note was the necessity of having an environment in which to fight to discover and define that self. Our families must be that right and natural environment in which that fight can be safely joined.

Lauren has been in school for three days, and Mom misses her. She has had word from the teacher (or to put it more accurately, she pried words out of the teacher) to the effect that Lauren is a little homesick, that she has been seen to put her thumb in her mouth, that she is having problems adjusting. At least that is the way it comes down to us by way of Lauren's mom, Sandy.

"How was it today, darling?" Mom says on picking up Lauren at two-thirty. "How was she today?" she asks the teacher with slight catch in throat. "Well, she seems to be adjusting," comes the response, "but she still misses Mommy"—the last a bone thrown to satisfy Mommy's needs.

"Was it lonely there without Mommy, darling? Oh, Mommy's girl . . ." It goes on until Lauren and Sandy are back in the warmth of the house.

After one more report that Lauren wasn't absolutely giddy over school, Sandy decides that it is far too early for Lauren to be away from home and hearth. Maybe Lauren is a little immature, a little too close to Mommy. The year at home will probably be just what's needed.

Three years later, Sandy can be heard complaining about Lauren's clinginess, and the kinds of arguments that result between Sandy and her husband.

Noah is twenty-six and a talented musician. He picked up his older sister's violin when he was five and did a Bach transcription from ear. At thirteen, he had abandoned the classics for rock, in which he was quite inventive. He had the full support of his parents. "If Noah wants to . . . If Noah thinks"—(fill in the blanks)"then it's all right with us." Sometimes people thought that his parents overindulged him, but they were wrong. He had bought all of his own equipment with money earned from playing gigs, had repaid anything he ever borrowed from them, and was immensely grateful for the rent-free situation that allowed him the years to compose and record some difficult music. He is now ready to move to California, where three recording companies and three agents are interested in his career. Everyone is excited for Noah's future, not least of all his parents, yet Noah's parents are depressed, as well. Noah's mom most profoundly.

Mom's depressions are not funks, however, but very active ones. She picks at everything that Noah does. "Did you close the refrigerator door? You dope. You know it sticks. It needs to be pushed shut. Aren't you old enough to . . ." All of this shouted toward his bedroom on the third floor, where he is probably well protected from the sounds by earphones while he audits a tape he made earlier in the day at a state-of-the-art studio. The other members of the household are not so blessed, but since they are a parakeet and a fox terrier, they get no vote. When Noah is not insulated from Mom's assaults, he responds as gently as one can imagine, except about every fifth time it turns into a donnybrook of accusation and counteraccusation. Within an hour or two of the latter, Noah has a migraine and cannot play for three days. One line in Mom's repertoire may just be the kicker: "When you are gone, mister, I suppose you know my life is over!"

Dad, on the other hand, is the facade of stoicism, except that whenever Noah talks about his music, Dad manages to change the subject. This gets Noah to say, "Hey, how come you never listen anymore?" and then a quiet little struggle takes place between Dad and Noah, a quiet little fight in which Noah often capitulates to Dad's suggestion that they jog together. If there is one thing Noah is less than rapturous about, it is jogging. He has lousy knees, particularly the right one, which he hurt in sophomore intramural football; it aches like the devil after the first half-mile on the macadam. When Noah declines, which he does from time to time, Dad's lip curls slightly while a smile is maintained, which gets Noah right in the sinuses. And when he runs with Dad, the latter's smile seems particularly broad and genuine as Noah painfully keeps pace.

Noah has grown too self-centered, perhaps, and hasn't been paying quite enough attention to the needs and rights of others in the house, we might say. As for Lauren and her mom, well, it is difficult for kids to adjust to school after being in a close-knit home, and was there any other reasonable solution for Sandy? As for the fights that occurred later, well, Lauren has to grow up some time. These are easy readings of the surface, but in each instance what was operating were problems revolving around separation.

Separation is the stuff of songs and poetry. It may be lamented or craved, but whatever the response, being physically apart from others is both painful and important. In terms of healthy maturation, it is an absolute necessity. It is also the first thing that happens to us as we take life, begin to breathe on our own. As much as we want to merge with those we love, to replicate that experience of total immersion in another, it can never be.

We need to be alone, to create our psychological and physical boundaries, rejecting, in a certain limited sense, those who have nurtured us in the past. We need to learn that we can survive on our own. And we do that within the family through asserting ourselves, finding those moments of solitude—a boat trip to the middle of the lake, a walk around the block, even locking the bathroom door behind us, thus putting ourselves beyond the immediate influence of those others whom we love.

Not surprisingly, then, issues surrounding separation cause many family conflicts. The locked bathroom door can be an affront to the parent who sees it, unconsciously, as an act of rejection, while the person on the other side of the door may feel it as a first free and adult act, a symbolic act of self-liberation. Sandy saw Lauren as needing her mommy, as still too immature to be away from home for so many hours a day, so she kept her home, not allowing that first separation between parent and child, school attendance. The fact, however, is that *Sandy* cannot stand the separation; Sandy is not ready to feel the pain of letting go or to have to observe the normal reluctance on Lauren's part to be away from her mom. Sandy's decision comes to haunt her, we see, and she begins to resent Lauren's clinginess and excessive dependency on Mommy, which interfere with Sandy's activities once she finds herself ready for separation. And there is tremendous potential for interference in the husband-wife relationship over time. Thus, a game has been set in motion that will require some hard work and introspection to understand and to change.

Noah is in a similar situation at a much later age. While there are indications that he is ready to fly from the nest, he still has a great deal of reluctance to disappoint parents who have been so supportive of his efforts. Mom is acting out all over the place, and Noah knows it; but knowing does not keep him from taking the bait and going head to head with her when he hears her aggressive comment about his behavior. Nor does it keep his head from aching. Dad is very different in his reactions to the impending separation. He won't recognize it, avoids it, but instead inflicts a certain amount of pain on Noah through the jogging scheme. Noah's going to fly, all right, but there are going to be some pitched battles and a lot of aspirin in the meantime.

In particularly close-knit families, the parents want to keep their children close to the nest. The kids, on the other hand, if they are generally healthy and thriving, have a natural drive in the opposite direction. Parents need to encourage kids to move away without driving them to do so, while kids growing toward adulthood need to find ways of moving away without breaking or damaging those bonds of intimacy and caring that have served them so well within the family. This is the stuff of life and of drama, whether in the plays of Eugene O'Neill, the prose of Thomas Wolfe, or the ordinary strivings of each of us in our own families.

Excessive focus on separation, of course, can lead to a deep and abiding sense of isolation from humanity and the inability to connect with others. Almost all of us from time to time have felt that "the world is too much with us," and have dreamed of the hermit's life, but who among us has pursued it? At the other extreme lie the even sadder specimens of humanity, those who have failed to move away, to know the pain of separation, and in their failure have not achieved change and growth. People who are unable to experience pain are also unlikely to experience the joys of growth, but you—and Kahlil Gibran—already know that.

"I tell you, Dad, I felt like throwing up. It really scared me, you know?" That's Daniel speaking with his father about having passed a serious three-car accident on the way back from a day at the beach with a friend's family. Daniel is fifteen.

"Mmm-hmmm." That's Jeff, Daniel's father.

"God, there were ambulances coming, and you could actually see people lying on the side of the road . . . it didn't look good. It was really scary and—"

"By the way Daniel, did you see the keys to the lawn shed? Can't seem to find them."

"Nope." Daniel starts to walk out of the room.

"Now, wait a minute, young man. You're not excused. Just wait a minute. Did you do the lawn last? Yes is the answer. Well, then, nobody in this household uses the shed but you and I; therefore, you must have had the keys last—I certainly did not—and you must know where they are."

"I don't know, Dad, I don't know where they are!" Daniel's response is a little sharp and harsh, maybe a little emotional.

"I don't like that tone of voice, Daniel, and I expect you won't like my dealing with it by suspending your—"

"Jesus!" Daniel explodes, his face flushed. "That's all you can think about, where the damn keys are and—you drive me nuts!"

"To your room. We'll talk when you're calmer."

Daniel goes, jerkily, agitated, confused.

And then there is Terry, and her mom and dad.

Terry has been having night terrors for several years. She has been to the doctor for tests, has had brain scans while sleeping, diet changes, lights on and lights off during the night, door open, door closed, warm milk, empty stomach. The night terrors persist. She is eleven.

Today Terry is going to go to the summer house of friends for a week. She is very excited. "Gee, Mom," she says, "I am so excited. Which bathing suits should I take? Did I pack enough towels? Do you think I will need more than one pair of sneakers? I can't wait!!"

"I think everything's fine, Terry. We take care of things the way they should be taken care of. I don't know what all this noise is about, it's only a week at the lake," says Mom. Dad trots in behind with, "Young lady, if you don't stop your bouncing around, I'm going to have to ask you to leave the room. I'm trying to read." Dad is referring to Terry's actual bouncing around with excitement over the week to come. "Yes, dear," says Mom, "be still. Someone would think there was something wrong with you. It's only a week at the lake. Can't you stop fidgeting?"

"Janice," says Dad, calling his wife by name, "if you can't keep her still . . ." He gets up as if to go.

"See what you've done. Fidget, fidget, fidget!" Janice says as she squeezes Terry's arm hard enough to leave fingermarks when she lets go. Terry winces, gets quiet, lowers her eyes and head. Dad goes back to his paper. All is well.

Daniel's dad and Terry's parents have something in common. They are not comfortable with emotions being paraded about in public. Dad does not want to know that Daniel was scared, that death is scary, that Daniel thinks about it, that Dad will actually achieve it one day. Better not to discuss some things, is the philosophy; they'll go away, is the conclusion. Rather than recognize Daniel's fears, his father uses a ruse to distract Daniel from his feelings, which in turn allows Dad to drop his own fears through the trapdoor of "Where are the keys?"

Terry's parents are scared because they don't know what Terry's night terrors are all about, and lots of medical time and dollars have brought no answer. Fear of the unknown is real, but dealing with the fear is submerged in "Stop fidgeting."

At the base of all such stories is the fear of the unknown, of death, of being "out of control." It is human, it is understandable, but it is wrong, for not to be able to express and explore the way we feel is to be emotionally constipated.

Emotional openness To grow and change, we need to engage our brains, we need to think. We make discoveries, we figure out the way things work and are pleased by the process and the sense of intellectual mastery. But thinking is only one part of growth; we also need to feel. We need to know discomfort so that we can enjoy comfort, despair to know joy. We need the emptiness of separation to realize the special qualities of reunion. And in our families, we must have permission to feel and share those feelings without fear of retribution.

There are people who do not give affection easily, there are others who are "touchers," always making physical contact as a manifestation of emotional feeling. Some of us talk with our hands, others of us manage to talk without moving our jaws. Some of us overemote, some of us err in the other direction. But common to all of us is the *fact* of feeling. We feel! We have a sympathetic nervous system, we take in information with our senses, we process it with our brain (no matter how minimally in certain situations), and we have a response that we have given a name and its name is "emotional." If there is no permission to display one's emotions and feelings, to discuss what is felt by family members, there will be conflicts about all kinds of surface things unrelated to the fact that one is emotionally constrained. Those emotions have to go somewhere, and will return in any number of guises from irrational nitpicking to physical punishment. There is a film loop of ironies here: I fear emotions; thus, I have an emotional response to your articulation of emotions, so I have to shut down your emotional response because it makes me anxious, because I am afraid of emotions . . .

It need not be so, however, if we are willing to create an environment in which we can each examine our own fears, admit our own anxieties, acknowledge our own emotions. If we do so, we may well find beneath the layers of "Stop fidgeting" or "Where did you put the keys?" our very own fears about fears, which once admitted, once aired, will make us and those we live with freer to express who they are.

Dorothy and Jim are seeing a therapist about their daughter, Mara. "Mara just isn't performing. She is such a disappointment, we don't know what to do. She is twenty-four, she has a first-rate undergraduate education, she's still living at home, she has every reason in the world to go on to graduate school, and she won't do anything about it. We have offered to pay her way to law school, but there she sits, wasting her life working for an insurance company in some dead-end job. We're disturbed, a lot of quarreling is taking place, it's tearing us apart, Dorothy and I are at each other's throats for no good reason at all. . . . What are we to do?" That is it in a nutshell. Jim, a very successful underwriter with a large insurance company, has an MBA. Dorothy is essentially a housewife, which she professes—at least on the first visit to the therapist—to enjoy and to do very well. On the second visit, without Jim, she allows that she had always dreamed of being a lawyer, but it just wasn't in the cards. At one point, she says that being a housewife is demeaning, but maybe that's all she was meant for.

"Mom, Dad! Hey, *Mom, Dad!* MOM, DAD, COME HERE!" The increasingly loud cries come from twelve-year-old Todd. His parents rush to his room and see there a pile of rubble in the center of the floor that was once Todd's collection of space vehicles, glued, painted, and proudly displayed by their industrious maker, whose rage at this desecration has him near tears. Mom and Dad agree that this is awful; oh, my goodness, how could this happen, and "Where is Steven?" Calls for nine-year-old Steven go unanswered. Somebody remembers that Steven was going for a bike ride with the Robbins boy; in fact, he had left some time ago. "Had to have been Steven," Todd says. "Must have done it while I was showering. Wait till I get him!"

Around lunchtime, Steven returns with bike, some flowers picked by the bank of the river for Mom, and a look of unblemished snow about him. "You rotten . . ." etc., is Todd's greeting. Mom and Dad quiet Todd down and talk to Steven. After a long time and probably as a result of knowing that he and Todd will be alone in the house tonight because Mom and Dad are going to the movies, Steven fesses up. "Yes, I did it, and I would do it again," he blurts out. He reddens, tears stream, he looks enraged—almost demonic with anger against Todd. Even the much taller and stronger Todd is a little frightened. Nobody knows quite what to make of it.

Mara's mom goes to the therapist with her husband to consult on the problem of her daughter and stays to talk of the problem of herself. She doesn't feel good about herself. She is dependent, she is *only* a housewife, she has no degrees, she would have liked to have become a lawyer, but maybe she would not have been any good at it, anyhow. Here she is with a daughter who doesn't want to make anything of herself: like mother, like daughter. I'm not very much, she thinks, not very much at all.

In the case of Steven, after a lot of talking, everybody

involved learns about the way that Steven has felt about himself for many of his nine years. Todd bullied him, often in secret, and Steven acquiesced. When the bullying became more public, Mom and Dad shrugged it off as big brother/little brother relating. "Boys will be boys." What anyone ever saw was not all that terrible; Todd was too clever a bully for that. Steven figured that he wasn't much of a guy, anyhow. If I let this brother dominate me—and I do admire him, he thought—I'm not very much, not very much at all.

A middle-aged mother and a nine-year-old boy, feeling lousy about themselves for not getting what they wanted. In response, the mother sees the daughter as a failure because she does not do what the mother would have done in her position. Steven held his rage at himself, his unworthiness, as long as he could, and then he let it rip, reducing to rubble months and months of work on his bullying brother's part in an effort to make a statement about himself, that maybe, just maybe, he did not have to tolerate all that his brother could dish out. That maybe he was just as good.

Self-esteem, the perception of ourselves in positive ways, as people worthy of love and acceptance, is basic to human growth. Without regard for ourselves, we find it hard to regard others well, and when we do not feel good about who we think we are, the world can become a gloomy, challenging place to be. If we don't feel essentially positive about our lovableness, we find it hard to love.

A lot of problem behavior results from concerns about worthiness and lovability. In the case of Dorothy, she projected her feelings about herself onto her daughter, hence the conflicts, and thus the problem was not that of the daughter not conforming but of the mother wanting her daughter to fulfill the mother's own needs. With Steven, it was having allowed himself to become a doormat for his brother that made him feel so negative about himself. The ultimate problem was not his destructiveness, which was a one-time phenomenon, but his feeling worthless.

When there is a problem in a family that seems on reflection to revolve around the issue of self-perception

and self-esteem, there can be a secondary parental battle
about who did the right things, who did the wrong. Such
a battle is fruitless, involves much guilt giving and guilt
taking when none is justified, and dissipates energies that
might best be used in restoring and reinforcing that which
is positive. The important thing is to recognize the problem and then restore a sense of worthiness. Nothing else,
after all, matters.

"So, why don't you put the garbage out? It's almost
nine-thirty, close to bedtime, why don't you do it, huh?
It's your turn. You think you are too good to put out the
garbage? I'd put out the garbage. Sure, yes, in a minute.
Okay, so it's been a minute. Put out the garbage. All
right, so you're not going to put out the garbage, huh?
Then *I'll* put out the garbage. Oh, no, not now, it's too
late. I'll have to get dressed, I can't put out the garbage
in my slippers, they'll get ruined. No, I insist. I like
putting out garbage. Or let's put it this way, I like seeing
to it that the garbage gets put out, okay? It's a responsibility, you know; maybe I can spell it for you. So I'll do
it, don't you. . . . I'll do the garbage. See the rest of the
lousy movie. She dies in the end, anyhow."

"You know I hate to say it, Doctor, but he/she is so
much like my father/mother that it is uncanny. He/she
was nothing like that when we met. He/she was sweet,
thoughtful, always sought my opinion. We never wanted
to do things separately, always together. Oh, some people
thought we were too much in each other's faces, but I
never could get enough of him/her. We were idyllic, if I
must say so. And then . . ."

If the above scenarios seem familiar, it is because they
are familiar. They are replays from the great cinema in
the sky where all of the bad and repetitive movies of our
lives are archived. In monologue number one, we have
two kids, duplicating a conversation that their parents
have undoubtedly had, as have the grandparents and the
grandparents' grandparents. It is the "All right, I'll fulfill your responsibilities for you, but . . ." gambit, the
one that reads like a game today but will breed tomorrow's resentment, just as it has historically. In this par-

ticular instance, the quiet kid is nonviolent, has been through this movie before, and is not about to get himself or herself heated up over the garbage, particularly since the result of that movie is already known. Monologue number two is the "How did it turn out this way? I am aghast . . ." gambit, the one about never wanting to meet a woman/man like Mom/Dad and then carefully going about selecting someone who has all the potential to ultimately be a clone of the fearsome figure. (Or the reverse, where you overlay the image of the loved parent on the spouse, and when the facts do not support the dream, blame the victim.)

The surfaces are clearly imitative, dependent on history, a playing out of events from the past. We could conclude that the behavior was totally surface, the cause and the effect running simultaneously. But the facts are often otherwise. We play out these old behaviors because we have not really assimilated them ourselves. We run them by just one more time—unresolved feelings, and conflicts, memories and dreams not understood, snares in our relations with others—hoping now to gain the understanding that was lacking in the past.

Repetition, when it is negative, is not at all funny, but on the surface, as in the instances above, it can seem ironically amusing. We do find ourselves repeating things that our parents did, things that we were sure we would never be party to: the choice of partners, the style of child rearing, the relationship to siblings, the way we think about possessions, prestige, etc. The important things to remember, however, are that some imitation is inevitable, all imitation need not be negative, and a willingness to be self-critical will help alert us to those repetitions that may be essentially negative and antigrowth.

There is a kind of family memory, much like the Jungian concept of the collective unconscious, where experiences from the familial past reside. We may wish to reexperience certain things that we fondly recall or that were related to us by a parent or grandparent. We take our children to a park we loved as a child, we read them books we loved, we search for ways to duplicate experiences from our childhoods that were positive. There is a richness in those experiences, if they are played out to our expectations, for which there is no warranty. There are also negative experiences that we may see ourselves playing out, and that should trigger, if we are vigilant, an ''Uh, oh! I saw this movie and the ending wasn't too hot'' response, and thus short-circuit the behavior.

As we have already seen, our ability to identify a problem does not mean that it will go away. Despite our knowledge of what is in operation, we may still feel the need or compulsion to play out old scenarios from the familial past. But we can work toward at least turning our awareness into a pause in behavior, and the pause into a longer pause, and the longer pause into a redressing of the issues that underlie the behavior.

These ''notes from the underground'' are hardly exhaustive, but are offered as signposts, reminders that there is more to our lives and our conflicts than mere surface. We have a responsibility to ourselves and to our families to be careful, to watch for the signs, to use our minds and our memories to make connections between the surface of the moment and the ongoing and perhaps unresolved issues that each of us carries with us. We will see later in this book specific instances in which awareness of the subtext of our conflicts can lead first to insight and then to change.

4

Stalemate and Tools for Unlocking It

In chess, stalemate occurs when a player's next move would result in that player moving into checkmate, that position from which there is no move except into another checkmate position. While neither player wishes to have his or her game end in a stalemate, it is also true that if neither can win, neither can lose.

In the anatomy of a fight, stalemate occurs when one or the other party to the conflict is stuck and acknowledges that fact. Nobody has won, nobody is ready to capitulate, and while each participant may really want to knock the other's block off, outside of the presence of continuing anger and new frustration, the only other feeling is one of being too tired to go on. It is at this critical point of stalemate that one or another party to a fight can begin to see some of the ties that bind as well as those that divide, and to make that realization a basis for using one of the important tools for problem solving.

Collaboration may sound antithetical to the process. We might think that if people in a fight could collaborate, they wouldn't be in a conflict in the first place, and to a certain extent we would be right. Yet if we are willing to accept the notion of stalemate, wherein we are too tired to go on, too frustrated to keep attacking-defending, then we can recognize in collaboration an opportunity to at

51

least rest our frazzled selves. We might also begin to make real strides toward harmony.

Here are some ideas that are at the very center of collaborative efforts. They may sound trite and ordinary, but they are often the first things that people and countries forget when a conflict begins to heat up. So if they seem familiar and commonsensical to you, just think back on the last time you saw somebody use common sense in the heat of the moment.

1. Understand the enormous importance of saving face. People want to look good—competent, strong, proud, effective—and they will go to great lengths to maintain that appearance. The angrier people become, the more determined they are not to look the fool in their own eyes or in the eyes of others. Biting off the nose to spite the face is how our parents may have characterized this unredeeming pride. Just the acknowledgment that this desire to save face is normal human behavior will help us to move away from the brink.

2. Look for ways to change a position without losing face. Sometimes that change of position can be a physical one. As international and labor negotiators have discovered, simply moving the discussion out of immediate public view allows for more tractability, more room for real compromise. In the family, it may mean Mom and Dad taking their spat out of the living room and into the bedroom, or Dad and Junior taking a walk together to hash out their differences instead of putting on a dog-and-pony show in the living room, where everyone in the house can see and hear. Being in the spotlight makes us self-conscious and increases the sense of necessity to not lose face at any cost. We get the opportunity to posture less and give more if we can take the extra heat of the klieg lights from our conflicts.

Sometimes a new formula can be brought to a situation that drones on without any signs of stopping. If Bruce and Fred have been at it for fifteen minutes about who gets to go first in Parcheesi, a new computer game, or the bathtub (not likely!), the intervention of Mom and Dad with a flip-of-a-coin solution breaks down the loss-of-face problem, for now the Fates are in control. It also saves Mom and Dad, because they did not have to make the decision but allowed the rules of chance to govern.

3. Try going first. Once a stalemate occurs, why not be the one who first extends the hand of friendship? "Why me and not him?" doesn't work because if both people reason the same way, neither will receive any satisfaction. But by taking a chance, by risking ourselves in this way, we gain both prestige and points as a "good guy."

The trick is to give something that the other side will appreciate, even though it may have not cost us a lot for having done so. When John Kennedy proposed to destroy NATO missile silos in Turkey in 1962 in exchange for Soviet assurance of the removal of their missiles from Cuba, Kennedy succeeded because he was able to give something of apparent value to the Soviets at very little cost to the United States, particularly in that we had already decided to destroy the missiles in Turkey as outmoded! If you can find a way of making the first move without leaving yourself feeling humiliated or endangered, you will have started on the road to the cessation of hostilities.

4. Show you can be trusted and are trusting. If we are trustworthy (that is, if we have not given our opponent reason to believe that we will react in the worst possible manner), our opponent will feel that he or she has an opportunity to look for ways to compromise, to go first. Likewise, we must not suspect our opponent of only the basest motives—we must be trusting, too.

If we think we can make concessions without losing face, we are more likely to look for ways to get out of stalemate. If we can't trust, we are reluctant to risk such behavior. If we behave in a way that suggests untrustworthiness, the other person is going to be reluctant to compromise. Trust, confidence, forgiveness, and willingness to risk ourselves are all important in finding the path away from conflict and toward a reasonable and equitable resolution. The temptation to throw the last volley after a cease-fire is present in the family as it is in the Mideast, but we can learn from history and stay that foolish impulse that only leads to reignition of a fire that destroys human harmony.

5. Take the historic view. Living together day after day allows family members to see each other's behavior and to learn how to react intelligently to it. It is clear from family conflict, however, that we don't take advantage of that daily exposure as we might.

Observing and understanding the repetitive nature of family fights takes time and reflection, the kind of reflection that does not flourish in the middle of a conflict. Such times have to be created. Parents should set aside time to discuss how the family is getting along. There can be family meetings involving the kids, as well, and they need not be formal or regularly scheduled. What they definitely should not be are autocratic opportunities for the local bully to pick at everybody else's sores and go off feeling smugly untouched. Yes, a lot of this is common sense and folk wisdom. We know this. But how come we're still fighting? We need to remind each other that the five simple, collaborative steps, and more, certainly, toward creating an environment in which collaborative efforts might begin, are available to us.

Negotiation is a second very useful tool that can be brought to bear on the family fight. This one we know from the daily papers, even though the negotiations are non-negotiations much of the time. It's simple: You give this and I give that. Trade-offs, negotiated settlements, whatever the term, it's the same thing. One Ted Williams baseball card for two Mickey Mantles and a Stan Musial. Giving for getting, and other clichés, but a wonderful tool.

Not every situation is negotiable, of course. If you believe in the right of women to have children out of wedlock, while I am adamantly opposed, negotiation from now till the millennium will not change our views, for we are dealing with underlying values. But negotiation thrives in the world of behavior, where there are many things that each person can give, accept, or do for another.

For some people, the term *negotiation* has a heartless, mechanistic, and crassly businesslike ring, with two or more people giving and receiving offers, moving step by step from some extreme positions toward something somewhere closer to the middle. ''Sounds dull, sounds homogenized, don't like it. We all give up something and we all settle for less. . . .'' Yet there is another way of looking at it, as in, ''How can we work together to solve this latest problem in ways that we each find satisfying?'' So, how do we do that?

1. Increase the number of options. We sometimes get stuck in a negotiation because we have not taken the time to devise options other than those already on the table. If pepper-steak sub and escargots en croûte are the only items on the menu, it may simplify the server's job, but doesn't give the vegetarian much choice except hunger.

In the world of policy, we saw in the Iran-contra hearings an interesting example of expanding the negotiation menu so that everyone felt a winner, or at least not exactly a loser. One faction wanted to allow Colonel North to give his slide show and rationalization for contra aid, while another was absolutely opposed to his using the hearing as a forum for his personal political views. Just when everything seemed stuck, or stalemated, a solution was found: Let him give his talk but not allow the slides. Each side of the issue felt enough of a winner to agree.

There is always one more option that can be offered to make a stalemate into a resolvable situation. What is required is the will to find it.

2. Expand the pie. Jack wants to play stoop ball, while sister Karen wants to have a catch with her friend. Two people, two sets of game preferences, one ball, conflict. Lots of conflicts in families are such ''fixed-sum'' arrangements, where the more one person gets, the less there is for someone else. One solution: Get another ball. Expand the pie; make it possible for both to get what they want.

Parents often like pie-expansion schemes because they make possible a bit of peace between warring kids by giving each his heart's desire. We must keep two possible problems in mind, however. First, not everyone can afford to expand the pie. If two kids are fighting over the use of the family car, it may not be possible or advisable to rush out and get a second car so that everyone will be happy. Then there is the possibility of increased greed. Give Ricky a new toy today to placate him for the spat

with Sally yesterday, and tomorrow he can be counted
on to ask for yet another. Give 'em an inch . . .

3. Exchange favors. This is the famous quid pro quo: I
promise to do something that you want, and you agree
to something I want in return. It is not that we want to
scratch each other's backs, but if it is what we have to
do to get what we want, then so be it.

4. Logroll. As any good lumberjack will tell us, when
there is a logjam upstream, the best way to get the logs
downriver is to get some loggers to stand on different
logs and then roll off in coordinated fashion. Politicians
are said to logroll when they agree to support, or at least
not actively oppose, another's piece of legislation in exchange for a reciprocal show of support on another issue
later on. Family members can be said to logroll when
they yield on certain issues. It is a little like the quid pro
quo, but it is different in kind because it does not relate
to immediate and opposing needs/wants. I want to go to
the movies tonight and my friend wants to go, not particularly tonight, having planned to read, but what the
heck, he'll go. Since there are no passionate opposing
views, but rather indifference, logrolling fits the bill.

5. Cut costs. Sometimes options in stalemated situations
cannot be generated because of "shortages." The pie
can't be expanded, logrolling seems impossible given the
circumstances, and it is even hard to think about reciprocating favors. Each party must chip away at the reser-
vations the other has about the agreement.
   Kate wants the car to go to a dance. Mom and Dad
had already decided to do something that required the
car. Impasse? No. Mom and Dad drop Kate off on the
way to their dinner, and Kate gets transportation from a
friend or calls home for a return ride. Nobody gets exactly what they want: Mom and Dad are inconvenienced,
and Kate is, as well. But both got what they wanted most.

6. Trade this time for the next. This seems like logrolling, but there is a real difference. In logrolling, you
get what you want on *this* issue in return for my getting
what I want on *that* issue. Here, it is I get what I want

this time, but *next time* you get what you want. This kind of turn-taking is a simple notion, certainly, but it often requires the person proposing the idea to be willing to let the *other* go first.

7. I cut, you choose. Mom selects five possible places for dinner, Dad chooses. Joe proposes five games, his friend Walter chooses. Simple, evenhanded, and particularly applicable when resources are involved. It creates incentives for agreement and in general does away with trust as an issue. So whenever there is concern about the menu offered being loaded, the resources not being fairly divided, the door can be opened to a trade-off of responsibility and function. "Fine, if you are the one to cut the pie, I do the choosing."

Negotiation may not be *the* answer, but it is often *an* answer, a way of getting out of stalemate, of getting unstuck, of moving from negative to at least neutral ground. In order for it to be effective, however, you must understand your own needs and those of others with whom you negotiate. Sometimes we, and international negotiators as well, focus on the stated needs rather than on underlying needs and real interests. "If I don't get to bat first, then I am going away with my ball, and nobody gets to play." Clearly, the would-be batter is sacrificing his wish to play ball for a silly, superficial, and bullying reason. Effective negotiation is built on understanding the wishes and needs of oneself and the person with whom we are negotiating. Effective negotiators learn to deal in practical realities rather than in subjective mythologies.

Some final words on negotiation. Try to deal honestly, empathically, fairly. In so doing, you will more often than not be able to move toward a reasonable negotiated settlement, saving face for one and all. It is not a panacea but a tool, and like any tool must be well maintained and used when the job requires it. Properly and wisely used, it can help bring order and agreement out of the chaos of conflict.

Communication is also a factor in family conflict. All right, you've heard this all before, but . . . Many family fights are the result not of genuine disagreement but of poor communication. Communication is a two-part process composed both of talking and listening. Unfortunately, we often fail to say clearly what we feel, need, and want, just as we often fail to hear the needs, wants, feelings of others.

Harvey came home from school one day upset. His mother was unable to get any clues from him at all. Everything was fine, according to Harvey, but his withdrawn, quiet behavior communicated something else. When Dad came home, he tried to figure out why Harvey was so obviously upset, but with no success. A few days later, however, Harvey came to his parents to tell them that there had been a disagreement at school. Some kids had really gotten on his case, and he had punched out a few lights. He prefaced this "confession," however, with some remarks: "Now you're not going to get mad, huh? I didn't want to tell you because I thought you'd really get mad, but . . ." As it worked out, Mom and Dad took it in stride. They could see Harvey's agitation, his real concern about how they would react, and thought it was better to talk through the event than to castigate him for impulsive behavior and not revealing the truth instantly on demand. Harvey felt good about his parents' attitude and the parents felt good that Harvey was finally able to talk to them about his problem. Everyone felt closer as a result, and communication would probably be even easier in the future.

The Harvey story contains certain elements that make for effective communication:

1. Identify. See yourself from the other side of the bargaining table. Do you appear intimidating, vengeful, sympathetic, closed, open, too fragile to take bad news or disappointment? Do you look like someone you would want to meet in a dark alley? Now try to put the other person's words in your mouth. Are they comfortable, do you understand why that person would utter those words given the opposition?

These are good exercises in putting yourself aside so as to identify with the other person's view. Harvey's parents could see themselves as Harvey might see them: pressuring, authoritarian, entitled, critical, potentially punishing. Recognizing this, they let up on the psychological throttle, and it worked. Harvey felt relieved and found the right time to talk.

2. Read between the lines. That's what Harvey's parents did. His behavior suggested a problem as well as a reluctance to discuss it at once. They gave him the room to become comfortable before the day of revelation.

Kids are often fearful of parental disapproval for good reason, as when they have experimented with drugs, alcohol, or sex, and correctly understand that their parents will be rightly concerned and critical. As parents, we need to be sensitive and to read dispassionately between the lines. No, we shouldn't play detective and give our children the third degree, but should get at the feelings under the behavior before attempting to confront it—or judge it. Sometimes the revelations are surprising or shocking, but before we scream or react, we must spend some extra time figuring out what our approach to the problem will be.

Although they have been dating for several weeks, Anne finds something unsettling about Darrell. She can't put her finger on it, but it's quietly driving her up the wall. Tonight she decides to pay particular attention to Darrell's behavior; she even hopes that "it" is all in her mind, because there is much that she admires and loves in this man. Over dinner she excitedly tells Darrell about her first and recent trip to Mexico. She rhapsodizes while Darrell maintains a smile that seems more the result of will and muscle control than genuine pleasure. As Anne reaches her fourth minute of excited dissertation, the will and the muscles begin to relax a bit, and Anne detects a strong intake of breath on the other side of the table. Could this be a prelude to an interruption? Out of deference, Ann stops, and Darrell says, "Gee, that sounds really neat. I love Mexico. But you know what's *really* great . . ." Off he goes on automatic, holding forth endlessly on some other topic. At this moment, Anne discovers the unpleasant news: Darrell is not a listener. If a long-term relationship with this man is to be possible, he will have to learn something about communication, which is something quite different from talking.

Moral: Put at least as much energy into listening as

into talking. In the process, we may eventually discover what the real problem is.

3. Talk about needs and feelings, not just about positions. "I want to go to that movie tonight, not tomorrow, not next Wednesday, tonight. It's tonight or to hell with it. You are always like this. I want to go now, and you don't want to go. What's the matter with you, anyway?"

This person is talking about a position.

"I want to go to the movie tonight, not tomorrow, or Wednesday. I really get the sense that you don't want to go because you are annoyed with me, that maybe I ask too much, that maybe I don't take into consideration that you've had a hard day, too, and would rather not go out. But, really, I sometimes feel so alone, and so want you to be with me outside the house, and we don't get to do it very often, you know. It would be so gratifying just to be out together. . . . Sometimes I feel I'm getting stale, and . . ."

This person is talking about needs and feelings.

In the first instance, the speaker is setting up a grid on which all play must take place. It is rigid and stultifying, leaving no room for face-saving or compromise. In the second example, the speaker is exposing some basic insecurities that underlie the simple wish to go to a movie, not later, but *now*. To which position could we most comfortably respond? The latter, most of us would answer, because there is something to respond to. In the first instance (and *position*), we are confronted by accusation and disdain, and are likely to become defensive and overlook the real concerns that may underlie the attack. When feelings are honestly expressed and vulnerability confessed, it is easier for members of a healthy family to respond generously.

However, you shouldn't use the rationale, "But, honey, this is how I *really* feel," to commit mayhem with destructive words. "I thought you should know that nobody in the office can stand you." "I've never really loved you, but there are the kids to consider. I thought you would want to know." No, those are not recommended communications. Which brings us back to our first suggestion, identifying with the other. If we put ourselves in the other person's position and hear those words directed at us, we would not even consider speaking them.

4. Separate listening from action. Too often we respond to someone else's words with action. Often that is the last thing that should occur. If Harvey's parents had responded quickly to the nonverbal communication from their son that something was amiss and had stormed in screaming, ''What can we do, darling, let us help! Oh, what can Mommy and Daddy do?'' then Harvey might have reacted quite differently than he did. He might have lied, stonewalled, built a barrier between his parents and himself that would take a lot of intelligent communication to break down.

Cool it. Or, unlike Robert Frost's traveler standing at the fork in the road, look down both pathways and decide to go no farther. In short, think, reflect, think some more; then act or not.

5. Know when to hang up the phone. Talking can sometimes be the cover for emptiness or a will of steel. In the former instance, the speaker just plain doesn't know when to stop because the recognition of the lack of content is not within the speaker's reach. In the latter instance, it is talking as a weapon, an exhausting, debilitating one that finally results in superficial if insubstantial surrender on the listener's part; the listener feels not talked *to* but talked *at*. Inaction—not talking too much, not revealing all in a torrent—can be just as valuable as action in resolving conflicts.

Hanging up the phone is not cutting the wires, but rather a ''down time,'' when we get an opportunity to rest, to reflect, to recompose ourselves and to return refreshed in mind and viewpoint to work at settling something, not in vanquishing the opponent.

Are these all the things we need to know about communication with each other in the family? Hardly. We will all find our own additions to the five suggestions above through our experience with each other. But the five points are important, and when honestly applied in the appropriate circumstances will help us in making something positive out of a family conflict.

Building Positive Momentum is the final tool in our kit.

Joe and Marge were in trouble. They had been married ten years, had two children, lived in the suburbs, and led independent professional lives. In fact, their lives had become so independent and busy that they barely found time to talk together. After years of this pattern, about the only time the couple talked was when they wanted to tell each other how dissatisfied they were with the way things were going, each blaming the other for being unavailable. Although Joe and Marge loved each other, you would not know it from overhearing their angry fights and recriminations.

But then one day Marge had a smart idea: Why not put aside one night each week—Wednesday, it was later decided—for the two of them to be alone. Maybe they would go to a restaurant for dinner, to a movie, for a walk; what they did was not the point, only that it would be their time to be together, with one caveat: It had to be positive. No arguing!

Over the following months, they kept their promise to each other, and Wednesdays became so great a success that they dubbed that day of the week MPW—Marriage Preserving Wednesday. It allowed Joe and Marge the opportunity to unwind gradually, to rediscover their good and playful feelings for each other, to focus more on what they liked about each other than what they didn't like. While the marriage continued to be an intense and sometimes stormy one, they had created a device that helped them to cool down, to rebuild a positive relationship. Eventually, MPW was no longer a necessary day.

What happened here was that a couple recognized a problem, agreed to do something positive about their relationship, worked at maintaining a schedule that allowed them to work on that relationship, and then set about doing it. They created positive momentum, a cycle in which positive move begat positive move, until in the end the positive feelings that were generated in the context of MPW took on a life of their own.

Once more we can say, ''It's simple.'' But as is often said, everything is context. How do you notice the problem, how do you start, how do you get the downward spiral stopped by the ''one little candle'' theory?

1. Try to start with easy issues. Family problems are often complex and entangled, so as a result it is easy to lift our eyes to the heavens, lift our palms in helplessness, shrug, and do nothing. But if a single, soluble issue among the many is isolated and dealt with, the positive momentum that results can spill over onto the next and presumably knottier problem. But how do we recognize the easy problem? The answer: *Follow the path of least resistance.*

We should look to those issues that pose the fewest problems and stumbling blocks, that seem the least loaded with symbolic importance for the participants. In one family, there may be a problem with Dad or Mom becoming housebound and cranky because there is no child care available. If the financial resources are there, the obvious solution is to have some help, thus breaking the cycle of irritability, and to move forward on the momentum gained. In another family, there may be a problem with kids' antisocial behavior; there we might think about providing a positive structure one evening a week that will, once more, break the cycle of negative behavior and provide momentum for further change.

2. Make constructive commitments. If we can get ourselves into binds by hardening of issues and stances—essentially making *de*structive commitments—we can just as readily get ourselves unbound through the hardening around positive and constructive commitments. Regularized, ritualized pleasurable experiences can replace those maddeningly negative ones that we often fixate on. We could replace the perhaps excessive grousing or the "grounding" of a child over "yet another" faulty report card with an afternoon or evening doing something with that child that will reinforce the child's competence. That positive step might be worth a great deal more than we can even imagine. Creating a sense of shared and positive history can help us to improve our feelings toward each other.

3. Help the other members of the family feel competent, cared for, and effective. Clichés are often clichés because they have stood the test of time and are accurate in at least a limited way. "If you haven't got anything good to say, don't say anything" certainly fits that category. In the family, this cliché suggests that we focus on what family members do that is right rather than wrong. Praise achievements with more gusto than you would employ in pointing out faults.

Sometimes we can get into that pattern of needing to show strength, as does the bad business executive, by expecting only the best and commenting only on that which is less than the best. This puts pressure on family members to perform to ridiculously high standards and then only receive praise inferentially by the absence of complaint. The "strong" one thinks he's setting standards, but like the bad business executive he's creating a tense and volatile environment. A kind and supportive approach, treating the positive as an achievement, will lead to a more congenial (and productive) atmosphere. (Time for another cliché: You catch more flies with honey than with vinegar.)

4. Apply standards of equity. When family members are in a stalemate, we need to find a way out. The application of an external standard can help. If two kids are arguing over the relative size of pieces of cake ("Mine's smaller, how come?") and there's a kitchen scale available, the question can be settled by the objective, external standard provided by the scale.

Decisions based on objective data, by reasonable discussion—in short, by principles of fairness or equity—will be more readily accepted than decisions made subjectively. Everyone may not be pleased with the result, but at least the objective manner in which a decision was reached cannot be faulted.

When you solve specific disputes with objective standards, the "hot" issues of competence, love, weakness, strength—all of those loaded issues that heat up fights—have no place in the equation.

5. Consider applying the rule of change. Perhaps the most important and simplest piece of advice that can be applied is: When in doubt, try something different.

That is what Joe and Marge did in the MPW program. This is what we all should do when we discover that the old stuff isn't working anymore. When the twenty-dollar watch stops and the works show forty dollars' worth of repairs are necessary, we don't continue wearing the watch hoping that suddenly our wish for it to keep time will result from our will; we throw it out and get a new one. Exactly so with life situations and the "solutions" of the past that have not worked. We should not rail that "if only you would . . ." or "if the world would just . . ." but should examine what we have tried in the past and make a new attempt at getting from stalemate to something much more positive. Threats may not have worked with a particular problem in the past, so why apply them again? Try something else and something else and something else until there is a positive response. The name of the game is not conformity to preconceived dogma but getting things unstuck, getting positive patterns going, getting as much happiness and cooperation and usefulness out of our lives in the family and beyond as is possible.

So that's the toolbox, which can be added to what we have already learned about our families' inner needs, the surfaces of our conflicts, and the fact that fighting is normal, necessary, and growth-involved. In the next several chapters, we will explore the specific problems of our lives from early marriage to childbirth through adolescence, empty nest, and beyond, applying what we now know toward the resolution of the common conflicts we all experience.

Part Two:

THE TIMES OF OUR LIVES

5

Courtship, Marriage, Here Comes Baby

Two people come together into the dance called courtship with dreams and expectations, hopes and fears, and a Western tradition of romantic love. We also come with a history, not just of ourselves but of a family, with attitudes and beliefs and wishes, half-conscious, half-submerged, that make our courtship by turns fiery, blissful, dramatic, dull—the works. It is at once both a magical and a terrifying period in our lives. Some of us would wish never to live it again; some others of us would prefer to live *only* it again . . . and again, and again. If adolescence is *Sturm und Drang*, then what is courtship but *Sturm und Drang* to the tenth power? But all its sitcom charm aside, courtship is a truly pivotal time in our lives, for courtship is about making choices, choices we hope we are making for life.

We select a person who in turn selects us for marriage or some other permanent relationship in which we will be intimate over a long period of time; someone with whom we will sleep, eat, share fears and dreams, whom we will care for, and be cared for by; someone with whom we will share power and to whom we will cede power; someone with whom we will be both literally and metaphorically naked, and whom we can trust with the knowledge and vulnerability of that nakedness. Choosing, being chosen—choices fraught with both wonderful potential and unknown pitfalls. Given the unknowns, it is a wonder that we do it at all.

It would be comforting if we could now parade out a set of rules and add some graphs and comparative charts that would together provide us with a foolproof way of looking at our intimate family relationships. Unfortunately, it doesn't work that way. While our experiences certainly have commonalities, each family is unique, with its own history, its own sets of problems and ways of solving or not solving them. Therefore, it will be more useful and to the point to look back at our family history and discover some of the roots of our ways of relating within the family, and to change those ways if we think that to do so will make our lives together better.

Cliché time: Those who do not learn the lessons of history are doomed to repeat it. Alas, the cliché is true, for in the world of human relations, the psychological world of family and self and those outside, we have a pretty good shot at repeating some of that history whether we like it or not. But we can learn and change destructive patterns.

Paul hates to get haircuts, but his hair is pretty shaggy, so he is going to the barber because tonight he is seeing Frances. They are pretty serious. He has been confessing idiosyncrasies he didn't even know he had, testing her for what may be a lifetime commitment. "Just clean up the edges, please, not too close, okay?" "Sure. Nice day." Clip, clip. "How about those Indians, huh?" Clip, clip. "Yep, some game." Clip, clip.

Paul would just as soon dispense with the small talk, never has been good at it, but that is not what accounts for his current state. His fists are tight, he is breathing scarcely at all, and if a thermometer were introduced into his mouth, he would either break it with his teeth or show a temperature above the norm. He is ablaze with apprehension. How come?

"Hi. Nice to see your face," Frances says to him as they meet at her door. Paul pecks her on the cheek and abruptly says, "Are you ready to go?" "Sure, almost, just one more minute," she says as she heads toward her bedroom to put on shoes and give a final brush to her coiffure. Paul sneaks a look in the hall mirror, brushes his hair, jaw tense, mouth downturned. %*## barber! It's too damned short, he thinks. I look like a choir boy at an Easter service! Frances comes out with a big smile and high expectations for the evening. Paul's face suggests a small storm in the offing, but she ignores it and says, "All set?" "Yeah, I guess so. You're really going to wear those shoes?" "Yes, don't you like them?" "I hate them. The color is no color at all." "I've always liked them; in fact, you were with me when I picked them out. How come all of a sudden—." "They are really ugly shoes. Can't you wear something else?" "Well, I suppose, but frankly . . ." "They are really, really ugly. Sometimes I wonder about how you can be so smart and yet do so many stupid—" "Say good night, Paul," Frances says. "Huh?" "Some other time, some time when you don't have a chip on your shoulder, all right?" With this said, Frances starts pushing Paul toward the door while he stumbles around some halfhearted apologies while still holding that "you've got to admit they're pretty ugly." "And when you learn how to talk to a woman with some sensitivity, you can call me," Frances says as she closes the door on a conflicted, confused suitor.

Frances has called Paul on his bad behavior. He is angry and embarrassed at the same time. He is vaguely aware of what might be going on, but after a while he decides that Frances really has terrible taste and needs to be shaped up. It was that and that alone, he decides, that was the problem between them that evening. He'll just have to be a little more circuitous in his "teaching" her, he figures. That is the text.

But the subtext is that Paul is angry because the very act of being shorn dredges up the anxieties of childhood surrounding haircuts. Sometimes he can recall why trips to the barber make him so uneasy; at other times, the apprehension just around haircut time seems inexplicable and unrelated to going to the barber. Paul's family was poor, and haircut money could translate into half a pound of sliced luncheon loaf, mustard, and a loaf of Wonder bread, so the longer the periods between haircuts the better.

"Get it very close. And I mean close! And if it's not close, I will send you back, and you know I will." He knows. He has been sent back before, felt humiliated. "My mother says . . ." The barbers smirk. "Okay, back up in the chair." His fists are tight, his breathing shallow.

Paul's mother, a woman, being humiliated, a day in the barber's seat, anxiety over the haircut. Disobedient, too, for he didn't get it very close. . . . "Just clean up the edges." Angry with Mom, angry with the situation, humiliated, feeling disloyal, unfit, angry. Ah, those shoes! A perfect reason to act out, to strike back at Frances (a woman), to be in charge, to make demands, to humiliate someone who humiliated him, for his mother was a woman, too.

How can Paul resolve this fight and bring peace back to his relationship? He might realize that, good taste or bad (in his mind, at least), Frances is too important to him to let this incident fester and drive a wedge between them for good. Thus, he might break the stalemate by initiating a positive move, such as making a strong and clear apology for what even he must see as boorish behavior. It is also possible that, although the responsibility for reconciling is clearly not incumbent on her, Frances might try to bring Paul around to at least exploring the underlying issues that led to his inappropriate reaction to her taste in clothing. By giving him no venue for his abusiveness, she handled the situation well, but she also might have chided him affectionately and amusedly, yet seriously about that response. "Hey, what's this all about, Paul, huh? I don't get it, and from the look on your face you don't either. What's under your nails, huh? Something get to you today?" Her guidance might lead him into the territory where he is really hurting.

Whichever approach is used, this situation should not be allowed to deteriorate by charge and countercharge, accusation and cross-accusation. If the fighting continues, there is still the chance for one or the other to stop it by building some positive momentum, which can be as simple as a large apology or a small bouquet, something that will break the string of negatives that get built up when there is an issue at the center that everyone has forgotten but that keeps people apart.

This is just one example of the type of baggage that comes to courtship. It can take many forms more and less dramatic than this one. The problem is that the one who carries the baggage shares it with his or her partner in courtship, whether the other wants to share or not.

When we get into a fight, we should examine what gets it started and the behavior surrounding it; we will often see connections between past and present. When we see them clearly, we have a good chance to modify our behavior, weaning ourselves from old, stale responses to conditions and situations that have their real meaning in the past.

The family, of course, provides the major model for learning how to relate in intimate situations, so it is reasonable that some of our behavior during such an intimate and yet tentative time as courtship and early marriage will be based on ways of relating we learned in our parents' house.

Liza is on her absolutely sparkling best behavior during courtship and the first two years of marriage. She gives the sense of being insecure, too willing to please, perhaps, but that is also her charm. She's funny and warm and pleased to make William comfortable, although she has repeatedly asked William, in as many ways as possible, just how much he *really* loves her. After four years together now, Liza is secure in Will's feelings. As a result, she is no longer so anxious to please, her wit has dried up, and that little edge of insecurity has been replaced by a tiny bit of arrogance.

A great admirer of her dad, Liza was a good unconscious observer, for her story was his. While she was not there at the beginning and too young to have seen the change when it occurred in her parents' marriage, she read well between the lines of her family's life and Mom's reveries about those early days. Mom was great and giving, although she always seemed a bit disappointed in the way life had turned out. But Dad sparked the romantic imagination of his daughter, having achieved any number of things and once having achieved them walking away from them. Fortunately, he did not have that attitude toward his family, but his own wife, whom he fought so hard to captivate and capture, was another goal that, once achieved, lost compelling interest for him.

Liza, however, armed with self-knowledge, has a chance to turn the situation around so that neither she nor William will be cheated of the fully reciprocal giving and receiving that makes a marriage more than an economic unit.

There can be the exact opposite result from the same circumstances, as well; Liza might have resolved never to maintain anything less than intense interest in her chosen partner, vowing never to inflict on another the sense of rejection that her mother has known. The permutations can be many, but the facts remain that our ways of behaving in courtship or marriage are very much affected by the history of the family, and that the nature of our fights and the manner in which we pursue them will likewise be significantly determined by our previous history. We must be willing to look at ourselves in the context of our relationships with our parents and siblings, to be aware of how they have dealt with conflicts in *their* lives, what behaviors of theirs brought conflict to the door. We must have the courage to identify those things in them that we are repeating and that are causing us problems.

"M.B.? It's Dave. Oh, you recognized my voice. How nice. Thought you forgot it about eight-fifteen this morning. What do you mean, what do I mean? You know what I mean. We have the weekend together, the first one in a month, and you get up this morning and languorously shower, spend hours brushing your hair and fussing at the mirror and all that stuff, you barely speak, and I walk down to Penn Station with you and I get a peck and a goodbye and you walk away and you don't even turn back! That's why I'm surprised you know the voice. Dave who?

"Aw, come on Mary Beth, let's forget it, but geez, it is so weird, and that corridor is so long, and I stand there and I can see you and it's like you're walking forever, and it's as if I'm not there, as if I don't matter. I know. Yeah. I know, I love you, too. Yeah. Great. Yeah, next weekend, I'll come up. Sure. I *do* feel better. I already said it, yeah, I love you, too. Right. Just one thing before you hang up, okay? Thanks. Hey, next time, will you turn around, please?"

* * *

This not-very-imaginary monologue is typical of one of the precipitators of conflict among suitors, and married people, as well, the how-much-do-you-really-love-me question that takes many, many forms. Its roots, however, are often the same: the search for proof of one's self-worth. It may be that search that sets us off in the first instance to find that someone who is willing to take part in an exclusive dance with us, with us alone. The danger is that we search for the perfect symmetry, the exact equality of fervor and ardor, the exact quantity of love for exact quantity of love. Why do we put so much emphasis on the equality of caring? The answer is that equality of caring implies equality of vulnerability and dependence, and it is scary to think that the other is less open to hurt than oneself. It is a risk, of course, that we all must take in one way of another or be alone, the question of worth still unanswered. It is uncertain if that question is ever fully and definitively answered for most of us, so it is best if we learn to live with the resulting existential angst.

Are there steps that we can take to relieve some of the anxiety that is inherent in situations like the one described above? In the instance of Beth and Dave, it is clear that there are different priorities and different emotional levels that have to be considered. If Beth requires a lot of quiet time before setting out for the day, Dave should honor that and help to build extra time into their schedule. If Dave requires a reaffirmation of love through attention, then together Beth and Dave might build in some ritual that would satisfy his needs, as well. Each must become aware of the needs of the other, become responsive to them while also acknowledging their separateness. For most of us, the maturity shown in that balance between our needs and those of the other comes only with some struggle over time. It is within our reach, however, and only requires our attention to the fact that each of us is different. In acknowledging not only our differences but also our right to our separate identities, we can be well on our way to a less anxious and more rewarding relationship.

Your career or mine? It's one of the key debates that couples have in the eighties, particularly because it encompasses morality, sociology, and finances. Tough topics, all of them.

Flo is an accountant and Roger is a junior adjuster for an insurance company. She has the opportunity to become a CPA and work for a large firm, but it will eventually require a move to another city. He has grown up here, he doesn't want to leave. In every other way, they are compatible: They love movies, particularly the English postwar comedies; they attend horse shows together and hire horses for organized trail rides in the country with friends; they both want two or three kids (both come from large families, so neither sees child raising through the rose-colored glasses of Ralph Lauren advertisements); they both overeat a little and don't get on each other's backs about svelteness. A marriage made in heaven. But this career thing is significant both as an opportunity and a stumbling block.

Flo is more excited about the opportunity than Roger is, so she begins to find fault with little habits of his. His specific and not irrational timidity about making a change (we are nearly all conservative in that respect) becomes a symbol for her of his overall lacklusterness, a quality of his she has never noticed before. His indifference toward clothing styles, the way he balls up the towels after a shower rather than hanging them up properly, become issues where they were not before. He feels challenged and a little inferior in the relationship. She has been singled out to go to school by her employer and will be in a position to make considerably more money than he. His job is okay, he has no particular desire to be the world's greatest insurance adjuster or president of Wewin Insurance Corporation, but now he feels guilty about his lack of ambition. Rather than turning on himself, however, he starts to chide her for being big-headed, too darned proud. Every once in a while during the hour of mutual criticism, he suggests that maybe they were really mismatched. "Better to know now, right Flo?"

Here is a problem that is less existential, less built-in than those described earlier, where often the best advice is to at least be aware of the inner dynamics of the situation and try to deal with it in a mature and creative manner. This practical problem is one that can be addressed in terms of collaboration. If the problem is immediately put on the table, and the anxieties separated from the facts, perhaps the sniping will stop and the practical center can be addressed. If Roger acknowledges that he really does love Flo and concedes that his "helpful" suggestion that perhaps they were mismatched was pride speaking, his way of backing away from a threatening situation, he can approach the discussion with less emotional bravado. Balancing out his pluses against his timidity, Flo may decide that there is more than enough to make some collaborative or negotiated settlement desirable.

After Flo and Roger discussed the practical ways that a move like this could work, a lot of the anxiety diminished. He began to get excited about living in another city after talking with friends who had moved for job reasons. He also realized that it was not absolutely necessary to be the spear-bearing hunter bringing down the dinner meal with the strength of his arm and the accuracy of his eye. So if she was happy in her job and was contributing more than himself, fine. A little discomfort in adjusting, it seemed to him, was worth the pleasure of being with the woman he enjoyed being with. As for her, she made it very clear that some of her sniping remarks and downgrading of him had been nothing more than mean-spirited, for she felt stifled. "I love you, and if it is not possible for you to move away, then to heck with the job." (This might have been used at an earlier time as a way of breaking out of stalemate. We have to be prepared, of course, to follow our words with actions, so it had better be true that he was more important than a job, prestige, etc.) Maybe she meant it, or maybe she knew it would have the desired effect. He felt whole and competent and a desirable male again, and from that position of strength it was easy for him to be magnanimous.

Had the desired result not been forthcoming, they might have used some negotiation techniques, agreeing that Flo take the job on a trial basis while Roger stayed behind until it became clear that they could live apart or that they must be together, in which latter case a formal negotiation of who moves where would have to take place. This would increase the options, thus giving a greater sense of control and choice. "This choice is mine, the next is yours" might also have been added to the negotiation menu. The important thing is to either make the relationship possible and let it flourish or to discover at this point that it is not possible to maintain the necessary flexibility and/or stability that the two require to maintain their partnership.

The potential for conflict when two people live together is endless. Some differences are relatively small, such as the joint checking account at my bank or yours, sleeping with the windows open or closed, bathroom politics, leaving lights on in rooms when not in use. But if these topics are seen by us as control issues, or as symbolic of what we fear most in our own selves, they can be serious precipitators of conflict.

Ted has a fit if the lights aren't doused upon leaving the room. He considers it wasteful, something he learned at Daddy's knee. Ted is serious when he says to Catherine, "You forgot to put out the kitchen light," and then gets up to put if off, giving signs with his heavier than usual footfall that this is important to him. It makes good sense to do what Ted suggests, but few of us always do what makes very good sense. Ted might not be so concerned himself if those glowing lights were not symbolic of his repressed desire to light all the lights and stay up late and raise hell and thumb the nose at Daddy, the very thought of which he finds terrifying. Ted's unresolved anger with a controlling father who made his son feel irresponsible as a result of his "light-bulb behavior" is spilling over into the relationship with Catherine. Both of them ought to be aware of this repetition of family history, and try to resolve it through confronting it. The chances are that Catherine's ignoring it, in the light of Ted's repeated insistence, will not make the problem go away. The more of these little issues that are unresolved through courtship and come finally to roost around the marriage bed, the more difficult it will be to maintain a good, positive, growing relationship.

Beverly thinks Tom is just terrific. They have been seeing each other for eleven months, and although he hasn't read any of the books that are so important to her and that she has pressed on him with so much enthusiasm, she figures there's a lifetime ahead of them. He is so gallant, he dresses so well, he's such a good lover, he never presses her when she would prefer he not. . . . Tom is going to have a surprise when they get married, because she has mapped out a new regimen for Tom; a whole Tom Reform Act is in the making. She's really going to turn him into a book-a-week man. Oh, boy, she can hardly wait!

If the road to hell is paved with good intentions, the road to misery in marriage is paved with wishful thinking. Issues that are bothersome or unresolved ideally should be dealt with in this period of courtship, for they will only by intensified when the idealization and romanticism of that period has ended, and the real daily intimacy of lives intertwined is upon them.

Other common forms of this disease: 1. I am going to make this poor person's life complete and happy for the first time. 2. "Could you turn that down, I hate loud rock." ("But what about all those concerts we went to when we were dating?" "I didn't want to disappoint you.") 3. Well, I have a lot invested in this relationship, and I am not going to go out and start all over again. 4. He'll relax once we are alone. 5. I know she has a tremendous capacity for warmth; she needs some time to develop it.

It is amazing how we can project our own desires and interests on to other people. The key here is to be careful. Not careful in the way of the compulsive who can never share intimacy so he or she carries a checklist of the necessary attributes for a mate, knowing full well that the odds against such a combination are nearly infinite; but careful in that each potentially serious concern is dealt with and resolved before the public commitment involved in marriage takes place.

"What a crybaby you are. Can't have your own way, so you're in a snit. There's more to life than play, you know, Samantha."

"I can't believe it. How did you so something so stupid, anyhow?"

Everett and Samantha have been giving a lot of thought to marriage. They have moved into Samantha's apartment because it has a better view than his place, and is rent controlled. While their midwestern city is not on this year's list of hot real-estate markets, it is a lively and desirable city, so the idea of five rent-controlled rooms with a good view of the river is more than simply attractive.

Ev is a pretty driven guy. He runs the parts department for a large car dealership and loves to be on top of his inventory. For him to be caught with his parts down is something he takes very, very personally. Being the best is important to his identity. He could have a job in any of the other dealerships any time at the best salary a parts manager can get, but he is very well taken care of at Smith Motors. In order to perform as well as he has been able to, he has had to put in many extra hours, some of which have involved tedious work like physical inventory, but some of which also meant installing a parts-inventory program of his own devising. The latter took the best part of half of a year, but the result has been terrific. It is almost impossible for a part available from the manufacturer, and by statistical analysis likely to be needed in Ev's area, to be out of stock.

Samantha is a junior buyer at a department store. She likes gloves and hats, but she is not defined by gloves and hats. She sees herself as Samantha who has a job as a junior buyer of hats and gloves, who loves Everett who is brilliant at his job, and who likes to listen to music, to cook fairly elaborate meals, take drives into the country on a weekend, perhaps stay at an inn and take walks. Hats-and-gloves *senior* buyer is not something that is at the front of her mind. In fact, at this moment when we meet Samantha and Ev, at the front of her mind is a pretty little inn north of their city that has a very good pianist on the weekends and some voice students who do operetta in the front parlor. On a cold winter weekend like this, it would be ideal, she has just finished saying, only to discover Ev can't do it, because there has been a major glitch in the system at Smith's. Some customer who has been promised a new carburetor was disappointed. Not only was there no carburetor, but, according to Ev's program's statistical analysis, there was not likely to be a call for a carburetor for seven weeks. Ev is depressed because one of his self-built identity props has fallen over. Samantha is angry because her dream person who can do what he does so well and still be the weekend romancer under eiderdown quilts is not available to fulfill the dream!

Here are two very nice people who are at a kind of crossroads. They have been very happy together, but they have also built their images of themselves and each other, to a certain extent, on insufficient information and/or wishful thinking. The perfect computer-inventory system has failed. With it has gone some of Ev's self-esteem. Samantha's perfect man cannot be there with mulled cider in hand and Gilbert and Sullivan in the air. Reality has intruded.

Both are thrown for a little loop. This has never happened before. For statistical reasons, they have never experienced either the weekend being blown by work or the work-defined self in trouble. Now, whammo: both at once. The result? They are both acting out a bit. Here are two people who have built images of themselves and/or each other on a run of good luck. They may get through it, because it is not a major contretemps, but it illustrates how we build little boxes for our own selves or each other. These little boxes of identity are nicely labeled and stacked away, but when the thing inside does not perform as we had anticipated, we are angry at that thing, which may be ourselves or our mates.

This same situation *could be* the beginning of the end. It may be that the myths they had built of and for each other, once having been shattered, will shatter the relationship itself. If that is the case, it is better that it happen now than one and a half children later. But rather than throw in the towel on this relationship, what alternatives might we discover that will allow for reality adjustment and reaffirm the basic feelings two people have for each other?

Since they don't have a long history together that would provide information or glue to repair the breaches, they must invent as they go along. In order to break out of stalemate, Ev could apologize for screwing up this weekend and make amends by planning a special weekend two weeks hence, something that would be "writ in stone." That would communicate to Samantha the value he places on her needs and expectations. On the other hand, Samantha could indicate her willingness to trust and to understand Ev's situation, and demonstrate her willingness to be realistic about changes in plans caused by work. This does *not* mean that his obligations within the relationship should not have their own gravity.

Using the concept of *negotiation*, perhaps Everett could work as long as it takes to set things right on Friday night, still leaving them the time to get away on Saturday morning. In return, Samantha might find something attractive closer to home, take on the driving chore that usually falls to Everett (Samantha likes to read during auto trips), and structure the time so that Everett might get some extra hours of sleep. If that is not practical, it is not unreasonable that Samantha acquiesce but, in the style of *I cut, you choose*, making plans for the next trip without consultation with Everett, but with his acquiescence on that point.

It is also possible that a more abstract but still useful discussion might take place that focuses on something that is very important to Samantha, something with the same weight that Everett's work has for him. With the acknowledgment of such, they are applying the "standard of equity," a step in building positive momentum. Once it is established, they can try to get the most out of the moment. Instead of being annoyed with each other, Ev for Samantha's "unreasonableness," Samantha for Everett's "callousness" about her desires, they might fix on the moment, upon the process of living, rather than on the goal of "finding the glitch" in the system or "getting away."

Throughout courtship, there are themes that are constants, that are the very essence of the world of the couple: intimacy, exclusivity, commitment. We want those things. We want to share with one another. We want that sharing to be there tomorrow as well as today. We want that kind of relationship with just one other (although there are some of us who need to replicate that sense of intimacy again and again and again), but to give and to seek that intimacy and commitment is to put oneself at risk. It is terrifying. "What if . . . ?" What if she doesn't care as much, what if he cheats, what if she takes advantage of my showing my vulnerability, what if he is only using me, what if it's just for my body, my money, the sex? Endless fears, it seems, and not at all surprising given that we have opened ourselves to another in the most intimate ways, for love—or *is* it love? With luck and maturity and the passage of time, we discover the truths. Often they will be the right things for the right reasons, but there may have been in our courtships, the early moments of marriage, right things for wrong reasons.

I know he will complete me, for he has the hard edges and assurance that I do not have. I will be whole.

She has the motherly gentleness that I never knew as a child and that will make me a better and gentler man.

He is so organized, it will be good for me.

It is fine if our perceptions are accurate, but often they are not, for we see what we are looking for in the least likely places. Sometimes we unconsciously choose those partners whose behavior and responses will duplicate an old experience that is still unresolved. If we have not resolved the basic difficulties within a relationship, the decision to have children can be less than a happy one.

Molly and Seymour have been married after a long and tempestuous relationship. When they were not fighting over your place or mine, a movie versus a concert, Chinese food versus a cheap burger night, they were ecstatically in love. He was never quite sure if she cared enough, she was never quite sure that he meant it when he said "I don't care" when it came to choosing clothes or furniture, but they were really in love. The rules have been followed. They have been scrupulous in their looking at themselves and at each other, have communicated honestly but with empathic care. They split up for a trial period and decided they were happier together than apart. The wedding—neither as small as Seymour had originally proposed nor as large as Molly had initially suggested—was a perfect example of trading for the sake of the wishes of the other. Eleven months have passed, and lately there has been some peripheral discussion about a baby, but nothing too direct. Both of them are scared of the responsibility. They are both quite serious about being superb parents, which makes thinking about it pretty difficult. When you set your standards so high, are you riding for a fall? each of them wonders, but neither really talks about it. So they go out and get themselves a dalmatian named Brenda. Brenda is their trial baby.

Over several months, they work the bugs out in the care and feeding of Brenda. If it is raining or snowing or 4 degrees, Brenda still has to be walked twice a day. She has to be fed, has to get to the veterinarian for her shots, worming, and all the rest. She has to have some regular exercise, because she is an energetic dog. Despite the fact that neither member of the couple is a dog person, they have shared well. They have groused, fought, compromised, exchanged responsibilities when necessary, and each of them has the idea that the other gave more than 50 percent of the time to the venture, but they both agree that it has been a success. Now, they think, just maybe they might be able to cooperate as parents.

Typically, men can become ecstatic over the notion of a human being "in there," while simultaneously resenting the lack of participation for themselves, particularly if the woman becomes quiet and peaceful—and to him, smug—in her pregnancy. "The giver of life"—that phrase itself is a pregnant one that can make a man seem rather insignificant, and simply a facilitator. If the sense of who you are is insufficient, the coming of a child can overwhelm either a woman or a man who may not feel prepared for the responsibility. A wife's pregnancy may challenge a man because of his status as outsider, and exacerbate the insecurities of both parents-to-be. We can negotiate little here. We can only hope to know enough about ourselves as adults. Know thyself. Be realistic. Know what you want and expect for and from each other. There is little else to say, except to hope that we come to parenthood as good and functioning human beings who can provide in the necessary ways for a new person.

6

And Baby Makes Three: Birth to Two Years

The arrival of a child is an extraordinary event. Together a couple will have experienced love, its consummation, and then the remarkable growth of microscopic matter over nine months into a real person. What could be more natural yet amazing? The new human being is named, doted over, looked at for familial traits and characteristics, shared, dreamed over. It is rightfully a time of hope. Two people have shared this wondrous thing, and now there are three. Three. A funny number. Three's a crowd. A two-seater. "We used to be able to . . ." Like it or not, and no matter how mature we are and how in love with our children, there are moments when there just seems to be one person too many. But just like family fighting, that feeling is normal.

"Katrina. I can't find that layout I did for the bookstore. Have you seen it?"

Somewhat distracted, a response: "Unnnhh-unnhh."

"What are you mumbling about, for godsake? What did you say? Can't you talk anymore?" There is a hint of jocularity here, but only a hint.

"No, no, Leo, I haven't seen it. Did you look under the—" Katrina doesn't get to finish as Leo loudly exclaims, "Dammit, I can't find anything around this place anymore!"

Leo and Katrina live in a city where space is at a premium. They have a Pullman flat, front to back, probably once upon a time somebody's third-floor bedroom and dressing room; but those days are gone forever. Now it is the entire kingdom of three people. Eleven months ago, one of these people was not there.

Leo works at home a couple of days a week so that he can share in the care and feeding of Leo, Jr., while Katrina puts in two days at the job she left four months ago to prepare for Leo, Jr.'s birth. Leo likes the arrangement, and the baby is a pretty good sleeper, which makes it easier. Since Leo is out of his office two days a week, he has to make up a fair amount of the work at night at home. Graphic designers like Leo often take on freelance work both for the money and the challenge of something outside the usual daily agency stuff, so taking work home is nothing extraordinary. The problem is, now that Leo, Jr., is on the scene, Leo's work space has been cut down by two-thirds.

Katrina doesn't touch Leo's work, and Leo knows that. But if Leo's work is not immediately visible, which is often the case now, since he has to work in a smaller space and winds up moving it several times before it is finished, he inferentially goes after her. Katrina has told him that he's really getting difficult and "bitchy." Leo denies it and just turns it back on his wife, saying, "I certainly am not hiding my work on myself!"

The fact is that there is competition between Leo, Jr., two months and four days, and Leo, Sr., thirty-one and a little large for the limited physical resources in the old brownstone, third-floor walkup. Leo loves his son and namesake and he loves his wife, but he is having a hard time adjusting to the new physical circumstances. He would rather pick on someone his own size, so instead of making mean faces at Junior, he throws barbs at Katrina, who, thank goodness, can talk back, thus making his grousing worthwhile.

Solving the broad physical aspect of this problem may not be easy, or even possible. This may be a case of the pie not being expandable because of income levels, job locations, housing stock, any number of factors. Katrina's recognition of the problem being rooted in a new limitation placed on physical resources would be a positive first step in bringing things back onto some rational plane. She might argue that the loss of space is more than made up by this new desirable somebody, the baby. But if this is not a shared view, the practical problem still exists. Discussing alternatives to work space and work storage rather than escalating the tension by snappishly responding to her husband's equally snappish comments would be productive. The discussion of increasing options is essential. Maybe Leo needs some help in getting organized. He could do it for himself, or what seems more likely in this instance, he could be helped by Katrina. They could choose a space for his work to be stored so that when he needed to return to it, he would always know where it was. That would eliminate the necessity for endless discussions of the number of square feet in the apartment. It is also possible that work *is* getting lost, that Katrina's innocence is masked passive aggressive behavior obscuring her anger at Leo's lack of involvement with the baby.

If the conflict continues, Katrina and Leo should also take time to discuss the problem as equals in a marriage. They should define their feelings about the apartment and the allocation of space, and how the baby has affected their lives both practically and psychologically. In the process, they may discover some important things, like Katrina's resentment of Leo's apparent noncaring and Leo's slow and mulish adjustment to having to share with and care for another, subtexts of their conflict.

Rationalizing the argument around the purely physical aspects on the surface of this fight is an important step. It is practical, nonthreatening, and will take the fire out of the fight. The second step involves getting at the feelings underlying the conflict and could be more volatile in the long run. The conflict may be one of those that will disappear with the passage of relatively little time. It is not uncommon for men to show resentment of a newborn who has "stolen the light" from a husband who until the pregnancy had been the center of a wife's life. Chances are that Leo will recognize his immature response and back away from it. Leaving room for face-saving in this instance is important. However, if there are not strong signs that this is happening, a deeper discussion focusing on the subtext is definitely called for. If the conflict persists, some professional advice should be sought.

"You coming to bed now?"

"In a while. Just go ahead, I'll be along." A minute passes.

"What are you doing."

"Just watching him sleep."

"For goodness' sake, I know the kid is wonderful, but it's late. And you'll have to be in the field at five if you expect to get that hay in before tomorrow's rain. Supposed to come in about four, I think."

"Yup."

"Did you check on the calfing?"

"Yup."

"Have you called the vet for the horse? I'd think he'd have been here by now. Did you forget that, too?"

Silence.

"George? *George?*"

Marie cannot hear George because his son's crib is down the hall two rooms from theirs, but if she were very close, she would hear an annoyed snorting sound as George teases the insides of his cheeks with his teeth.

George and Maria have a dark-haired son of nearly two, who shares their large Iowa farmhouse that has been in George's family for three generations. George is real happy about this son because for a while it looked as if there wouldn't be any kids, but then along came this miracle. Marie was a very pleased mother when carrying and nursing their baby, and she is still pleased as can be. During the day, she talks to her son constantly, telling him stories and showing him things and singing to him. He's a great and animated companion, staying awake most of the afternoon now, never seeming to need a nap anymore.

When George comes in from the barns, though, Marie is ready for some adult attention. And when the baby is down for the night, she really would like some of George's very fine romancing, but these days George is transfixed by this growing boy who has that signature dark mop of hair and who appears to be almost a miniature George. Nearly every night ends like this, it seems, with George in the baby's room dreaming and looking at his son, Marie calling for him, George not coming, Marie bringing up a list of "must do's," George biting his lips. It's like a little war, one that usually ends with Marie's surrender to sleep when she would much prefer surrendering to George's passions.

Once more we see competition for limited resources, this time for *time*. The list that Marie brings up is not the subtext but the text of the "fight." George does not rise to the bait in a verbal way, but he does get annoyed. The short-term problem is simply annoying, but the long-term effects could be more significant, with Marie thinking that she is just being treated like a cash cow, resenting the child for alienating her husband's affections; or with George deciding that Marie is a nag and putting his energies into something else besides their relationship. Marie wants some of that old romantic George who helped produce that son they both love. George is filling himself up simply breathing in the air around his son's crib, adoring him with his eyes. After the years of waiting and a long day on the family farm, he takes great satisfaction from that experience, but he is being shortsighted.

Here is a situation where improved communication would definitely be useful. If Marie were to declare straight out that George is a wonderful lover as well as husband and farmer and father, and that she misses him in that way, she would be speaking to his pride and ego, clearly two things spoken to by his son. She needs to know that she is fulfilling another's needs, that her motherhood has not made her less desirable, that she is attractive and not just "Mommy." George will probably be flattered and respond appropriately. A specific time for the parents to be alone together might be worked out, providing a context for renewal of positive momentum, a time for something special and pleasurable so that an essential part of the relationship does not fall into disuse.

Negotiation is *not* a factor here. Marie does not simply want to have George make love to her but wants his attention, which has been diverted. She wants to be appreciated as a woman and as an attractive one, stretch marks and all. She wants George to really *care* again.

* * *

There are any number of ways that competition for resources can lead to fights, but there are other areas of competition that too can start skirmishes, breed resentments, and start a couple acting out in ways that can become habitual.

"Leave the baby alone, don't you see he is cranky?" she says just minutes after her husband comes in after a business trip. "He's been beside himself all day. My head is ringing from his crying." And just then, baby stops crying. Wife turns from her task to see father and son cooing contentedly into each other's faces. If her husband didn't look so pleased, she would really like to go over there and smack him one! Instead, she says, "What are you doing, you haven't even washed your hands. Put that baby down and get upstairs and . . . " Husband's incredulous look stops her from going on, and she sees the foolishness of her jealousy, but sometimes she just gets furious.

Or another situation with a different couple. The baby is an all-day screamer. The husband returns from work, lifts up the child, who almost immediately calms down and coos, while the mother, who has comforted and cleaned and loved and sung all day, stands looking on. "I don't know what it is," he says, "certainly not my charm. I just think it's a matter of how much contact there is, you know. Maybe he's just not getting enough, dear," the last spoken in a tone of voice reserved by the Latin instructor for the perenially late and somewhat slow scholarship boy at a pricey school.

Both of these situations come under the "Whose Baby Is This, Anyway?" heading. In situation one, the mother is up to her ears all day with a colicky child. No matter what she does, the baby cries. She adores the child, feeds and changes it with reverence, talks to it, cuddles it, lets it sleep when it wants (not very often, alas), and for all her efforts is rewarded with cries from sunup to sundown. When Daddy comes on the scene, and for no discernible reason, baby quiets down. In this instance, the mother finds herself annoyed by the unfairness of it, sometimes sufficiently annoyed to interfere in the indirect manner she did here—sending her husband away in retaliation. But then she catches herself and tries to smile.

Yet Mom is definitely jealous of the child's responsiveness to the father.

In the second situation, the husband becomes the aggressor, indirectly attacking his wife as incompetent. He's getting his innings in, claiming the turf called Timothy. He goes off to the office all day, and Mom gets to have Timothy's company all day, and "I'd be as good a mother as anybody," rolls around in his head somewhere. Mom must really be annoyed here, given that she tries so hard, only to be made to feel somehow inadequate, wanting, less fully a woman.

These little skirmishes are fairly common, and people can move beyond them quickly. It's normal to be jealous. A father who sees a child so seldom may lash out, resenting that he's being denied one of life's great pleasures. A mother who is exhausted after tending to her child's needs and tears is understandably frustrated and annoyed at the serendipity of a child's amiable coos when absent Daddy returns. Self-esteem is threatened. The last thing a mother needs is her husband's second-guessing. There is danger here, for issues like this can polarize people over the issue of "ownership" of the baby. It can make a child feel like a piece of property on a Monopoly board; it can also lead to resentment of the child on the part of the parent who feels denied or less than fully competent.

Sometimes there are colicky babies, sometimes a child will respond favorably to a voice or a smell of someone rather than the full-time caretaker, sometimes one parent is home with a baby all day and has the enviable experience of watching its seeming minute-by-minute growth—and that's just the way it is! These facts do not give us a license to be cruel, to attack another, to act out our jealousies. Over the years, there will be plenty of opportunities for each to feel temporarily jealous and excluded. With a growing child, there is reassurance in this: At different stages in his or her young life, the parents will alternate roles. In infancy, a mother is almost inevitably the primary caregiver, given the limitations of nursing and the extreme attachment a new mother feels. But as a child grows, this world will, if the mother allows it, more flexibly include the father. Furthermore, there are certain periods in your child's life (which most of us know about, thanks to Freud) where either the mother or father will find it easier to communicate with son or daughter.

Parents find that there are different ages in their child's life that they enjoy more. One may be a baby person, while the spouse may not be. What's important here is to take advantage of one's spouse's strengths, be thankful for them, and know also that no matter what happens, in a few weeks the young child will be completely different—and this may be a stage you'll feel more comfortable with.

"If you do that, Julia, he'll be up all night. Here, give him to me. There now, see, he's taking the bottle fine and he'll be down for the night. Believe me, I know. You may remember dear, I raised you and you turned out all right, didn't you?"

"Let her cry, Harry. No child ever died from crying. She'll stop when she wants to. It may break your heart to hear it, but believe me, I know, you turned out . . ."

"Well, John, my mother said that it's the only reasonable way to treat him. Otherwise we'll be faced with a spoiled brat, she says."

"I don't give a damn what your father said, Jessica, he's our kid, and if we want to bring him into bed with us so that we can get a few winks, then that's what we'll do!"

"There, now, he'll love this _____ (fill in the blank)."

"But, Dad, I . . ."

"Yep, he'll love this and . . ."

"But, Daddy . . ."

This is the other important part of "Whose baby is this, anyhow?" and it is called the parents and in-laws part. While relatively few of us live in the extended families of the past where Mom and Dad were always there at our sides as we raised our children, we still have parents, and aunts, and uncles, to deal with on a sometimes basis. And of course they have had children who are now fully grown and who should be grateful for the sage advice of experienced parents. We turned out all right, didn't we? Well, let's not address that question here, but rather turn to the more practical one of what to do about the grandparents and other family members who decide that the baby is theirs.

First of all, they are wrong. The baby is not theirs but their babies' baby. Second of all, the couple who begat this child are the people who are going to be responsible for it for now and forever, amen. It is wonderful to have the advice of those who have "been the route," as it can be wonderful for children to grow up with engaged grandparents and other relatives who have the child's welfare in mind. The intergenerational connections are enriching if they are good connections, but we must take the responsibility upon ourselves for our children's care. This does not exclude the judicious consideration of advice from others, so there is plenty of room for grandparents and others in the family to share their knowledge. Once again, awareness of the kinds of problems that can arise is essential.

Having a child can be nearly overwhelming in both the physical and psychological sense, sometimes sufficiently so as to cause one to lean heavily on the advice of a parent. If a husband is tentative about his wife's grasp of motherhood, and uncertain of his own role as father, he may rely too heavily on his or his wife's parents for advice. For a woman who is herself tentative about her role as a parent, she may be relieved to have the weight of parental responsibility lifted, abrogating her role to parents or in-laws. The kind of passive parenting that is bred in such a situation will only later be resented when one has regained strength, learned from other parents in one's circle, etc., and will likely lead to intergenerational strife. Setting limits for parents is essential to short-circuit later conflict. Just as with children and with ourselves as part of a couple, we must delineate the roles in an adult and responsible manner without needlessly ruffling feathers. If feather-ruffling is a necessary by-product, however, it is better to rustle them than to deal with our children in ways we think inappropriate merely to avoid conflict with our parents.

Where only half of a couple is heavily dependent on parental advice and then tries to enforce that "outsider" point of view, there is obviously great potential for conflict. This extraordinary time in the life of a new family is a time for listening, for talking about the issues as they arise by deciding methods of dealing with the dozens of new problems—sleep scheduling, feeding and cleaning chores, how to deal with crying, whether or not to take the baby into our bed—that come with the bassinette. It is not easy, given the prevalence of two working parents, to schedule our lives, but it is far easier to do it without what either or both of the new parents see as "outside interference" than with such complicating help. While the text might be "The baby mustn't come into the bed with us at night," the subtext for the other partner might well be, "There's his damned mother again! It's *my* baby!"

The voices are conversational and the sounds civil, but the words are something else.

"Okay, Jimbo, I've had it up to here with you. You are going to have to start pulling an oar or this little ship is going to sink or . . . or else."

"What are you talking about, Nora? I damned well do my share. This case I'm preparing may distract me a little, but I don't see where there's any more that I could do. I mean, Mrs. Beach comes in to take care of Lucia every morning. I set that up, if you recall. The cleaning service comes in every other Wednesday; hell, I don't get it."

"That's the problem, Jim, you don't get it. I want a little more cooperation, a little dishwashing, a little cooking, a little sharing, dammit. I can not work full time and be expected by some chauvinist lout to be the stout Victorian housewife/mother. I am not going to do it. You are going to learn, believe me, you're going to learn."

"I do the lawn and I don't complain. I also do the bills."

"The lawn! It's miniscule, and that's probably eight times in the five or six months of the season. Oh, you are going to learn, starting tonight, because I am going to cook just enough for me from now on. Welcome to the world of nouvelle cuisine." And with that, she smiles satisfyingly at Lucia, who lies there in Nora's lap, her eyes having just opened after a little nap.

"You're being silly and I have reading to do. See you in bed."

* * *

Jim and Nora are both lawyers. Jim is in litigation and likes the opportunity to perform in the courtroom as much as he does the trial preparation. Nora is in the somewhat less glamorous practice of real-estate law. They love their work. Both want to do well in their professions, hope to make partner within the next three years in their respective medium-sized firms, and in their dotage be both financially secure and proud of their accomplishments.

They really wanted a baby and were happy when Lucia came along. They felt from the beginning that they could handle careers and a family without the child or children being shortchanged. They have been lucky in the baby, for she has been a self-regulator, needing just one midnight feeding and then sleeping through to just before Mrs. Beach's arrival. As far as Jim is concerned, everything has been going pretty well, until recently. Nora has really become a pain, a nitpicker, he thinks, bitching about his not doing enough. Sure, there is a lot to do when there is a child, but she has to understand that he has to take a lot of time preparing for court and, well, his dad never . . . Nora, on the other hand, is quite grooved in to both the parent and lawyer aspects of her life. Both these aspects have their problems, but both are wonderfully satisfying. The problem is that she's exhausted by three in the afternoon. Her work involves a lot of detail, which in turn requires a lot of care. A $3-million real-estate deal should be perfect in its form. You don't get to be a partner with sloppy paper work. Thinking about her new irritation with Jim, she connects it with her exhaustion and realizes that she is doing all the work at home. She gets some emotional support from Jim, but no significant sharing of household responsibilities. No wonder I'm tired, she thinks.

Sharing is a very big issue in the life of a family. When a couple works and has a child, sharing is of enormous importance. Without it, a relationship becomes lopsided, exploitive. Agreeing to do more for specific reasons and specific periods of time can make sense, but the one who wakes up one morning to discover that 85 percent of the household work has been done by her or him can become enraged. It is not a matter of precise mathematical equity, but it is a matter of what is fair and equitable in the broader sense.

Nora seems to be doing the right thing here, letting Jim know how she feels, telling him that he has to share, demonstrating to him, by not cooking his dinner, that there is no free lunch—or dinner. Furthermore, if he wants to eat, he's going to have to cook. If he wants clean clothes, he's going to have to take his to the cleaner. If he wants a clean house between every other Wednesday, he's going to have to learn vacuums and mops, the whole string. The object lesson just might work. On the other hand, it may only baffle the otherwise agreeable and sensible Jim. "My dad never . . ." may have been a significant clue to his behavior. He had no model for that kind of cooperation in a household, and for who knows what reason, his mother didn't seem to mind or act out some deep resentment in any way. So for Jim, this is normal!

Given the nature of their work and their mentalities, it would be very useful for Nora and Jim to draw up a list of grievances toward a collaboration/negotiation session. In those terms, the lawyer couple might be able to approach it relatively dispassionately and bring about a reasonable result that will go beyond the threat, that will not bring resentment "because I am no longer being taken care of." This puts more of the onus on Nora, it seems; alas, this is often the case. But one person does have to give, to find a way to save face for the other, get some real dialogue going. Without it, there is the danger of Nora's own resentment becoming so deeply rooted that there might be less probability of turning back from the brink of continuing conflict. So, too, there must be some acknowledgment of what each is giving to the marriage. Even if with slightly gritted teeth, Nora could acknowledge that Jim is not without his pluses, that he does contribute to the house by his grounds work, and with that said, and Jim feeling less defensive, perhaps the basis for negotiation would be somewhat firmer. Anything that takes the other partner off the defensive is useful. Communicating along these lines can be nothing if not felicitous in getting freer and more open communication going and getting the collaboration/negotiation under way.

If Nora has phrased it right, Jim will respond by coming up with constructive solutions of his own.

* * *

"Patrick, dammit, you're never around when I need you, you know that? Donald is an incredible handful, and I just can't keep up with him, he's just too much for one person, and, dammit, I'm not going to do it anymore on my own. You're just going to have to find more time to be here, that's all there is to it!"

"What the heck are you talking about? You're lucky to be at home with him. Most women we know are working at least part time, and you've got this luxury of watching him grow. I'd give my eyeteeth for that. You know I have to get this business off the ground and have to put the hours in. Come on, Mary . . ."

"You go to hell, you selfish rat!"

This would seem an unusual outburst to people who have known Mary over the last thirty-six years. Usually, she is pretty mild and easygoing. When she gets down she gets quiet, maybe a little depressed, you might observe, but raising her voice and aggressive behavior—this is not the Mary most of her friends know.

She was the oldest of six pretty closely spaced children, and as a result of her seniority she got to be assistant mother. Her authoritarian mother was a bit of a cold breeze, and had little nurturance to give to Mary. Dad, on the other hand, was a warm man, and Mary was his favorite, a "Daddy's girl." Patrick had been his mom's favorite in a family of three kids, so when Mary and Patrick married, they transferred to each other the warmth they had for their respective favorite parents. Mary was subject to a little mild depression from time to time as a young adult, but with Patrick's warmth, and their long evenings of talk, sharing the day's experiences with each other, she was supremely satisfied and happy.

Seven years into the marriage a son was born to them, just at a time when Patrick was starting up his own business and thus had little time to share with Mary. When he was home for any extended period of time, mostly on shortened weekends, he spent a lot of time playing with their child. Mary was infuriated. All of the old resentment connected with caring for her sisters and brothers was brought to the surface. She didn't really want to nurture, but wanted to be nurtured the way Daddy had nurtured her, the way Patrick has nurtured her before this baby came, before this business started. Mary felt herself as the odd person out in a threesome.

The text here is clear: This kid is driving me nuts and I need your help, because I can't go it alone.

The subtext is that, not having had a nurturing mother, Mary doesn't feel strong enough as a nurturer without Patrick's nurturance of her. The old feelings of being trapped in a family as caretaker of children comes back, and she panics, yells, attacks, threatens a seven-year-old marriage.

While Mary's problem may be such that she would probably benefit from some therapy, there are certainly steps that she could take to begin an honest dialogue. Mary could talk about her feelings, rather than about her position vis-à-vis child rearing "on her own." If she could do that, she might remove the "either/or" argument that seems to be at the center of her text. Chances are that Mary doesn't understand that this situation reminds her of her youth, and such a discussion might lead to increased self-knowledge. Patrick might find a way to put aside an extra half hour every day so that he and Mary could have some private talking time as in the past, time that so gratified both of them. By listening to Mary, he may learn how needy she is. He should go out of his way to reassure her on a daily basis—especially in times like this, when there is so little time.

Patrick might examine his own behavior and see that, yes, he is spending a disproportionate amount of time adoring their offspring, some of which might be spent nurturing the good relationship that the couple had before their son's birth.

In general, the father's understanding of and support of the mother's needs for nurturing is a vital part of the loop that goes from father to mother to child to father to mother to . . . It is a tremendous responsibility raising a child, and despite the two-job couple, the main chore tends still to fall to the woman. If the woman feels supported and nurtured, she will find it easier to support and nurture. A child well nurtured gives back a good deal of nonverbal satisfaction, which feeds the father to feed the mother to feed the child, and so on.

* * *

"Louis doesn't even know that Ben exists, sometimes, I think. Some father!" So speaketh JoAnn, Louis's wife of seven years and mother of nearly nine-month-old Ben. Until two months ago, they were having some pretty strong disagreements. Because of her own experience with a cold parent, JoAnn was not about to subject Ben to an iceberg father. "This can't go on, Louis," she warned.

Unfortunately, Louis's disinterest spilled over into more practical areas of their life together, as well. While not a traditionalist, per se, he behaved like one during this period, and JoAnn was forced to take nearly all of the weight of changing, feeding, cleaning, responding to cries—all of the normal jobs that come with an infant.

All during the pregnancy, Louis had been pretty excited about the coming child. He would listen to the organic sounds, ear pressed to JoAnn's belly, would chuckle and smile and generally have a good time of it. He was also very thoughtful, almost treating JoAnn in that stereotypical manner of the father-to-be in movies of the forties and fifties. When Ben appeared, it was a dramatic moment. Louis cried over his son's cradle the first night Ben was home. But after a couple of days, Louis seemed to lose interest. Nine months and four days seemed to be about the time limit on his ardor for offspring. For the next nine months, his interest was relayed by small smiles of semi-approval, "uh-huh's" to JoAnn's daily recitation of the super achiever's achievements. He would look at the baby with interest, cuddle him a bit from time to time, but it seemed as if he had lost real interest in Ben. It infuriated and troubled JoAnn. Then Ben started holding his head up like a real person, and the light came on in Louis's eyes.

He bought a baby back carrier, and at six-thirty in the morning Ben and Louis could be seen walking the streets of the city together, the little warm papoose on the daddy's back, no wobbly head, little sounds of discovery, a little wetting of the parka from time to time, and a real sense of communication with his son on Louis's part. The problem had disappeared. But for every action there is a reaction.

Mom was pleased, but . . . Now was the realization that she was no longer the sole caretaker, that, indeed,

there was somebody else very connected to Ben and that
the exclusiveness of their relationship had ended. She felt
a sense of some loss and sometimes overfussed about
these early morning sorties. "I don't think he's warm
enough, Louis. He looks awfully tired this morning. He's
going to get an awful cold." These were the kinds of
roadblocks, or at least hesitations, that JoAnn put forth.
But she was a realist. The game of solo was over. She
knew, too, that she couldn't have it both ways: an involved and helping husband/father and Ben all to her self.

The text is that of the dad who sees a kid as a novelty,
like this year's batch of TV shows. The other, and
minor, text is that of the mother who worries about the
child's well-being *ad nauseum*, but that was so short-
lived, it was not a major issue.

The subtext is that Louis didn't think he had anything
to give to Ben until Ben had some kind of independent
relationship with the world around him. He felt he could
not nurture while JoAnn did nothing *but* nurture. He felt
shut out until that moment of the possibility for exploration with that erect neck and more animated responses
to the world were possible. Now is my turn, he thought.
He also started doing his share of the work around the
house without prompting.

Louis and JoAnn had not had serious fights over Louis's
behavior, but if Louis's lack of interest in Ben had continued, or if JoAnn were more hotheaded, or if Louis
hadn't found a way to give to his son, it could have become a very serious problem between them. As it turned
out, Louis found his niche before JoAnn lost her patience.

What could the partners in this marriage have done to
clear the air? JoAnn might have directly confronted Louis
with her concerns about his detachment both from the
baby and the daily grind of caring for him. Louis might
have talked about how he felt, detached, a bystander
watching a baby grow and have all of its needs taken care
of by his mommy. Instead, he kept his feelings to himself. Trite as it may sound, what were called for were
improved communications and a discussion of feelings.
JoAnn might have negotiated a division of responsibilities with Louis, which would have as least addressed the
practical issues and might have made Louis feel involved

enough to then participate in the baby's nurturing. Either one could have tried to identify with the other: Louis realizing that JoAnn must be tired after carrying that baby for nine months, going through the birth experience, and now working full time at being a parent. JoAnn might have stood in Louis's shoes, considered how frequently fathers feel left out. There were several ways to approach this unhealthy situation. In this instance, not creating a major confrontation worked, as the father discovered his own place in the sun, but in many situations a more active approach would be appropriate.

Problems do arise, when parents question their own or their partner's ability to nurture. The primary caretaker of the child needs to feel competent, and that the competence is rewarded not only by a happy child (although if you draw a colicky crier, it might be a little hard to tell), but by an approving spouse, as well, and by that extended family of parents and in-laws. If the competence of a partner is in question, the manner in which the subject is broached is everything. If a discussion of such import takes place, it should be in the context of identifying with the other, and should be approached in the manner that will save the most face for the person whose abilities are being questioned. To do otherwise is to make a battleground of family life that not only threatens the couple, but the child as well.

"Eat, Melissa. That's a good girl, open. Open, Melissa. Melissa, open! Eat for Mommy, honey. Yums. Nice. Melissa. *Open*."

"Listen to Mommy, Meliss. Eat. Open your mouth for Mommy and—yech, that's disgusting! Can't you stop her from smearing that all over? Woops, grab that spoon before . . ."

"Now, Melissa, that's naughty; now open, honey. Open for Mommy, like choo-choo going into the tunnel, that's . . . oh, God, all over my shoes.'

"I'm going upstairs to get some work done, Alice. I can't stand this chaos.''

Alice sits very erect, very tense in her chair, a tight smile on her face, but tears are spilling. Melissa is dribbling pureed something or other in an interesting pattern on the dining-room floor, and seems to be having a good time.

Alice and Rob have been very happy with their marriage and with Melissa. Cuddling this baby has meant a lot to Alice. She had her all to herself, and the baby was very responsive to her. It made Alice feel whole in a way that she never had before, and Rob was pleased because Alice was always so "high" over their daughter. Then, at about six or seven months, Melissa started being more individual, more Melissa. She didn't always do what Mommy wanted her to do, particularly at mealtime. She started being messy, and as Alice said on one occasion, "Messy is no fun, Melissa, messy is yucky." But Melissa didn't seem to agree. She was really into those textures of pureed everything. Hey, you could draw with this stuff, too!

The very same things that Melissa apparently liked about playing with food, Alice did not. Something had gone wrong. Suddenly, this lovely little tractable and cooing baby was doing all these mischievous things that were not at all pleasant. Alice's sister's baby was a good baby and didn't make all these messes. This fact was not lost on Rob, who admired the tightly run ship that was his sister-in-law's house.

Alice became angry with Melissa for her eating habits, habits that sent Daddy running upstairs and made Mommy feel like a fool. "Messy baby, yuck" soon turned into "I don't know why she is so stubborn." Before long, Melissa was the stubborn child, Rob was the dad who didn't know what had gone wrong, didn't know why his wife couldn't get the baby to comply, and Alice was constantly nagging at the stubborn child. The marital relationship was tense, and this made Melissa nervous and whiny; she began waking up several times every night.

The text here is the stubborn baby who is driving Mommy and Daddy apart. The subtext is that Alice and Rob like a controlled environment, and a baby who is on the way to becoming an individual does not turn off and on by remote control the way a television set does. Alice is threatened by her baby growing up and not doing what

Alice wants her to do. Rob doesn't like the fuss or the mess and blames his wife.

Novels, movies, and poems address the "letting go" of adult children, but it has its roots right here in the dining room or kitchen. The increasing autonomy of a child is one of the major parental traumas. The baby-doll, playing-house part is ended. This child's dependence is slowly being eroded, and the loss of control over another being is presaged. If we are, as Alice is, a controlling person, the inability to will order is threatening; and in the case of a child who does not eat at command, the label of "stubborn" might be affixed.

Both of these parents have got to take a more than superficial look at their behavior. The more mature of the two will have to make the first move and face the fact that Melissa is becoming a separate human being. Instead of being threatened by the separation, they should look for the positive aspect of it, that they are privileged to be "present at the creation," as it were, of another human being. Both parents have enough rigidity (both for order, and she for direct control of her child's behavior, and a fear of separation) that they might seek some outside counsel. On the other hand, they simply might spend more time with other parents who can share kid stories, thus allowing Rob and Alice to compare their experience with others. Right now they are in a vacuum with Alice's perhaps overorganized and controlling sister as the worst possible measuring stick of reality in the world of kids.

It is also unfair that Alice has to take not only the flak from her husband but all the responsibility for the mess and the behavior. Alice would be well served to confront her husband with a fairer division of responsibilities. "I know both of us are upset by Melissa's messiness. It is a phase perhaps, or it may be that she needs variety, another voice, *your* voice and attention. It is fascinating to see how kids respond differently to different people. It might be really enriching for her, and for you." If she can get herself off the hook for *all* the responsibility for her daughter's life and behavior, which is how it seems here, she might feel less stressed, less guarded and defensive, less upset by messiness, and more of a *partner* in this family rather than the child raiser. It might give

Rob some insights into his own self, strengths, and weaknesses, and an appreciation of how damned hard it is to "control" another human being's behavior. At the very least, some tolerance would result.

It is unfair to expect a child to conform to our abstract notion of "child," of course, but it is also unavoidable for a time. Just as we idealize those with whom we are in love, at least for a time, so do we idealize our children. When they do not conform to our ideals, the disappointment is often with the children, when it should be with ourselves. From the first, we set ourselves up for the fall, for never was born the child who could measure up to the expectations his parents have for him.

Reaching out to each other, and to others with more experience, is necessary. Honest discussion of expectations, refusal to place blame, and exchanging roles might help, as well. Most important is to fulfill parental responsibility to that child, that messy Melissa who, with two good and loving and understanding parents, will have the opportunity to grow and become, not without fighting for it, as good and as happy and as useful a human being as she might be. And on that hopeful note, let us go on to the three-ring circus called toddlerdom.

7

Toddler and PreSchool

The growth of a child from the moment it takes those first tentative steps in its first walking shoes until it is exploring every inch of the world it can reach is nothing short of amazing. The happy amazement that so small a person can be so motivated to discover everything in just one afternoon can turn quickly into frustration, fear, and exhaustion. The saying "They sure are a handful" could not be more accurate, except to add that they are "a mindful," as well. When not in sight, the toddler is never far from mind.

The ordered, adult world of objects placed where they seem most aesthetically appropriate disappears for the duration. The world must now be child-proofed. The raku bowl may no longer be on the low table in the living room. The stairs are barred, those pleasing windows that go nearly to the floor become the stuff of nightmares, and the cookie/cracker/cereal trail now knows no bounds. Books appear mysteriously on the floor, the two lowest shelves of a bookcase now often bare.

Balanced against this "giving up" of things, and the exhaustion that overtakes us after a day in this growing child's presence, is the window we have on the child as it discovers its powers. To know that is to know the meaning of pure ebullience. Surely it is a time like no other in the life of the family.

The nature of conflict changes with the child's verbal

and ambulatory growth. Gone forever is the smiling, relatively compliant, portable, controllable infant, to be replaced by the "terrible twos," and "tumultuous threes," and "ferocious fours," and the "fractious fives," one following the other with lightning rapidity.

"It's not my fault that he fell!"

"Well, I couldn't very well have prevented it, since I was downstairs doing the laundry. Can't you at least keep your eye on him? I don't ask a lot, you know, but . . ."

During this, the baby is howling, the "egg" on his forehead rising, both tears and nose running at nearly equal rates, the unfairness and unexpectedness of such an event clear in his face. In five minutes, the baby will have forgotten this event. He will have had his face scrubbed up, which he will not like, his diaper changed, and his shoes retied. He will be making a beeline for the couch when he will trip on the rug, fall into its cushiness, and lie on the floor giggling like the two-and-a-half-year-old he is.

Mom and Dad, on the other hand, are tense. Mom thinks her husband is not sufficiently responsible, that the baby should not have fallen, that disaster may come if we are all not ever-vigilant. Dad feels bad that the baby had a fall, feels worse that he is called incompetent by his wife, and is more than a little angry at her for making him feel guilty for the inevitable falls of childhood. The child's physical activity should be a signal to rejoice, not to drive a wedge between parents, but underlying the feelings of both parents is the primitive fear that a child will be harmed. The text here is the responsibilities of adults toward the incautious and enthusiastic exploring toddler, and the subtext our deepest fears.

The subtext cannot be dealt with, for it is simply a given, but the text of who is in charge, who will take responsibility, how much sharing there will be, can be dealt with so as to create an equitable situation that should go some way toward preventing "blaming" for the inevitable accidents of childhood. Now is the time for Dad, in the case above, to tell his wife that he feels personally attacked and that he is just as sorry that the child fell and hurt himself as she is. But he should not attack her in retaliation. He should express his views of the inevitability of accidents and he should do what he can to negotiate agreement about the extent of vigilance that each can reasonably expect of the other. Perhaps in this instance there can be some new physical accommodations to the toddler: no more slickly waxed floors, no unanchored scatter rugs; maybe some shoe sole scratching to help keep this dynamo from tumbling so often in his headlong rush to discover everything before next Tuesday. Given that Mom just did the laundry, she may be feeling a little martyred. If so, this is the time for giving expression to that thought, and negotiating a reasonable sharing. It would be simple to propose ''me last time, you this time.'' This way there is more equity and more experience on the part of both people. In particular, and this applies to nonthreatening situations as well, Dad can *take* more responsibility, negotiating with his wife times that their child is in his care. This is more equitable, obviously, and as a result Mom should develop more confidence in her husband's abilities to deal with a lightning bolt of a child. Some parents, of course, do not want to have the relief that comes with such equity, but like it or not, it is both healthy and necessary to have to come to terms with the fact that no one parent is indispensable, and that others can care equally well for our children. Supermoms and Superdads suffer—often needlessly—and they torture their spouses. They also undercut the relationship that can and should be developing between the child and the other parent. If Mom feels that there is not enough equity and that she has to find a way to get Dad more involved, she might propose to Dad as he goes out for a walk that he take the child along. Since he is already going out, her suggestion cuts the cost to him and makes it more difficult for him to say no.

''I don't seem to be very important around here anymore.''

''Hmmm?''

''Well, that proves it, don't you think? I say I'm not important around here, and you don't even know what I'm talking about!''

''Be right there, Fran. Okay. What did you say?''

''You can go to hell, Larry. Right now.''

With that, Fran goes off to her study and tries to read a book she put down months ago, but the story doesn't interest her anymore. Chances are that no book would distract her. She's fuming.

Larry and Fran both have very satisfying jobs plus a daughter named Annette who is almost three. Annette is a very active and charming kid who talked early and is the apple of her parents' eyes. Larry loves to talk and gambol with Annette, and often does so while completely ignoring Fran. After having taught English all day, Larry says, he finds Annette's company wonderfully stimulating. So does Fran, but Larry really overdoes it, she thinks. Besides, Fran's job in a research lab is absolutely solitary. She may not say twenty words to another human being all day, child or adult, so she would like at least a little warm-up session in the evening so that her vocal chords don't atrophy.

A couple of things feed into Fran's notion that she is "being ignored" as well. For the first couple of years, Annette might have been a mushroom to Larry, but when she started to talk a lot and Larry discovered that she could be clever with words, at least three-and-a-half-years-old clever, he really took over. The fact that Fran is a scientist and he the literary man—and clearly his genes have dominated in the lovely Annette—sets up another antagonism. For Fran, it seems as if she had done the hard stuff and now Larry is going to reap the goodies. When Fran tries to take part in the evening revelries, Larry gets "snitty" and closes her out by one or another method. She has become the third for tea. Not only is she annoyed with her husband, but she is beginning to resent her daughter. Larry's nonrecognition of the problem caused by his selfish and, at this point, boorish, behavior is no help at all. These are not great conditions for any of the three in this triangle.

Fran needs to be straightforward in declaring her feelings to her husband. Not her positions, as in, "You get in here now, I want to talk with you, you lunkhead," or "You go to hell," but her feelings. She must explain that her needs as a functioning adult are not being met, that she likes Larry's company, but that this feeling of being locked out is making her jealous of her daughter, and that as a result she is concerned that she won't be an effective mother. Larry *has* to listen to her and make accommodations, because his taking over of his daughter's time for his pleasure is selfishly destructive. It is touching, too, of course, but not in context, and it is also selective, since he did not participate in the preverbal years.

An appropriate negotiation of the division of household and emotional resources should take place. This family needs balance, and that means everyone has to share equally.

In situations like this, one person often has to initiate the discussion, which doesn't seem fair. Often it is not, but the alternative is a continuing cycle of unhappiness for one member of the family; and since the family is a system, everyone ultimately suffers. Often, too, it is the woman who is called upon to bring some order and rationality to the process of making a family. While that may seem unliberated in the context of these "enlightened times," it is, in fact, the woman who has historically been the nurturing one, the one who raised families. The advent of the Pill, which allowed women to take greater control over their lives, and the relative sensitization of men, all of which have happened only within the last quarter of a century or so, cannot be seen as the antidote to centuries of history of the female as the major nurturing figure. It will change, of course, but it will take time. One day men will take a more substantial nurturing role in the life of the family.

While we need to let our hurt and vulnerable selves be seen, to show ourselves in all of our honest pain to those we love, it is sometimes hard. But for Annette and Fran and Larry, it is important for Fran to take the initiative toward negotiation.

"Larry," Fran might begin, "you really make me feel horrible. You don't pay any attention to me anymore in the way that you once did. You take over the baby when you come in, you ignore me, and we only happen to sleep in the same bed and eat at the same table. This is on my mind a lot. I need to talk about this with you or it's going to drive me nuts. I'm even getting to resent our baby, for crying out loud. That's unnatural! But it's happening. Larry, I want you to help me feel better about this and to get something going again between us." Clearly, Fran is angry, but the anger is controlled. Fran is also clever in bringing in Larry as someone she *needs* to talk to, and who can "really make a difference" by listening and helping. There is also a nascent threat in what she says, one that Larry would have to be even dumber than he sometimes is to miss. This kind of controlled blow-off can be useful in getting Larry's attention. (It's good to be angry and open about it, but it is wiser to *use* your anger to gain what you want.) Fran can use this moment to press for more *real* sharing. Perhaps there is room here for an exchange of favors, Fran insisting that she needs to get out and spend some time with friends on her own a couple of evenings a month. Larry might want a couple of nights off himself. If Larry has no wish to go out with friends, not unusual for men who do not keep intimate friends in the same way women do, another trade can be made. The result should be more immersion in Annette's ups and downs for Dad, and more variety and equity for Fran.

"How's your John doing, Beth; toilet-trained yet?" asks Evelyn. There's something in her tone that makes one suspect that she knows the answer, but . . .

"Well, it's an off-and-on thing, Evelyn. Some days, even several days in a row, he does real well, and then, I don't know why, he just forgets."

"Some of them are like that. My sister has a boy who was just like that. Thank goodness my Rachel, knock on wood, has been regular since the third month of training. But don't worry, John will come along. Some are just slower, that's all."

Brendan, Beth's husband, has been enduring a tedious discussion about the joys of military miniatures with Evelyn's husband, Timothy, but has been able to keep an ear attuned to what's going on at the other end of the room. He does not like to hear that his son is not winning the toilet training race.

The next weekend, Brendan takes John on a long walk, pointing out the changing fall leaves, and fallen crab apples, the moo-cows, etc. He meets Evelyn's husband and has a brief conversation with John perched on his shoulders. John *is* only three and a half, and the combination of the walking and the fresh air has tired him out. In the middle of his next sentence, Brendan hears a familiar sound of air expelled near his left ear, and nearly simultaneously feels a warm stream running down his neck and shoulders. John is a big boy, and the light "just-in-case" diaper is not quite up to the task. Brendan chuckles, and after a few awkward moments toddles off for home, wet, fuming, feeling not quite up to snuff.

When Brendan arrives home, he says something to the effect that "Beth's kid" really embarrassed him in front of "Field Marshal Tim," as he calls Evelyn's husband. After somewhat roughly handing John to Beth, he showers, changes clothes, and on entering the kitchen where Beth is making an apple pie to have with coffee later in the evening, Brendan begins to attack her mothering skills *and* her piecrust! This challenges Beth, who does not feel secure about her qualities as a mother. Later that evening, this will affect the way she talks to and behaves toward John, thus making John anxious, which will make his toilet training difficult, which will make Brendan act out, which will . . .

Talking and walking are certainly important developmental issues. Parents can be subtly or overtly competitive over the exact moment when a particular developmental task is achieved. Those parents who believe in an exact developmental time line, or who think that *earlier* is the same as *better* are setting themselves up for a disappointment. The swirl of conflict over developmental stages is never more obvious than when toilet training is involved. Perhaps it's that at this point a child seems to "take control," and control may be something we prize highly. Or perhaps there's a deeper reason that a parent may turn this anal stage into a crisis. Whichever, to allow toilet training (which is most likely based on neurological or muscular, not intellectual development) to become a point of conflict is absurd. Yet it often happens. So what are some of the ways we can deal with that conflict?

Brendan is upset and embarrassed by his son's apparent lag, and lets Beth know about it by questioning her mothering. Beth's response should not be, "Oh, goodness, what have I done wrong?" but "Let's look into this together." They could either read a child-development book together, talk with parents so far beyond the child-rearing stage they are objective, or ask their pediatrician's advice. In short, collaborate.

In this instance, Beth needs to know that her husband is feeling threatened by his son's "problem." His behavior should tell her that. She could attack him, saying that he is such a puffed-up and proud man that his son's toilet training (or whatever developmental "lag" might be involved) problem is his, because his mother told her that . . . Or she could avoid such an escalating response by quietly pointing out other children of the same or greater age—even gently pointing to herself or to him or a mutual friend—as a touchstone of "normalcy." She should not attack herself, either; getting herself out of the spotlight, taking the heat off herself by not making a quick and bickering or attacking or defensive response will do that, and thus allow her to take full measure of the "problem," which clearly has more than one face and which involves two or three people. By not attacking, you show that you can be trusted not to take advantage of the other's truculence. That attack would only lead to escalation.

The next step is to begin negotiating. "Brendan, that must have been awful. You must have felt kind of silly. Maybe you can help in training John. I think you could be very effective." This shows the empathic qualities of Beth and makes "the Problem" a shared one, not just one of "Beth's kid." Or she might point out the time spent in raising a child may be cutting into her cooking time and attention, so "maybe you can lend a hand, hon. I love that ratatouille that you make. . . ." The important thing is to generate some identification, some realization that this is not a war, this is not the boardroom, this is *life*, and to get through life with its structural and psychological complexities, people need to work together . . . or stand apart.

While "lags" in development can cause squabbles and self-questioning, developmental spurts bring with them a whole new set of challenges. We all feel ambivalent about our children's growth. Perhaps we discuss this with our spouses or best friends, but it's usually ignored. It is a nostalgic, perhaps "Garden of Eden" sense that the child's wondrous way of being in the world at a given moment will never be recaptured. It is natural that we will have these thoughts and just as natural that they should pass, as we help to prepare the growing child for the challenge of adulthood. But meanwhile . . .

"NO!" This is the hallmark of the forming person, what seems to be the knee-jerk oral response to almost anything at times, the signal that tells us that the child has discovered its own power to use words to control the world it inhabits. It is also the only two-letter word we know that causes such consternation on the part of parents, for until the moment of the no, the parents have had almost singular control in the world of words.

"Time to eat." "No." "Pick that up, dear." "No." "Mustn't touch." "No." "Give that to Daddy, dear." "NO." Not at all an exaggeration of what goes on in the time of the no.

"And she was so sweet. I don't know what went wrong."

"This kid's turning into a brat, you know that, Edith?"

"If you can't get him to behave, Philip, I'll . . ."

"Take that food *now*," he says, as he nearly pries the mouth open with a spoon while his highly individuated daughter sprays the room with essence of spinach.

People are saying and doing these things somewhere while you are reading this.

The "no" is a given and in moderation is a sign of health. It is a new word to a child and a word that tests the extent to which a child may be successful in controlling his world. Just as it would be unhealthy for a first-time bettor at a racetrack to win every race and to believe that he or she really could predict the outcome of so random an event as a race among horses, so, too, would it be unhealthy for a child to grow up thinking that each of his "no's" led to acquiescence or agreement. Limits must be set consistent with the situation at hand. At this point, it might be useful to specify what constitutes limit-setting, in general:

1. Be very clear and specific about expectations. (I want you to take some food/maintain some relative order/ not destroy the house entirely.)
2. Indicate the consequences of behavior. (If you break that, it will not be replaced. Throwing that vase will cause me to be angry and you to have a spanking. If that does not get done now, you will be sent to bed.)
3. No character assassination is allowed. (Do not say you are a wicked girl or boy. How did you turn out to be so cruel/stubborn/filthy, etc?)
4. Whenever possible, have agreements made with others in the family present, thus making the commitments on both sides public. (While some of this will not neatly apply wholesale to a youngest toddler, there is no reason not to begin to deal in this fair and rational way from the beginning. It surely beats screaming.)

Words will also sometimes be cruel, challenging the very reason for your being a parent, words such as, "I hate you!" "I wish you were Freddy's mother and his mother was mine!" "You are the meanest father, I wish you were . . ." Rarely are the words meant, but they can challenge a parent who is fatigued from a day spent trying best to feed, observe, love, help, protect a child and still maintain some semblance of order in other aspects of life. Those brief moments of a sense of time misspent are dark, and if the stress threshold has been breached, then it is no wonder that a parent might either lash out with an epithet later to be regretted, or fall quietly into a pit of uncertainty about vocation. It is only reasonable in light of the limit-setting above that one talk with a child, when it is clear that the child is old enough and receptive, about feelings being hurt.

"You're stupid and I don't like you and I wish you would just fall in a hole!" Thus speaketh Amanda to her best friend, Courtney.

Laurie, Amanda's mother, is in the next room with her best friend, Courtney's mother. "Give it to me, give it to me, you stupid—." Before another word can be uttered, Laurie enters the room, and Amanda, who has used these words before, buttons up rather quickly, but is still tugging at her Paddington Bear, which Courtney has appropriated at this possessive moment in the lives of the two four-year-old girls.

Laurie is rested, not having worked at the hospital on the weekend and having had Monday off, as well, so she uses her softest voice and tells Amanda that she really mustn't say those kinds of things to people. "You can make people very sad with words like that. It really isn't nice to call people names like that. You don't like to be called stupid. I never call you stupid. Sometimes we all do things that we shouldn't, but that doesn't make us stupid. Maybe you can share Paddington with Courtney, huh, do you think so? No. Well, fine, that's your decision, but don't call other people hurtful names, all right?" Then, turning to Courtney, Laurie says, "Amanda isn't in a very good sharing mood today, Courtney, but she still loves you, I'm sure. She always says that you are her best friend. But just now I think it is best if you let Amanda have her Paddington. There are other toys and there are other days for Paddington." Laurie returns to her friend, and the children to play.

A situation like this could play out quite differently, however, if the circumstances were different. Laurie could have demanded that Amanda share; there could have been crying and hollering and perhaps, for whatever reason (maybe simply "not a good sharing mood, today,") a refusal on Amanda's part to cooperate at all. There might have been a spanking, a torn bear, harsh words spoken to Courtney for "causing the problem"; and just possibly some harsh words between the two adults over "the problem." But one person took control in a responsible way, attempted to explain the inexplicable (who knows why children act out in a given way on a given day?), and made everybody feel at least a little bit better about a situation that could have been noisy, disappointing, angry-making. Laurie's action resulted in a DEAD END sign being posted; this behavior is going nowhere, was the ultimate message. Insisting on Amanda's compliance would have exacerbated things, and Laurie took intelligent action. She did nothing to encourage selfish behavior in her child, while giving room to her daughter and her daughter's friend to save face. Everybody is out of the spotlight and the situation defused.

* * *

"Dad. Dad. Dad.DadDadDadDad."

"Yes, Chuck?"

"Dad, I want a drink of water, please."

"Chuck, Mom gave you one a minute ago, and I'm busy doing some work right now, so why don't you just roll over and go to sleep, okay, pal?"

"But I'm really thirsty. Thirsty as anything, Dad."

"In a minute, pal, Okay?"

"Thanks."

Seven seconds pass.

"Dad. Dad. Daddy."

"In one more minute, I'm going to come in and . . ."

"Oh, George, come on, give him a break, he only wants . . ."

"I know what he wants. Can't he understand that . . ."

"Dad!"

"Okay, buster, now you have had it, stop being such a baby and a staller. Now take this and go to sleep and don't let us hear from you again!"

The last is rather to the point, because that is one of the hidden fears surrounding darkness, sleep, being alone: that you will never be heard from again.

A familiar ritual, this of the water. It is in the same lineage as "Just one more page, Mom, please," "I think there's something weird outside my window," and "I can't sleep with the light out." Another source of family fights.

We often respond to the "come and do something for me" pleas with annoyance at being disturbed. After all, we have done our day's work, our evening's work, and are relaxing a little or getting a leg up on tomorrow's work when the plaintive voice from the bedroom makes demands that we don't want to know about. Requests like "Leave the light on, please," or "Don't close the door, no, don't, I'll scream," are sometimes met with anger rather than annoyance. They don't discomfort us in the physical sense (like the others) but they do touch us some place where we don't want to be touched: wherever it is that we keep our fears.

For a child, going to bed can sometimes be scary. The scared that kids feel is the same scared that we felt when we were their age, and that is what gets to us: We remember our fear, we are embarrassed by it, and we try to deny it by asking our children to deny it in themselves. Sometimes our response makes a child feel even more scared, less protected, less cared for, particularly if parents or another child in the family attack the fear as "sissy" or stupid. Trying to get a child not to be fearful in exchange for not being spanked, for instance, is hardly a negotiated trade-off; yet it has been a tool in family arsenals for generations. We need to identify with that child through that child in us, and to remember the world as it was when we were four or five: large, complicated, sometimes strange. And remember lying in this place in absolute darkness, imagination alive, sounds of life around us, building creaks, listening so hard we can hear our blood pulsing—another sound added to the others that we cannot quite identify. If philosophers argue the question of whether or not a tree has fallen if there is no human witness to the event, why can a child not be allowed its skepticism at being enveloped in the darkness of the night and the closing of its eyes?

As annoying and unreasonable as we may find such demands, we must emphathize, for the world is a complicated place. When you are a young child, there is so much that is unknown, it is reasonable to be scared. Beyond empathy there should be agreement between parents as to how such nighttime "ruses" or real fears will be handled. We must be careful not to use the "good cop, bad cop" routine, where one parent is the conciliator and the other the heavy; nor should we use the conflict over "giving in" or "talking it over" as ways for Mom and Dad to work out their own little fights over authority. Either of these methods of dealing are at the expense of the child's concerns and the need for a stable environment where the adults are reasonably consistent. Instead, the calming influence of a parent's touch or voice should be used when a child is frightened. If there is more than one child in the family, but only one shows the inclination to stall or be fearful, we should look at how we distribute our time, attention, and praise among the kids. We might discover that there is some inequity here and that the "noisy wheel" is getting too little grease.

Sometimes there are strong, and to us, inexplicable, fears in childhood, fears and night terrors that we can do nothing to lessen. When they appear, it is reasonable to explore them with pediatricians and other professionals whose experience and insights may be useful in determining their cause and their mitigation. There is no clear-cut answer in some cases; they just happen, and then one day they stop. But whatever the case, we must use our kindness, our sympathies, and our memories of childhood, not our fears of our fears. With this and some good sense, we can keep a balance between the privacy and leisure we need to function and our children's growth.

We can also do some negotiating in this area, with some problematic behavior responding to quid pro quos. After the dentist warned Charlie's parents of incipient mouth problems that might result from his pacifier, Charlie was weaned through a reward system. For every day he went without it, he would get a star on the week's calendar, and for every seven stars in a ten-day period there would be a small but desirable reward. And when three weeks of stars appeared back to back, there would be something that was truly coveted by Charlie. Over four months, it worked out. He got his most-wanted toy and his mouth shape was saved. A rational discussion with Charlie probably would have been useless, and threats and anger would have likely fed into whatever insecurity underlay the behavior in the first instance. Instead, Charlie was able to feel more in control of himself through the discipline required to get the reward that was clearly of more significance than the old habit. Everybody got something out of this negotiation, which is exactly what we should hope for in the best-case scenarios.

Some parents balk at this kind of trading to modify behavior. It is "buying" a result, they feel, and it is not satisfying. Yet we do it all the time in our own lives. Companies give bonuses for sales increases, department stores give discounts for purchasing at specific times of the year when business is generally slack. If it works and is not so frequent as to encourage negative behavior the moment that good behavior isn't rewarded, there is nothing inherently wrong in such negotiations. The important thing is that the behavior be changed and that the result be lasting.

* * *

"I don't wanna, I don't wanna, I don't wanna! I want to go home, I want to go home, I want to go HOME!"

The voice is hysterical and very, very loud. The parent is beet red and trying to comfort or appear oblivious to the event while browsing through a rack of sale sweaters. The third variant is the parent who is showing remarkable composure, understanding, and a tight smile while talking quietly to the child, saying that this is not nice behavior, that it must stop, and that Daddy/Mommy is really surprised by this outburst. Here is a full-fledged temper tantrum and three ways of dealing with it. But where does it come from, and what can we do about it?

Mark is five. He has not been to preschool because his parents decided he was too immature to handle it. When he went to nursery at temple, he didn't play a lot with the other kids. "I think he's immature," Ellen said. "Uh-huh," said Barney. When he didn't want to sit with all the other four- and five-year-old kids in the back of the pickup truck decorated like a big flag for the Fourth of July parade, Ellen said, "I think he's immature." Barney said, "Uh-huh." By the time Mark threw that temper tantrum in the sweater department, he had been diagnosed by his mother as immature on so many occasions that he might have responded to that word as to his name. "How he is ever going to be ready for school, I just don't know," says Ellen." "Huh?" says Barney.

Temper tantrums can cause tremendous embarrassment. The tantrum thrower is *out of control*, and out of control tends to scare us (we wouldn't want to be out of control, would we?) and holds us up to scorn by all the rest who are apparently *in control*. A tantrum is also scary because we wonder if there is anything really wrong with our child. Often, however, and really more than just often, a child uses a tantrum to control a parent who spends too much time trying to control that child. If we stop and think about it, it makes sense. A child is too small to be on its own, so if it is frustrated by the restraint that is inherent in an overcontrolled situation at home, it will find a way to pay back the controlling parent. Sure, it could be bed-wetting at five years, embarrassing behavior in front of company, silence (Oh, my

God, can't he talk? Is he retarded?), or other kinds of
withholding behavior. But what can be more upsetting to
a parent who hungers for order and predictability than to
appear to be completely out of control in a public situation? Not only does it frighten Dad or Mom, but it gives
a child a peculiar feeling of freedom, freedom that is rare
with a controlling parent, plus that slightly perverse
"Gotcha!" feeling of getting even in a meaningful way.

Let's look at some ways our overcontrolling behavior
can lead to temper tantrums. (We refer here to genuine
temper tantrums that cannot be stopped by negotiation.)
The circularity of the problem, if more than a fleeting
control phenomenon, is unhealthy, of course, the tantrum being the symptom of what is probably a family
problem. Long term, it is best dealt with in concert with
an appropriate therapist.

"That's nice, Lauren, really nice. But more like this.
Here, let Daddy show you."

"No, you can't. And sit up straight. Not your left hand,
your right. Can't you do anything right?"

"Yes, dear, that's just beautiful. But don't you think it
would be prettier over here? No? All right, but let's just
try it here. Oh, I like this much better, don't you? No?
Oh, yes, let's ask Daddy, too. See, Daddy says so, too.
You're going to like it very much there, Sandra, really."

Each of the above monologues suggests the desire to
control. If they are rare events, we probably can pass
over them, but if there is a consistency of this kind of
behavior toward a child, we should be concerned.
Whether we are repeating behavior from the past, or are
immature and need to give ourselves a sense of being in
control, or fear our own potential (we all have it to some
degree) for being out of control, matters less than being
aware of our behavior and taking steps to change it. If
we are able to recognize that kind of behavior in ourselves, of course, it is ideal, but often we need the help
of a mate in order to confront it.

"Have you noticed how nervous Tim gets when we
have company, Doris? He can hardly wait to get out of
the room. What do you think it is?" Pause, response. "I

wonder if it's because we are too hard on him sometimes. You know, about his room being neat, insisting that he always look like a department-store mannequin. Maybe we have to let up a little bit, huh?'' Charles does not even directly confront the occasional temper tantrums that cause great ructions in the Lewis household, because he thinks that is too charged a subject to go at directly.

''Maybe you're right, Charles. We have to give him a little more rein, perhaps. Now I do think that a child owes his parents . . .''

Charles has given Doris the opportunity to share the blame, even though he may not behave in a controlling way toward his child. He understands the importance of saving face. Doris seems willing to share the ''blame'' with her husband, and thus not feel talked down to and thus *out of control*, herself. She also is not going to give up on some issues right now, as the ''a child owes his parents'' addendum suggests. But it is a start.

In another possible scenario, Charles's need to control those around him might be directed at his wife, so conveniently close at hand; and a frustrated and downtrodden Doris, in turn, might be controlling toward their child. His controlling behavior might take the form of ''suggestions'' and ''mild'' criticisms, as in, ''*That* dress?'' ''Wouldn't you prefer the couch over there?'' ''I wouldn't do it *that* way.'' ''No, I want to see the other movie.'' In the process, which is a cumulative one, Doris is made to feel inadequate, and her response to this awful feeling might be to behave toward Tim as Charles does toward her. This recycling of frustrated anger is obviously to be avoided. Since it is not likely that Charles will wake up one morning a changed man, the prompting once again becomes the responsibility of the more adult person in the relationship to take charge, to recognize the cycle of conflict, to see the negative results in the family system, and then to take steps to bring about change in as nonconfrontational a manner as possible.

Doris's first move might be to delineate for her husband the differences between them, and to let him know that those differences are not really life- or identity-threatening for him, but they can be for her and their child. When Charles next says, ''Oh, no, not that dress,'' Doris should want all the more to wear that dress and no other, not as an act of defiance but as an act of *defining* the spaces between herself and her husband. Perhaps asking his advice as to the shoes that go best would be another face-saving device, one that says both "I don't know everything" and "I do cherish your advice," while the choice of dress says, "I start here and you end there." This is really the negotiation gambit of increasing the options in another guise. The system will become more balanced, the need for Doris to control Tim will be diminished, and positive changes in Tim's behavior should occur.

Remember that the temper tantrum or other embarrassing behavior is likely as not an act of control on the part of a child. It is often the child's way of getting even for our real or perceived misdeeds related to control. Think about it: If somebody manipulates us in a way that takes our freedom away, that makes us feel less whole, we resent it. If that person has a great deal of authority over us, it may be that we cannot directly flout that authority or even have a reasonable discussion about the manipulation; but we can throw our little darts at a critical moment when the object of the darts cannot effectively fight back. So when that kind of acting-out behavior surfaces, we should not look first to the child for the answer, but to ourselves. There, in all likelihood, lies the key. (Curiously, terrorist activity, while quite different in detail and consequence, takes impetus from the same impulse. Feeling thwarted by superior powers but righteous in their beliefs, terrorists make a large fuss to gain a sense of control over their lives and do so in a very public way.)

If the temper tantrums are of the superficial and infrequent variety, the child might respond to the same sort of reward system that Charlie's parents used with the pacifier. Yes, we must be careful not to be trapped into bribing for good behavior, so a reward system might need to be balanced by a lack of reward. As in all such systems, consistency is terribly important. That, at least, is in our control.

"I will never, ever forget the day that I brought the firstborn to nursery school. It was thrilling, of course. Here it all began, the socialization of the child, the absolute thrill of this little person, rather formally dressed, now that I think of it, making his way in the world starting this very day. He was going to be in a room with eleven relative strangers about his age, and with two really wonderful and caring women who had all the credentials the world required, and more. And yet that day that I left Dave in that room, I smiled, I waved, and then walked briskly back to my car, where I sat and felt my lips quiver and my face wet with tears as had not occurred since I had heard the news of my brother's death in Vietnam. The best of times and the worst of times in that moment. It is so hard to let go.''

Todd goes off to nursery school every morning at 8:45 and gets picked up by his sitter at 1:00 P.M. Dad gets home at 3:30, the sitter leaves, and at around 6:00 P.M., Mom returns from work. Todd likes nursery school and seems to be flourishing. The parents have different views about the children Todd is meeting in school, however, and that is a bone of contention. There are little words Todd now utters that neither Virginia (the mom) nor Greg (the dad) are nuts about, but Virginia figures you can't insulate yourself or your kids from everything. Greg thinks otherwise and is trying to convince Virginia to take the next couple of years off from work and stay home with Todd until he is old enough for the kindergarten of the private school he will attend. Heck, no, says Virginia. I have a career, I'm enjoying the contact with diverse people, and I would go nuts at home. Greg insists. Fortunately for Virginia, she is strong and holds her ground. I love Todd at least as much as you do, but he is not going to grow up under a bell jar, because out there, she says, indicating the world beyond the window, there are no bell jars.

Greg's nose is definitely bent out of normal shape. He was attracted to Virginia for her strong individual ways, but enough is enough, he thinks. The staff at work don't talk back this way, so Greg isn't, nor does he want to become, used to it. Are children who speak that way the kinds of children we want Todd to be with for four hours a day? he asks himself again and again, and the answer is always negative. So the battle goes on, slopping over from time to time into slight and then overt attacks on

Virginia's virtues as a mother. It finally gets to the point where Virginia suggests that if Greg feels that strongly about it, he ought to give up medicine for two years and stay home and keep Tim out of the influence of "them." Greg is shocked.

There are a number of things going on here: Greg's fear of Todd being influenced toward the ordinary, his inability to see that his wife's career is just as important as his, his lack of faith in the resiliency of kids. Greg's wish that his wife give up her career, which would definitely suffer from a two-year leave, can be seen as a possible hidden agenda, for does a significant career and the kind of independence it brings with it not threaten a man who tries to control his environment the way Greg seems to? Or maybe his motives are quite innocent. But what is *truly important* to note is that now that Todd is out of the direct sphere of influence of his parents or chosen baby-sitter, Greg overreacts to any changes in his son. He wants to control his child directly or through his spouse; that, and the inability to let go (and this is where that process of letting go becomes so important and graphic) are threatening him. Todd is adjusting to school, Virginia is adjusting to some of the verbal behavior that she would prefer not to deal with, but Greg is having a very hard time. He is also sharing his hard time by creating little weapons with which to "persuade" his wife to relieve his anxieties over separation by staying home.

Once more a center of conflict requires that one heroic person figure out the situation and bring it to the attention of the other in a way that will not cause the other to lose face. Yes, Virginia, it's up to you.

Even if there is enough income to justify an "au pair," and assuming that she would be to Greg's liking (the baby-sitter is nice and neutral, and is only with Todd for brief periods of time, so she doesn't count), the fact of the matter is that Greg will forestall Todd's being "out there" for as long as possible if encouraged, so Virginia isn't going to bring up that possibility. Greg won't take "*You* stay home" seriously, so that's out. One change of nursery school might be possible, but from all that they have heard, and goodness knows they have researched it well, the choices available are not better choices, simply different ones. Perhaps the only thing that Virginia can do is to ask for Greg's trust in this matter.

"Greg, I understand, believe me, and I share your concerns for the future of this child we have made together. I have never led you astray, nor you me. We have been very good for and with each other. Todd is learning some words that you don't like and that I would just as soon not hear from a four-year-old, particularly *our* four-year-old. He is becoming more physically aggressive. Probably some of the kids there demand that, and it's a good thing that Todd has it in him to follow suit, otherwise he might get scrunched. But in light of the past, and how we have always been able to trust each other, trust me on this one. Todd won't become a thug between now and Farmdale. If they had a nursery, maybe that would be the answer. Maybe not, too. It is good for him to see some diversity, because at Farmdale he is going to be in something closer to a bell jar than to the world. Let's just relax on this one. I love you, I love Todd, but I would resent having to leave the bank at this point, and my resentment of the change might come out in my relationship with Todd. I swear, if he comes home with a switchblade, I'll quit the next morning!"

Virginia is going to have to find her own ways to get Greg to relax, find the right buttons to push. She could start with the daily papers, pointing out that you don't have to be an upper-class kid to plead guilty to manslaughter or a poor black boy to become a presidential contender as a man. With Virginia's promptings, Greg may come to recognize that contradictions of his clichéd view of the world abound, that Todd—genes, money, and Farmdale aside—is going to have to make it on his own. Holding on to Todd so tightly will not help him to grow. On the other hand, she might say, letting go of something is often the only way you can ever really have it.

Geoffrey is in the bathtub. Until a minute ago, he was quite noisy moving his boat from one end of the tub to the other, his mouth all puckered in imitating an engine sound. But now there is quiet, just an occasional lazy sound as movement causes the water to lap against the tub sides.

"What are you doing, Geoff?"

"Nothing."

"Nothing? Why don't you get out and dry yourself and get into your jammies, then?"

"In a minute."

Some more time passes, and Geoffrey has still not made an appearance, so Dad/Mom goes into the bathroom to find Geoff staring with interest at his penis, which is pink and erect from all the attention Geoff has given it since the power boat lost its fascination for him.

Varieties of response:

"Stop that this instant. That's yucky, dirty."

"Hi, Geoff. Want me to help you dry off? I have to go get something ready for the morning in a minute, but . . ."

"Do you do that a lot, son? That's not nice, you know."

"I/Dad have/has a penis, too, just like yours. All boys have them. They're interesting in the way that they can grow and everything, huh? Well, what do you think you would like for dinner, pal?"

A girl's vaginal curiosity and play is no different, of course. You could simply substitute *Jane* and *vagina* above, and all would be the same. Kids get curious about their bodies, and that is that. It's natural. How we respond is important, and how parents individually feel about sex and sex play vis-à-vis their children can be a focus of family conflict. If we are self-conscious about sex, it might be difficult for us to tolerate children's sexuality. That intolerance could be directed at the child: "Stop that dirty thing! What kind of a monster are you? You'll get . . ."; or it could be directed toward a spouse, for instance, and revolve around superficial issues, entirely unrelated to sexuality. So what are the problem-solving answers? More verities.

Sexual exploration is as natural as nine months' gestation, development of motor skills, putting your pants on one leg at a time. It happens. Yes, one can become fixated, but that is not common; in fact, it is more likely to become an issue for a developing child if we place too much importance on it. The best thing is to acknowledge such curiosity, talk about it a little, but with a casual sense of proportion. After all, toes are amazing, too, those little bones, those arched things that help move us, balance us, and that take so much abuse. Maybe it is worth talking about the miracles of toes while the vagina or penis is in the spotlight of the moment, as well.

We should hope to agree, as husband and wife, on what sex is all about: natural, another function, pleasurable, not something to be spoken about with embarrassment. If the subject is a loaded one for one of us, there should be some exploration of how to deal intelligently and nonthreateningly with that one of us who is not comfortable with the subject.

Kids outgrow the fascination at one point, and then later it all comes back with great force. We ought to know, oughtn't we? If we can remain aware of these things as our children explore the wonders of their physical selves, it will be useful in short-circuiting another area where conflict can lie.

The birth of another child brings with it the need for all kinds of adjustments for everybody. The night feedings, the wash, the flash fevers, and the worries are back. The physical, emotional, and financial demands are increased. Coalitions form, with Mom and number-one son aligned against Dad and new baby girl; or worse, Mom and Dad go bananas over the new arrival and ignore number-one-girl. Parents have both psychological and physical limits, of course, so when we are pressed with the needs of two demanding people instead of one, we can begin to show wear in the way we talk to each other and to our children. Do we have things to fight about!

Financial strains. The cost of having a baby, just in terms of hospital expenses and prenatal care, is phenomenal. If we are well insured, the burden is less, but there still remain the postnatal costs, the shoes, the sweaters, diapers, all the gear. When we are four, instead of three, a thirty-dollar day at the shoestore becomes a sixty-dollar day. Clearly, the financial demands can cause fights.

"There just isn't enough, Allan, and that's the truth. How am I supposed to run a house on what you bring home? Ilene, for instance, her husband . . .''

There is a real problem here: Right now there is not

enough in the bank account to make the car payment, pay the fuel bill, do the weekly grocery shopping, and pay the medical insurance. Something has to give. Yet it is clear, too, that in this situation Delilah is doing something wrong right off: She has presented a problem in a manner that attacks her husband, makes him feel incompetent, and generally causes him to lose face. Allan is being attacked where he lives, both literally and metaphorically, for his wife is saying he is not competent as a provider and she is doing it in their kitchen. With an approach like this, there is little immediate hope for constructive engagement on the subject of money, which in and of itself can be very anxiety-provoking.

How might Delilah approach the problem? Perhaps she could have made the time, or caused Allan to have made the time, to take a hard dollars-and-cents look at their lives. With that balance sheet, they could then sit down and see what can give, what cannot, and what must be done (if necessary) to increase the size of the pie. This brings together skills of negotiation and collaboration as tools in problem solving. No matter what the conclusion—fewer dinners out, money from their vacation savings to supplement for a period, and thus no trip this year, no more all cotton shirts that have to go to the laundry, but ironing lessons for Allan, an immediate return of Delilah to the work force—it *should* be based on mutual respect. Each should identify with the other's problems, concerns, and faults, cooperating and not backing each other into positions from which each would be hard pressed to move. Perhaps a new scenario might be written.

"Since we talked last week, Allan, I've gone over the budget as you suggested," Delilah begins, "and there just isn't any room in it. Here are the numbers and maybe, just maybe, we can cut out about thirty-two dollars' worth of entertainment expenses, but, outside of that, I don't see it. What do you think?" Delilah has started this conversation on a quiet weekend evening when both are relaxed and there are no interruptions. Her manner is straight-forward, nonaccusatory, and friendly; it is also no-nonsense.

"Whew. I guess there's no fat there, kiddo, huh? I don't know, honestly, I don't know. It's not always going to be this way. I expect that over the next two years I will—'' Delilah interrupts.

''I know, I know, it's going to get better. You work as hard as anybody can. These growing years are just damned expensive. What do you think we can do in the meantime to keep things from getting too hairy?''

''Well, I can't take a part-time job right now. There's too much going on at work now, and I have to put my time in for the future. Maybe I can do some Saturdays at one of the stores in town, maybe I can talk to Bob about a little moonlighting with him as a helper on electrical work; I still know that stuff well. But to tell you the truth, I really would prefer it if you could find some part-time work.''

''I don't have any problem with that. Frankly, I would feel better about pulling a little more oar. And being home with the kids all of the time does send me up the wall. I'm going to shoot for three evenings—you'll have to get the kids into bed those nights—and at nine dollars per hour, that ought to smooth out some of the bumps.''

This is an ideal kind of conversation on an emotionally charged subject with identities and dreams all tied up together. Both are willing to do what is needed, neither attacks or reproaches or tries to put a guilt trip on the other. It requires thought, not blurting out concerns, but real thought. The figures make the problem real, and then the participants can begin to make problem-solving contributions. They both show willingness to confront the reality unemotionally, to recognize each other's contributions to the whole, and finally negotiate a settlement. It nicely displays that financial problems are not *her* problems or *his* problems, but *our* problems. The images of the daddy as the hunter and the mommy as the cave sweeper should have no place in our thinking. If our discussion results in it being clear that a husband has to take a second job, and/or a wife start working part time, then so be it. Sharing responsibility is necessary, which is one of the historic reasons for formalizing relationships.

With a second or subsequent child often comes a sense of déjà vu. It is not immediate, but rather sets in after the excitement of childbirth, the homecoming, the packing away of the gifts, and the oohs and ahhs of friends and relatives have died down. Suddenly, it is once again real, just like the first time. The feedings, the interrupted sleep, the jealousy of the father if the mother shows too much attention to the baby, and a new problem not previously experienced: sibling rivalry. The bugs in the system had just been worked out, everything was going along fine, when whammo, says the firstborn, now I gotta share everything with this kid!

Derek, who is going to go to school next year, loves his little sister, but boys being what they are, he is a little bit more rough and tumble than Mommy and Daddy like. Sometimes when Derek tries to share a toy with Samantha, it almost looks as if Derek is trying to *hurt* Samantha. Or is that just my imagination? Maura wonders.

"Be gentle, Derek. She's just a little bitty thing, you know. And you're such a big boy."

Mom thinks that kind of praise about "him big, her little" will appeal to the macho in Derek, but it doesn't seem to be making a difference. Since Samantha's arrival, Derek has been having occasional nighttime accidents, although he had been pretty much toilet trained for eight and a half months. He also whines a lot and can be seen crawling across the dining room floor making goo-goo-gaa-gaa sounds that somehow don't ring true from the mouth of this really quite large four-and-a-half-year-old boy who appears to have professional linebacker potential. When Dad sees him doing that, he really gets annoyed. "Come on, son, get up now, you're a big boy." That's how it starts. More flagrant baby behavior follows. "Now get up, I said, *now*." "Goo-goo-gaa." The final *gaa* just makes it out when Dad stands, all six feet of him, walks to where Derek sprawls, bends over and rather roughly pulls his son to his feet, and says, "Now that's enough of that, young man. Come and sit with me and we'll look at the newspaper together." Now how could a child resist such an invitation?

Derek's dad and mom need to think a little bit about the baby from Derek's point of view; they need to identify. "I was king of the mountain and suddenly this one arrives and I gotta share! Well, if going goo and gaa gets Mom and Dad's attention, then it's goo and gaa for me."

Derek is going to have to learn to share or be sad, but his parents need to think about whether they are fairly sharing their limited time with their firstborn. Unless they do that and take steps to share more equitably, Derek may continue to be variantly ''babyish'' and hostile to the infant. If he continues to behave that way, he may be labeled babyish and/or aggressive by his parents. As we all know from experience, we often tend to fulfill other people's view of us, so, in fact, Derek may become that potential football player who exhibits babyish and later bullying characteristics. All the understanding in the world will probably not get Derek to be thrilled about his new rival being on the scene, for such jealousy is normal, but there is much that can be done to short-circuit arguments over behavior, not only with the child, but between Mom and Dad, as well.

Mom and Dad may argue because Mom says, ''He's only a baby himself, you know. Get off his case,'' when Dad treats the older child with disdain or does not take the child's point of view into account. Mom or Dad may identify with that child's behavior because of their own experience and form an alliance: ''me and him against you guys.'' No matter what the alliances or the reasons for their formation, once aware of the problem of the family as ''camps'' of interest, we should approach its solution the same way: Stop, take a hard and nonemotional look, and talk.

After describing our perceptions of the problem to each other and agreeing that it is, indeed, a problem, we should decide how we are going to deal with each of the kids in the future. Aware of Derek's jealousy, both parents might plan to spend some very special time with their son. In addition to spending more time with Derek, Dad could become more directly involved in the care of the new baby as an example of boys caring for others. He might even ask Derek to help, which would make Derek feel powerful and responsible rather than shut out and angry. If it's in the budget, a nursery-school experience for Derek would give him some special territory that he does not have to share with the ''new kid.''

Patience, vigilance, and dealing directly and consistently with the problem over time usually work. Kids do adjust to each other's presence, and eventually may even form alliances against us! But there are occasions when children are very slow to accept another child in the household. If our best and consistent efforts to short-circuit negative behavior—ongoing sullenness, pokes, pinches, slaps—fail, it might be time to get some advice from a therapist.

As if being a parent weren't hard enough, we are asked to measure ourselves against advertising- and public-relations-created mothers and fathers so plugged into life and so full of energy that the four kids, the fourteen-hour days at their respective offices, the two English sheep-dogs, and the hang-gliding near the weekend mountain hideaway where she cards wool and he paints are just the norm for "our generation." The fact is that if you get two kids close to each other in age, you get worn out. Period. Kids are exhausting. They devour our psychic and physical energies. These small and apparently tire-less beings requiring total maintenance over long stretches of time call on all of our resources and put in orders for some we don't even have.

One of the two parents will probably have more re-sponsibility than the other for the children's daily care and welfare, and that person is clearly going to be more tired, more anxious, more potentially irritable than the other. Given that realistic scenario, it is incumbent on the other to act as cheerleader, praiser, mollifier, work-ing to reinforce that primary caretaker's sense of com-petence. To praise is cheap. To divorce is expensive. To make relaxation time available for the parent who carries the heavier parenting load is nothing less than wise, yet nothing more than necessary. The resentment and/or ex-haustion that comes with that major care provider's turf will spill over onto the other, but the other must not respond in kind. Communicate, identify. Make construc-tive commitments. Apply the rule of change. Talk about equity. "Why don't I take two days off next month so that you can go visit with your brother and fish? I know you have been wanting to do that. You have really had the worst of it lately." Go out for dinner or do whatever it is that will please and distract and rehumanize the other who has been crushed temporarily by the burden of caring for the welfare of two or more very important but young and taxing human beings.

''Your son, do you know what he did today? He nearly killed himself with a bobby pin that he found somewhere and tried to pry out one of the plastic plug things—you know, those safety things—and then he nearly killed his sister, climbed up on the dresser next to the dressing table and nearly tumbled her over and . . .''

We could respond to the complaint with challenges and rejoinders. ''How come your vacuuming is so careless? I've told you to look out for my bobby pins. What do you mean, my son? He's just like your brother, old fat George. How did he get that much time alone to climb up there, aren't you watching, for #©&*?'' And there could be a full-blown, table-banging, and hurtful fight. Or we could listen and say nothing immediately, and when the bulk of the frustration and anxiety is played out, we could be very sympathetic, forget to attack, build positive momentum through making the other feel loved, competent, effective. Talk firmly but sensibly to the older child, find a way to get some time out for the other parent so that the burden of the moment will not overwhelm and make the life of the family unhappy. Turn that conflict into something positive.

8

School Days: Six Through Twelve

If sending a child to nursery school or day care is traumatic, it is here, when we give our children over to *an institution* that will have significant control over their lives for the next twelve years, that we begin to understand the separateness of our children from ourselves.

Remember. We were five or six, we were "dressed up," Mom or Dad—maybe even Mom *and* Dad—walked us the blocks, waited with us for the bus, drove us to that first schoolhouse, that feared, anticipated, mysterious place where we would be for a big chunk of the day. We loved it, we hated it, we cried, we embraced it, we did something, but whatever it was we did, it was between us as children and our schools. The first few days we came home filled with stories of triumph, anguish, or boredom, to be sure, but after that, it kind of dried up. We went to school. School was what we did. No third degrees, please. So here we now stand on the other side of the schoolyard fence, outside looking in, interlopers. It is no wonder that some of us cry on that day of giving over our children to the world "out there."

While that separation is the herald of what is to come, it is only the first item on the menu that can result in conflict.

A short list of possibilities:

    choice of companions
    achievement in school
    achievement in extracurricular activities
    camp
    kids' available time for us
    our available time for kids
    the big new budget
    kid fights
    eating habits
    family rivalries
    who gets what

The list is not infinitely expandable, although it sometimes seems so, but it is clear that there will be plenty of opportunities to test our skills at taking the material of problems and making of them a learning and growing experience. Let's begin at the beginning.

The same separation anxieties a parent felt when a child started preschool or nursery school will resurface when kindergarten begins. Though a parent may claim the child is too immature, on closer examination, it may be the parent's lack of maturity that is the problem. The roots are the same, the possible solutions are the same: Look inside, take some deep breaths, help your child to feel comfortable with the world out there. You have to let go sometime. There are other problems just ahead.

Tom was five weeks into second grade and showing signs that he liked it a lot. He was an early reader at home, using both sight and phonic techniques equally well, so he has been a bit of a star at the Deaver Public School, reading way ahead of the class. That makes Mom and Dad proud. It also puts some pressure on Steven, who is a fourth grader and doesn't like reading. He just isn't good at it and is going to have to work very hard just to stay even. On the other hand, Tom has for the first time discovered that he is not made of gold: He is doing very poor work in his numbers. Because he had previously received nothing but praise, Tom is really brought down by his poor performance in arithmetic, even to the extent of getting Monday belly aches. At the same time, despite the fact that he is not natively gifted on the verbal end, Steven slugs away at the reading, trying not to notice that Mom and Dad dote on Tom's ability to read fourth-grade stuff with ease.

Today, report cards have been issued, and as is the scheme at good old Deaver, the kids get to bring them home and present them to their parents. After having a peek at his, Tom decides he would prefer to wait to show it to his parents, if he really had a choice. The arithmetic evaluation is not good. There it is in black and white. Now he will have to share what he has known all along with his parents. If they have been so praising in the past, he figures, all seven years of him, they will find out the truth. And, boy, will they be angry. Errgh!

Steven gets his report from his fourth-grade homeroom teacher. He opens it with some trepidation and sees that the reading *has* improved, not a lot maybe, but enough to make him feel good about the effort he has made. Mom and Dad will like that, he thinks. The math is off the scale, of course. He never had a thought that it would be otherwise.

The kids go home to the baby-sitter and do what they usually do after school, except both of them are feeling a little excited about showing their cards to their parents. Tom feels bad-excited because he has graphic evidence of not doing well in math. Steven feels good-excited because he has shown improvement in an area he has done less well at before. Mom and Dad arrive together. It's Friday, and whenever possible they take the train from the city together.

"Hey Mom, Dad, got my report card today," says Steven.

"Great, good, let's take a look after dinner. Tom got his, too, I suppose?" That's Mom.

"Yep, we both got 'em."

"Great. Missed you guys today," she says, as Tom makes his appearance and Mom hugs them both.

"Hey, guys, what's this I hear about report cards, huh? Let's get a look." That's Dad.

"Hon, let's get changed and washed up and . . ."

"No, sweets, let's take a look now. Steve here's been having a hard time with the reading program, and I want to see how he's doing, you know? Let's see that card, Steve." There's something about the tone of the last that seems a little challenging, and Steven's neck is perceptibly withdrawn at the sound, but knowing that things are looking up, he marches over to Dad, whips out the card, and puts on a pretty good imitation of a suppressed proud grin.

"Uh-huh. Hmm. Still good maths, Steve. Effort, good. Good isn't good enough sometimes, Steve, you know? See you're making a little improvement in your reading." He hands the card to his wife and immediately says, "Hey, Tom, let's see those reading marks. Great. Terrific. Keep it up. I was just like that at your age, great job, keep it up."

After Mom has had her look at the grades, she compliments Steven for his improvement in reading and continuing good work in math. All other areas are fine, and both of the kids seem real happy. Mom is satisfied, but she says she would be glad to help Tom in his arithmetic.

At dinner, Dad tells stories about his reading skills as a boy, about how they prepared him for his work as editor of a specialty magazine of some reputation. He directs a lot of his conversation to Tom, who is pleased, particularly in light of the fact that he is Steven's "kid brother." Dad says that he had a hard time with math, too, and that he never really got much better at it over the years. "But that didn't stop me, old man," he says to Tom. "That's why there are magazine publishers and business staff. Let them handle the numbers." There is a hint of disparagement in his remark. Just about now, Steve's dinner doesn't taste so good to him. "What is this junk, anyhow?" he says, addressing the question to his mom in a tone that could curdle milk. "I can't finish this crap!" "Steven, get to your room and don't let me hear you use that kind of language again in this house, especially with your mother." Steven pushes his chair away with a certain amount of drama and goes off to his bedroom near to tears.

Over time, Steven and Dad often act out a dance around the unimportance of math and the primacy of language skills. Steven does little more improving in reading skills. What for? he figures, because his father is never going to be satisfied. Tom, at the same time, gets a lot of positive reinforcement from Dad and begins to be just a little bit more than a little arrogant. He puts the knife in, subtly of course, but he puts it into Steve's sensitive skin, and twists it. He grows closer to Dad and away from Mom, who is doing her best to tell Steve good things about himself. For all her efforts, she gets little in return, because Steven feels embarrassed by her efforts. They make him feel really spoken down to and second-rate. Instead of taking comfort, he takes advantage, getting concessions from Mom that he would not otherwise get. He learns to manipulate. And when he doesn't get what he wants, he acts out, like at the dinner table. He wants approval a lot from his dad and he isn't getting it, so what's the use? Since Dad doesn't think too much of Mom's career, which happens to be in stocks and bonds, and which revolves around numbers, he takes no comfort in his consistently excellent math scores. The only way he can react, it seems, is to be miserable, difficult, intractable. At least it gets me attention, he figures.

Fights ensue, escalating out of control. Mom gets blamed by Dad because she is too lenient with Steven when she should be leaning on him to work harder. Mom gets very angry with Dad because he is so lacking in understanding. She even begins to take sides against Tom, to a certain extent, despite the fact that she isn't getting much love from Steven now. The whole situation is pretty unpleasant, and nobody is very happy.

Let's get the subtext out of the way first. It is pretty apparent, having to do with parents identifying with children and using the achievements of children to reaffirm the self. It is as common as families. Here it revolves around academic achievement. It could be physical or extracurricular and play out the same way. Dad probably does not feel as positive about himself as the surface might suggest, thus the need to achieve through Tom, whose skills he identifies with. He also isn't good at tolerating differences. If he were, he would be able to see Tom as Tom and Steven as Steven, people with different strengths and different qualities as human beings. Steven is being attacked where he lives.

First, Mom and Dad need to sit down and talk about what is going on. The beginning of their discussion may be about Steven's behavior, but it should move as quickly as possible to the reason for that behavior. As usual, it is going to require the person with the head closest to level to take responsibility for directing the discussion. This comes under the collaboration heading, with the need for trust, awareness of saving face, leaving room for the second party to change a position without feeling weak. In order to do any of this, of course, time has to be set aside. The conversation might go like this:

"We haven't had any time together, Ted, so let's arrange to have my mother take the kids for a weekend so we can be alone, for a change. It's been so darned long," says Mom.

"Boy, am I glad you said that, Penny. Maybe we can even drive north and stay at the inn on that little harbor—you know the one. Now that the tourist season is over, it will be real quiet. I could use some of that. It can't be the weekend of the twenty-sixth because I have to put the magazine to bed then, but any other time in the next month is clear."

On the second day of the chosen weekend, Mom brings up the subject of Steven's acting out. "It concerns me a lot. He is such a good kid, you know, very loving, generally, very sweet, but for a while now he has been awfully hard to deal with and to get to agree to almost anything. Contrary. What do you think is bugging him?"

"Probably growing up, glands, I don't know. I do know that he has been a pain in the neck recently. And those school marks. How does he expect to get by on those kinds of grades? It's bad enough that he isn't doing any better in English, but even his math marks are down. I just don't know. Maybe more discipline, maybe . . . I don't know. Tom, on the other hand, God, he's so great . . ."

Penny gives Ted enough time to rhapsodize about his favorite, his second-grade alter ego, giving praise, as well. After a little pause, however, she leads Ted to the day that Steven's behavior seemed to have changed. "Remember that report card when he started to do a lot better in English? You know, I think he expected more praise from us than he got. It had been such an issue for him, particularly in light of Tom's exceptional grades in reading—reading at Steven's grade level, for goodness' sake—maybe we just didn't react positively enough."

Ted raises his eyebrows, makes a reference to favoritism on Penny's part, but rather than rising to the bait,

Penny agrees that there may be some. This takes Ted off of the defensive, and when she smiles and suggests that there just might possibly be a little favoritism toward Tom on his part—"my son, the writer," as she amusedly characterizes Ted's projections—she has left enough room for the relaxed Ted to fess up with a little smile. "Yeah, it just could be that I don't give Steve enough credit for what he does do well. And of course, when the credit isn't there, and you're ten years old, well, it can be pretty daunting. Come to think of it, I got my back up like that at home—I was around twelve, I think, and it was about baseball, at which I was less than terrific—and made life miserable for everybody for a while. My dad just wasn't giving any room for the fact that I was neither a Ted Williams at the bat nor a Jimmy Foxx in the infield."

Together, Ted and Penny map out a plan. In fact, knowing Ted as well as she does, Penny lets him do most of the work. If it is his plan, she figures, he'll implement it with more vigor. First, lay off the remarks about underachievement. Second, reinforce the good stuff. There is less of the good stuff now, but there is still some. Third, talk to Steve about his behavior and admit that maybe Mom and Dad have not been as fair as they should have been. The "we're-only-human" defense will be used. Take some responsibility for having created Steve's behavior and make it clear that his "only human" parents are not going to be so unreasonable in the future. (Penny is silent during this part of the presentation, trying to keep from blurting out the fact that *she* was not the one who reacted negatively to Steve, but she doesn't want to blow this progress just in order to save face. It's more important to get agreement.) Fourth, help Steve by praising his earlier progress and by helping him with his reading. "Who knows," Dad says, "maybe he got turned off of reading because he was the firstborn, I was relatively new and insecure at my job, and I was spending more time reading than I was being a father to him." Penny has made a nice weekend away into a remarkable one.

Implementing the plan will require a number of tools from the toolbox (Chapter 4), including the reapportionment of a very limited resource, time. This will have to be quite intelligently handled, because Tom has become used to more than his share of attention. The trick is to give Steven what he needs without shorting Tom and having him react negatively. ("Maybe I should act out like Steven, since it got him the attention" could be a line of reasoning Tom might pursue.) Steven's negative momentum, resulting from the lack of praise and reinforcement he had hoped for from his father, needs to be replaced by positive momentum, built on the making of constructive commitments, starting with the simplest issues. Dad might begin by admitting the shortsightedness of his previous reaction, maybe telling the story about his own father and his (Ted's) ineptitude on the baseball diamond. If he can show his son that he can be trusted to do what he says, there is reason to think that this deteriorating situation can be turned around into a positive one. Perhaps Dad should suggest going to a baseball game together, which is a very simple way to begin. This father and son have the potential to be closer than they had ever been before the incident of the report card. Dad could apply the rule of change by just de-emphasizing grades for a while. The absence of the dripping faucet may work wonders. In all of what goes on, however, the careful agreement of husband and wife is essential.

At the same time, it is important that the extra time that Dad might spend with Steven in compensation for the past be balanced out by Mom's taking more time with Tom. The attempt to keep the balance between two kids with separate functional and ego needs, as well as the same insecurities the rest of us have, is necessary and even essential to maintain the equilibrium of the family system.

While this story is a long one, there are a lot of things going on in it, each requiring some understanding and in response some modification of behavior on the part of somebody. Most issues *are* made up of more than one element. People are complicated, and families, since they are made up of *people*, even more complicated. This seems a particularly appropriate place to again mention the fact that the family is a system. As with a balloon, if we squeeze or push *here*, there will be a response *there*. In this instance, if there is a too-abrupt push of resources toward Steven, Tom may get out of shape and react. If Mom suddenly begins to suffer from Dad overcompensating (too hard a push) relative to Steven, she may get bent out of shape, as well. Unquestionably, change must occur, but the implementation of that change is just as critical as the change itself. Just remember the balloon.

"I don't want to practice. I hate the stupid piano, any-way. I want to go to Freddie's. I promised. Why do I have to?"

"Well,everybody else has a . . . How come I can't?"

"Frankie's father says he can go, and even Mrs. Dan-forth is letting little Brucie go."

"I can't wear something that looks like this. What are you trying to do to me, huh? I'll stay in my room, I'll never leave this house again!"

Conformity versus nonconformity. I don't want to practice because nobody else has to practice versus I have to have a pair of those seventy-eight-dollar boots because everybody else has a pair. Different but the same, for they put us into a no-win situation, and sometimes cause problems between husband and wife in the process. Would that it were as easy to talk about solutions as it is to posit the problems!

He remembers having to go, much against his will, to religious education classes. *Nobody* went to religious ed-ucation classes, he held. "Besides, we're agnostics," he said, "so why do I have to go to religious education classes? You people are phonies." A doted-on boy child does not take to being spanked with great equanimity. He tends to lose his historic sense, and some pride. If he has a lot of grit, he just might find a way to get even. But he was spanked, and it was clear that he was going. In a slightly less than normal hysterical moment, his fa-ther said to him, "This is for your grandparents. The grandparents who survived. This is for them, out of re-spect." Here, darling, do it for history, do it for the countless dead, do it for your grandparents who were lucky enough to survive a harsh and hostile world. Could they put it on a person's head, he thought!

The day came and he got dressed, really dressed, shirt, tie, suit, shined shoes, overcombed hair. Today he was going to Hebrew school for the first time. He went, but he was not happy. He "refused" to learn Hebrew, but despite himself he learned. He was flippant from the first, and he did not measurably improve over the years. In secret moments, he had rather purple thoughts about a girl in the secular school behind whom he sat and who was an early developer and he was almost certain that he could see straps that held God knows what, but something wonderful perhaps. The hormones were raging and it was bar mitzvah time.

Though he was an unwilling participant, his semiangelic soprano voice filled the temple with sound nearly on key, and the eyes of some of his relatives with tears of memory and hope. The years of fighting with this strongheaded boy over connecting to tradition "for the sake of the grandparents" seemed to have been worth it, or so the parents thought for a reason as much informed by wishes as anything else. The service ended, they walked across the temple lawn to the car for the celebratory meal at a nearby restaurant. A few minutes onto the parkway, his father complained of an odor. "What odor?" "I smell it as well, Harry. Perhaps . . . Perhaps we should stop for a moment and have a look at our feet. Maybe from the temple to the car . . ."

His father pulled the car over into the breakdown lane, and there, while automobiles sped by at sixty miles an hour, there was a procession of very well-dressed people from a very well-made car. What could they be thinking, he thought, as one by one they turned up their soles. There, there, it was: him. Even on this day he had found a way, his father thought—for father was at least as much a Freudian as anything else—he had found a way to repudiate all of it. Oh, this boy was impossible.

Communion, confirmation, bar mitzvah, bas mitzvah, daily reading of the Koran, accepting Christ through immersion—all of the rituals of faith may be subject to the "Why do I hafta?" of the child in this period. While religious issues may be fraught with particular meaning for the adult, to the child these fights are little different from the right ice skates, shoes, boots, winter coat, bathing suit, ballet lessons, piano lessons, karate classes, and/or the lack thereof. To the child, the wrong/right clothing, the having not to/to stay in for piano lessons, and the rest is the very stuff by which their peers identify them and by which they identify themselves. There are millions of fights revolving around these more mundane issues every day, all over the world. They are often the hardest conflicts to be firm about. We were children, and we did or did not want to have piano lessons. Mr. A says he is still angry with his parents for not insisting that he continue his lessons thirty years ago. Mr. B. is as passionately angry with his parents today for having "tortured" him with music lessons as he was when he was eleven. How do you know what is right, and therefore, what to do? You will be happy to know that there is no answer. This class of questions has to be judged individually, so let us take a stroll through some individual cases in this minefield of "I don't wanna and I don't hafta" and "I gotta."

Carol takes Georgiana to ballet classes every Saturday at nine-fifteen. Georgiana adores the lessons, and Carol is very pleased. While 99 percent of the kids who start lessons are going to be bored or otherwise employed within a couple of years of commencing lessons, every kid gets something from it, Carol figures. But there is a kid in the class who is getting nothing at all from it except grief.

Deirdra is constantly being spoken to harshly and publicly by her mother, Theresa. Deirdra is quite awkward. Her coordination is poor. It may improve with age and further development, but just now she is definitely not ballerina material. Deirdra is held up to ridicule by the meaner of her peers (never forget the "kids can be cruel" wisdom); her normally peaches-and-cream complexion is beet red for the sixty minutes spent in class, and not the result of exertion. Carol and a friend take turns driving to the school. If you pick up Deirdra you get her mom, as well, so you get to hear the litany of Deirdra's balletic faults on the way home.

Deirdra happens to be very good at so called "masculine" pursuits, however. She can throw a ball to there and back, can hit well, and in little kids' touch football, she is so fast and ferocious that her opponents often forget what it is they are supposed to do when they see her plunging toward them. But that doesn't count. Theresa has her heart set on a sylph-like Deirdra who will live her life *en pointe*, all delicate and terribly feminine, poised and assured.

There are not only the humiliations at ballet class, but there are knock-em-down fights at home, with Deirdra finding fault with almost everything that her older brother does, which results in his getting a little physical with her, but only a little. That brings in Dad, who screams at his son for picking on a girl, which brings in Mom on her son's side, if only because she is annoyed with Deirdra, which . . . and on it goes. You don't have to be Freud to know that Theresa is asking her daughter to fulfill a dream that Theresa has, rather than a talent that Deirdra has. But what do we do about this on the practical level?

The child is in the control of an adult, so we cannot expect Deirdra to suggest the answers. An adult in the family needs to recognize that expecting Deirdra to take ballet at this point is dumb. Her coordination is not right. Her size is not right. She would rather be playing soccer. So we have to lean on Dad for the insight and/or for bringing up the question. Mom will have to give up her dream and begin to love her daughter for what her daughter is and can do, not for what she wishes for her daughter. Her wishes may be simply an extension of wishes she has had for herself over time.

Theresa needs to use some of the skills from the toolbox. She should put herself in Deirdra's place through identification. She should learn to listen to her daughter's complaints about ballet, believe her eyes at ballet class, and realize that this person and this activity are not made for each other. Or at the very least change her expectations. It may be a relief for both mother and daughter. Theresa may also find that she is pushing her daughter to this precise and delicate activity as a stand-in for the young Theresa, who was equally poor at the same activity. While it is hard putting those little-girl dreams to bed, it is far better to do that than to create tension between parent and child based on a stubborn parent's unfulfilled wishes.

Theresa needs to get excited about those activities that Deirdra loves and excels at. Instead of Mom bitching about ballet, let her cheer over another activity, thus creating positive momentum for herself and her daughter, breaking the stalemate of this no-win position on ballet's importance in the life of Mom.

The same kind of situation may involve another motive entirely, that of the parent who wants to be the super-parent, who is constantly in competition with other parents, a competition that can only be decided on the basis of the achievements of their kids. Thus the hockey/ballet/soccer/you-name-it mothers and fathers who are omni-present, and who, as often as not, wear out their kids in the quest of affirmation of their own worth.

"How's your ankle? Must be a lot better, huh? Well, it's been nine days. Think you'll be playing Friday? Well, how bad could it be? Come on, pal. Don't be such a molly coddle, for goodness' sake. I remember when I . . .''

David's an eleven-year-old hockey player who seri-ously twisted his ankle in a scrimmage. His father and he were afraid it was broken, it hurt so much and was so swollen, but after a look by a physician it was clear it was only a sprain. Ice and rest brought the swelling down, but not Dad's anxiety. Dad really rises and falls on Da-vid's sports performances. He pushes Dave a lot, and it is apparent, so much so that David's mother, Kathryn, gets very annoyed with Vincent. There are two other children in line, too, Dorothy, who is seven, and Beryl, who is ten, both of whom are beginning to feel Vincent's breath on their necks as the school teams are made up, even as the local parks have foot-races and potato-sack races. If there is a winner and a loser, Vincent wants to be there. And he wants the winner to be one of his kids. The kids feel pretty anxious around Dad these days. They love their dad, but they hate having him so dependent on them. He actually turns affection off and on based on performance, and although the kids might not articulate it quite that way, they feel it. The result is that they get tense in competition and get hurt a lot, which makes Dad's anxiety level zoom, which makes them anxious for having "let him down," while at the same time they are annoyed with his insistence on their performance. And Beryl really couldn't care less about winning and losing.

She has a good time and is willing to leave it at that, but Dad won't let her.

Kathryn would like to break this cycle right now. She thinks it is nuts for David to skate with a sore ankle just because his dad is pushing him. She also loves Vincent very much and does not want to hurt him by direct confrontation, but she has got to do something. As if she had not heard anything of his promptings, she begins: "Vince, David is not going to skate this Friday, hon, really, is he? I think he would be nuts to do that, don't you? He has got to get some sense into his head. This macho thing of his at eleven is just going too far. I can't talk to him about it. He won't listen to his mother, but I'm sure he will to you, dear. He respects you so much." Kathryn has said this with speed and atypical force, so Vincent knows she is serious about it. He is now in the position of either going along with her request that he be the go-between in cooling David's "self-destructive impulses," or challenge her and risk being seen as the macho fool she just described. He also would have to fly in the face of a strong compliment. She has given him the opportunity to do right and to save face in the process.

Vincent needs to gain some sense of proportion related to sports, achievement, and worthiness, but that is a longer-term problem that must be chipped away at. For the moment, this first-aid approach seems most appropriate. On the other hand, if it does not give the desired result, direct confrontation and intervention, as in "He is not going to play, period," would be necessary, followed by a discussion allowing Vincent to open up about his own sports achievements . . . or his lack of them.

Confronting the longer-term question of weaning Vincent from this sports/achievement/worthiness cycle will not be easy. Kathryn must be patient, must have a strategy, and must be willing to implement it and wait for the slowly emerging results (and be convinced of the basic solidity of the relationship she has with Vincent to make it worthwhile, needless to say. Her own admiration and response to the less "spectacular" aspects of Vincent's achievements or qualities might reinforce that you don't have to love mayhem to be a man. Voicing admiration for the gentler qualities of males who are nonthreatening (writers, actors, and such, those who are by their distance not exactly reasonable rivals to Vincent) could be put to good use. If Vincent has a sense of humor, Kathryn might find times when she can poke fun at certain "macho" characteristics in males other than her husband . . . or in him, if his sense of the ridiculous is sufficient. She might want to balance some of this with an occasional jab at a female who is trying to out-macho the male of the species. This is essentially a reeducation process, of course, and can not be expected to have immediate and startling results. On the other hand, if the relationship is a strong one, if the participants know each other very well, and if there is sufficient resiliency, direct confrontation is certainly not out of the question. No matter what, if the process is informed by love and respect—and those qualities should underlie all important interpersonal relationships—the communication will be honest, given in good faith, and not intended to do harm.

Kids' fights, like family problems in general, have any number of roots and motivations. Deep resentments built on perceptions of favored-nation status for one kid or another, ownership of space or things, age differences (me big, you little), the need to assert oneself at a particular moment, differences in priorities, something that happened at breakfast, all these and much more can bring about conflicts that end up in fights. Whether simple or complex, these fights can drive parents nuts, if parents let them or if they haven't got the strength at the end of a day to deal with the issue at hand with the necessary detachment and perspective. We don't always have that necessary detachment, however, and the perspective is skewed by the other responsibilities of the day, even, forgive us, children, please, by our personal needs! So it might be useful to look at the daily kid fights and explore ways of dealing with them.

Who knows what it was about, but Bea overheard the following exchange on a Friday afternoon not long after getting home from her teaching job. The sparring partners were a seven-year-old daughter and a ten-year-old son.

"Oh, yes, you will."

"Get out of here, you creep, I will not. It's mine."

"Give it to me, now."

"I will not."

"Oh, yes, you will."

"Go get your own."

"Give it to me, *now*."

"I will not, you creep."

It might have been an audio-tape loop, because it went on like this with different levels of intensity of sound for what seemed to Bea a very long time, long enough, in fact, for Bea to want to take a vacation without telling anybody. However, she did not intervene by choosing sides. Nor did she insist that one party give over to the other whatever was being demanded, or that the other back off. She refused to get caught in the middle of the dispute. Instead, she did something simple: She calmly walked into the kids' room and told them to separate for ten minutes, not talk or even look at each other, and then begin their discussion again. It worked. The kids were not suddenly angels, but the senselessness and incontrovertability of their individual positions of ten minutes ago were modified by the cooling-off period, and their renewed "fight" became a genuine discussion. Bea had introduced the rule of change. Instead of letting something continue, instead of becoming enmeshed, instead of getting angry, when a fight has the quality of a broken record, enforced cessation of hostilities for a specific period of time is often the very best solution.

Breakfast is never an easy time at the Baldwin house, but it is not always as chaotic as it is this particular morning. Joe wants eggs, Mandy wants Cheerios, and Fred doesn't want anything, thanks, he's too involved with trying to get done the homework he said he had finished last night. Dad is cleaning up last night's dishes, Mom is making school lunches for the kids, and the dog is barking because he needs to go out for his morning walk.

"I don't want these now," says Mandy. "Joe's eggs look good. Eggs, Mom, two, sunny-side up."

"Okay, in a minute, honey," says Mom.

Dad tells Fred to go walk the dog, and Joe sticks his

tongue out at the clearly perturbed Fred. Fred kicks Joe under the table.

"OWWWWW. You rat. Mom, see what he did? Look at this, I'm gonna be all . . . I don't think I can walk!"

"Cut it out, you guys. Here are your eggs, Mandy."

"I don't think I can move my leg. Look, look . . ."

"Bring the dog out now, I said. We'll talk about picking on your little brother later, my friend." Dad's voice suggests retribution is on the dinner menu.

Getting up, Fred noisily thrusts his chair away and simultaneously propels his book toward the Cheerios bowl; the milk spills all over *French I*.

"Cripes! Now lookit," says Fred, as if the universe were stacked against him. On the way to the door, he gives a little slice to the air, teeth gritted, eyes on his kid brother (who is still moaning), steps on the dog's paw in his rush, which elicits a bark from the dog and a bark from Dad.

"See what he did?" says Joe. "He's gonna kill me, first my leg and . . . I can't go on the school bus with him! Mom, Dad, can't you do something about him!"

After walking the dog, Fred decides he needs a glass of milk before he goes on the bus, but finds the milk all gone, Mandy having had the last of it in the cereal she decided she didn't want.

"You jerk," he says to his kid sister. "Mommy's spoiled baby."

Both Mom and Dad need to get out of the house, too, so they are as anxious as one can imagine to have this drama over, and preferably never repeated. How can we deal with this much first thing in the morning? they wonder.

First, we need to put out the brush fires and deal with the obvious. Mom might have been better served if she had suggested that Mandy cook her own eggs. After all, Mandy is eleven years old and capable enough when she needs something to eat if no one is there to provide service, and being able to do for oneself is a symbol of growth. Second, separate Joe and Fred with a firm "If you're not eating, Fred, go study in the other room." Again, the rule of change. That would have done away with the kicking incident's escalation. Given the circumstances, it might be better for someone else to walk the dog.

Longer term, everyone would be better served if there were more organization in the household than there appears to be. Organization is not always easy, and it does mean some imposition from above, but it gives clear signals to all as to what is expected. Setting limits is how we do this. No books at the table, homework done the night before, establish who does the dog walking and when, who helps out in a pinch. When everyone knows what is permitted/expected, and what the results will be when the agreed-upon expectations are not met, some objective criteria have come into play. Consistency of enforcement is very important, of course, but so is the ability to maintain some flexibility in the face of special circumstances. The issue of physical aggression has to be considered, as well.

Dad might have put the dishes aside for a moment and taken his oldest son into another room when the arguments began and perhaps have discovered why the homework had not been done. Perhaps Fred is having a difficult time with French I, and that's why he puts off dealing with it. Removing Fred from the heart of the morning traffic with four others busily moving toward getting out of the house might have helped. Perhaps Mom and Dad are *too* busy for their own kids' good, which might lead to a discussion between the parents about priorities and then a family meeting. The issues may turn out to be less those of Cheerios and spilled milk, dog walking, and books at the table, than not feeling well enough loved and cared for by parents, or not having an equal share of their attention.

The Miller house, Thursday evening. Tomorrow is a holiday, and everyone gets to stay up later than usual. Everybody is particularly looking forward to the time together, because the year has been very busy, with Mom making a number of business trips out of town and Dad often working late at the office when mom was not traveling.

''Let's play Scrabble,'' suggests Francine. She's nine and a word whiz.

"Nah," says eleven-year-old Gregory, "I wanna play Monopoly. Come on."

Mom and Dad are just waiting for things to sort out and they'll go along, so they're silent.

"Yeah, Scrabble, that's fun," says Jennifer, who is only seven but manages to stay in there with the rest of the two- and three-letter words.

Mom says, "Well, that seems to be the choice, Scrabble, so let's get going."

Gregory is not tickled. After about twenty minutes and three challenges from Francine, who is right in each instance, Greg starts getting obnoxious.

"Got enough room, Francine? Keep your feet out of there, okay?"

"Listen, Greggie," she starts, knowing how much he hates being called Greggie, "you're just mad because I've got a lot more points than you. How many do I have, Dad, huh?"

"I don't think that's the point, Francine. It's a game, and it's just fun playing together." Mom agrees with Dad's view.

They continue to play.

"I said, keep your stupid feet over there, you dumb—"

"Come on, guys," says Dad, "cool it, will you? No name-calling, Greg."

Mom wins, Fran and Dad tie, Jennifer and Gregory are within points of each other.

"That was great. Let's play another," says Jennifer.

"What was so great, Jennie-Pennie, huh?" asks Gregory. "What's so great about that dumb word game, anyhow, pipsqueak?"

"What's the matter, Greggie, can't pick on someone your own size? Afraid that Jennifer is going to beat you this time?" asks Francine.

Greg storms out of the room, the teasing remarks of Francine following him, and little Jennifer joining in for the first time.

"Hey, that's not nice," says Dad. "Gee, it's only a game." Mom agrees.

Greg's door is slammed so hard that Mom and Dad are shocked. They talk late that night in bed about Francine's needling and their growing concern that one day instead of slamming his door Gregory will use his hands on his teasing sister.

There are a couple of things that Mom and Dad could have done in this situation. They could have limited the choices, knowing Gregory's weakness in Scrabble and Francine's strength; that would probably not have been a fair decision, however, or a realistic one. We often have to play "games" in life that we are not expert at, and to be protected from this reality is not very useful.

What might have been a better strategy would have been to suggest that each child choose one game to play that evening, thus increasing the options. This would have given each child a sense of control and have cost nobody anything. "I might lose here, but I have a good shot at winning there" might be how the two competitive kids would have viewed this negotiated settlement of the game question.

Francine's purposeful needling of her older brother seems to roll off the parents' backs, but clearly not off Gregory's. Perhaps a discussion with Francine on that account would result in her empathizing with her brother. Perhaps not, as well, because teasing seems to be endemic among children. It might be worth taking a look at *why* Francine teases. She may be doing it for the attention it brings from her parents, attention that she thinks she will otherwise not get. As can often be the case, her self-image may not be as strong as it appears to be; thus, she tries to build it on her brother's weakness. Whatever the case, confronting the specific issues is necessary in order to see that the growing anger that seems to be clear in Gregory's door slamming does not escalate.

Both of the boys are about the same size, but almost three years separate them. Philip Johnson is twelve and his brother Leonard is "going on eleven," as he puts it. The school year has just begun, and Philip has a heavy work load. Next year he is going to be in high school, having skipped a grade early on. Leonard is a fifth grader. The boys have been best friends from the beginning, but this year there is a strain being put on their relationship. Philip gets to stay up later, Philip gets to watch some "stupid television program" that precludes Leonard watching one of his favorite before-bed weekly shows, Philip gets to do a lot of things that Leonard doesn't, and "It isn't fair." Philip also gets more "stuff," according to Leonard.

"Leonard, could you just give me a hand with this for a minute, dear?" Mom asks.

"Go ask your little Philip," comes the answer. Mom is absolutely surprised. Where did this come from? she wonders.

"Leonard, did you hear what I said? I asked you nicely to come and help your mother. Is that a dumb thing for me to do? What's the matter, dear?"

"Nothing."

"Well, come and help me, please. I really could use your help in cleaning up this room. It will only take a minute."

"I've got to study."

Mom cools it, scratching her head over this curious response from her almost eleven-year-old.

A couple of days later, Philip comes out of his room looking puzzled. "Mom, did you see my tennis racket?"

"No, dear. Go ask Dad. He's in the garage fixing the mower."

"Dad. You see my tennis racket?"

"Nope. Ask your brother."

After a search, Philip finds Leonard throwing rocks at the pinecones, trying to knock them from the trees. Philip has never seen Leonard showing so much concentration or throwing so hard.

"Hey, Len. You see my racket?"

"Nope."

"What are you doing?"

"What do you think?"

"What do you mean, what do I think? I see that you're throwing rocks at the trees, but what are you doing, you know? Why?"

"Because I want to, that's why."

"Hey, what's with you?"

"Why don't you go bug off and leave me alone, okay?" With a very disdainful look, Leonard turns to his brother and then back to the trees.

A week later, the missing racket is discovered, along with the missing first baseman's glove. The strings are popped and the glove is water-soaked. After a few days of denying any knowledge of what happened, one Sunday morning Leonard goes to his mother and tells her the truth. Hugging her, he sobs that he is just as good as Philip, any day, and how come "you guys"—meaning Mom and Dad—"don't love me as much as you used to?"

Leonard clearly missed Philip. Philip wasn't reciprocating because he was very busy. Mom and Dad were as busy as ever, unaware that the necessary work, the extra attention, the extra television time for Philip to see a program assigned by his English teacher, would break the closeness that Leonard had felt with his brother. Once aware of the facts through Leonard's sobbed confession, his parents sat down with him and told him how important he was to them and how much they loved him, just as much as Philip, no kidding. While it is very important to be equitable with time and with other resources, it is not always possible to be absolutely evenhanded. Without question, the Philips of our lives will get more strokes from time to time than will the Leonards. But if we are aware of the important interdependencies within the family system, we can help to ameliorate the sense of loss or rejection that one child might feel as a result of the other having center stage.

Leonard's parents must now find a way to strike the balance between reassuring Leonard and preventing Leonard's ordinary human fragility from resulting in a further imbalance, as in "We can't do that or Leonard will have a fit." Leonard will have to learn that life is not always fair and that he must adapt to changes or else find life very difficult. Mom and Dad can help him to adjust to that fact, while at the same time making some special efforts to do things with him that he likes.

This situation was helped by the fact that Leonard felt comfortable with showing his emotions. By letting his parents know that he was feeling left out and less loved than his brother, his parents could then act. But if the family did not allow for overt emotional display, the anger and acting out might have escalated, and the life of the family would have been adversely affected.

It might have played out quite differently in another

family. There might have been accusations made when the broken racket and water-soaked glove were found, a ganging up on Leonard could have occurred, and the needy and locked-out (from his point of view) Leonard might have become ''Bad Leonard,'' caught in constant battle with ''Philip the Good.''

The story of Philip and Leonard makes clear the need to be sensitive to the family dynamic, to be able to empathize, to allow the display of emotion, to talk things out, to make strides toward equity. If we are aware of what's *really* going on in our families, if we learn to read between the lines, we have a shot at helping our kids grow while making family life more satisfying and happy.

She is going on thirteen, and next year is her last in junior high school. He is ten and finishing up fifth grade this year. For a long time, they were buddies, equals, but now she bikes off to her friends' houses and he has a friend or two from down the street come over to play, which is fine, except that now she is too busy for anything with him, and indignity of indignities, she gets to stay up later!

''What do you mean I have to go to bed? What about her?''

''It's time, sweetie, that's why.''

''What about her, huh? How come she gets to stay up and I have to go to bed? It's not fair. I'm not going.''

''Baby,'' teases the sister.

''I'll show you who's a baby,'' he says as he runs after her.

''Hey Mom, Dad, stop him! He's crazy, he'll hurt me.''

''Stop that, Daniel, right now.''

Daniel stops. Julia, the nearly thirteen sister, turns, sticks her tongue out, and repeats, ''Baby.''

The chase resumes and everything is repeated. In the end, Daniel goes to bed and Julia stays up to do homework. The next night may be no different. If there are three or four kids, the possibility of staggered bedtime schedules simply expands the possibilities for chaos!

While every kid wants to be at least equal in all ways to his or her brothers and sisters, it is not possible. There are age differences, differences in needs and interests, differences in size and sex. Kids are not generic. Each one is special. In that fact lies the key to lessening conflict built around ''Why him, why not me?'' Note the ''lessen'' rather than ''eliminate.'' The latter is as likely as a beach day in Vermont in February.

''Daniel,'' Mom says, ''what special thing do you want to do before you get into bed? Or maybe you'd like Dad or me to read you some of *Stuart Little*? If you want, you can watch one of the videocassettes. You still have a half hour before you have to brush up and get tucked in. Don't turn it up too high, though, your sister has a lot of studying to do, okay?''

It may not thrill Daniel that Julia will still be up while he is off to sleep, but the special time doing something alone or with one or both of his parents might make him feel special, which may be the nub of the matter, in any case: ''How come she's getting special treatment and not me?'' The inferential ''Oh, your poor sister is burdened with homework'' may work to make him feel thrice blessed.

''Hey, here comes bat breath,'' says Jake as his younger brother, Edward, comes in for lunch.

''Come on, leave me alone,'' Edward says as he tries getting to the refrigerator for some milk to wash down the pb&j that he is going to make himself in a minute. On his way, his sister puts her foot out to try to trip him, but he sidesteps that one. ''Off my case, Becky, will ya?''

''Yeah, you have the rottenest breath in the whole city, you know that? The cat is real mad at you, bat breath. She says she's not getting all her protein because of you. The school nurse says we need our protein to grow, but gee, bat breath, don't take Suzy's mice.''

''You're disgusting, you know that?'' says Edward.

''Oh, I'm disgusting, huh? Well, look at the geranium, it's tipping over, bat breath. Move your face away from it, will you?''

Despite his smaller size, Edward is getting really mad, mad enough to go near his older brother and start shoving him.

''What are you doing, pipsqueak?'' says younger sister. ''Watch out, or you'll get rolled up and put out with the trash.''

The scene can go on and on and on. Sometimes it does.

Edward has become the designated scapegoat in his family. It is not always easy to figure out why, but maybe because he is so close to his mother, the other kids feel a little left out. Or maybe it's because the oldest son is in the bullying stage, which may be a result of being bullied in a different way at home, or in the same way at school. In a certain way, it is less important to know the root of the problem than to see the behavior and try to address it.

"Jake," begins Dad in a private setting, "how come you get on Edward's case so? I know that sometimes it's fun to 'rag' the other guys—I did enough of it myself in high school—but, you know, it can really hurt someone. I think Edward feels real bad about the way you go after him."

"Did you ever smell his breath? I don't think he brushes, honest. What a slob!"

"Come on, Jake, don't give me that. Look at your fingernails. Look at your dungarees; I bet you could stand them in the corner. Hey, you're no paragon of hygiene, buddy, so what the heck gives?"

"I don't know, it's fun."

"Fun? Okay, if it's so much fun, I'm going to get on *your* case. Every time I see you, I'm going to say something negative. Maybe your famous slouch—yeah, that's it, the old slouch—that's the target. Old Quasimodo Jake."

"Aw, come on, fat buns, I don't slouch that much, do I?"

Despite the defiance in the characterization of Dad's rump, there is behind the bravado a hint in Jake's voice of not feeling fully approved of.

"Wicked bad. Wicked. Awesome hunchback," says Dad.

"You kidding me? Hey, come on, Dad, enough of the joke, huh?"

Dad goes on to talk about the object lesson, and how important it is for Jake to walk in his brother's sneakers for just a moment. He enlists Jake's help in stopping this ongoing ragging of Edward, asking him to help to turn

Becky around, too, because it's humiliating for a kid to have to take that kind of criticism from a younger child.

"Teasing is one thing," Dad says, "but enough is more than enough. Okay?"

Jake's nod is sufficient, and on the way by Dad gives him a handshake. On the way out of the room, however, he can't resist one more barb about Dad's spreading backside. Clearly, there is more work to be done, but there has been a beginning.

Later, the family can look at the subtext to try to discover some of the reasons underlying the behavior. Favoritism on the part of one parent, insecurity on the part of the oldest child, whatever, but at least for the moment the pressure on the developing Edward has been removed, which is a good-enough start.

If we feel the strain of not having as much time to give to our children as we would wish, there are sometimes things we can do about it, like reapportioning time. That is not always possible for very concrete economic reasons, and we must do the best that we can with the time we do have, leaving a trail of clues that we have as much love and concern for our children as they would want us to have.

Jerry and Kelly are both out flat most of the time. They like their work, all right, but more than that, the things that they want for their children, like a large-enough house in a town with excellent schools, cost a lot. Ben is seven, Moira is nine, and Malcolm is eleven. They come home from school to an empty house at the same time, and Malcolm is responsible for the three of them until Mom and Dad get home from work. Malcolm is good-natured, but enough is enough. He's beginning to get sick and tired of the responsibility. He also has some friends at school who are good soccer players and who would like to add Malcolm to their after-school games. But Malcolm can't go; he's got to be home with his kid brother and sister.

As good a big brother as Malcolm is, he is not enough for Moira and Ben. Some nights they have to be in bed before Mom and Dad get back from work. When they were younger, they think, they were happier. Mom and

Dad came to tuck them in, they played together before going to bed, Dad would read stories. Now, in this new house, they only see their parents on weekends, and then it's almost all work. "Can you help me with . . ." resounds all Saturday. Sunday is a special case. It starts out okay, but as the day wears on, the two younger kids get antsy, and start to pick on each other. By around 5:00 P.M., they are hollering at each other, and last week Moira hit Ben so hard that he actually has a visible bruise on that arm. Mom and Dad, of course, are pretty tired by now, having tried to accomplish a week's worth of normal house chores on the weekend. They come running when the Sunday screeching starts, lecture the kids about how they have to be nice to each other and how hard Mom and Dad work, and then spend the rest of the evening with the kids trying to keep them from killing each other. If only Malcolm were here, they think. Fortunately for him, he's off somewhere playing soccer or something.

Jerry and Kelly have bitten off a big chunk "for the sake of the children," and in so doing have tied themselves up in car and house payments that don't give them any breathing room. They work too many hours a week, and their growing kids don't get enough of them. The fights are nothing more than a reaction to that lack of time together, as well as a device to get it. The Monday morning sicknesses that Ben and/or Moira are now beginning to invent are further evidence that something has to give. But just what?

It may be that Mom and Dad have not only bitten off more than they can chew, but have been bitten by "the dream." Perfect house, perfect children, perfect schools. Having pride in their children's education is great, but there has to be consideration of the other parts of their kids' lives, as well. They may have to give back some of the dream and find some time to fill the need the two younger kids have for their company, counsel, closeness. Maybe they have to cut back in some areas. It may mean a smaller house or a slightly less impressive neighborhood, but something has to go. Perhaps a less drastic reapportioning of other resources will do the trick. Mom could spend the whole weekend with the kids while Dad does the necessary tasks and gives the time not involved with chores to the family; the parents could alternate weekends this way. Whatever the solution or solutions applied to the situation, the important thing to recognize is that kids need closeness with their parents.

Lynne and Bob have two kids named Kyle and Tracy, ages twelve and eleven, respectively. Over the last year or so, Lynne and Bob have been ''on our cases,'' according to the kids. ''I can't do anything right around here'' is how Tracy puts it.

''You call that bed made, Kyle? Get back in there. And I think that you better just hang around here for a while and help out a bit. We're not hired help, you know.'' Bob has a real burn on.

''You kidding me, or what? Let's see your bed, huh? Bet it isn't even made, that's what I bet. Come on, give me a break. I wanna go play ball.''

''Don't you talk back to your father that way, young man,'' says Lynne. ''I want you to help out with the windows. Seems I just washed—''

''*What?* Are you nuts. Cripes, I can't believe it. You guys are unreal!'' Tracy comes down the hall.

''I see they're on you, too. It's not fair, and they know it. If they were decent, they'd be ashamed. I'm not going to do a thing. It's just not fair.''

''Listen, here, young lady . . .'' You can imagine the rest.

Bob and Lynne are lonely. They are from big families and are used to having a lot of people around. When the kids were younger and spent most of the time at home, they loved it. They are good and creative parents, but they are too dependent on their kids for companionship. They need to work at taking pleasure in their children's independence. There are times in children's lives when they need to do a lot of testing of themselves by peers, and this is one of those times for Tracy and Kyle. The poorly made bed or the messy this or that of kids on the cusp of adolescence is sometimes only the superficial reason for punishment. The real reason can be that the parent feels abandoned by the child and needs to punish the child to keep it close in the process.

Instead of abandoning their own needs entirely, Bob and Lynne might be able to work something out. First they need to read between the lines of their own lives and words and see the needs that are at the base of their being on their kids' cases. Once they have identified what is really troubling them—that they miss the company of Tracy and Kyle—they can talk to their kids about their feelings. Maybe they can then negotiate a little by exchanging favors or doing an alternate deal of this-time-for-next. The result could be that Bob and Lynne will have some of what they want, while acknowledging that dependent childhood is on the wane, and recognizing that the kids have their own priorities to make, as well.

Letting go is a recurring theme in this period, and in the case of first-time campers, it is truly a two-way street.

Terry is preparing to go off to camp for the first time. Except for a week on a farm in Wyoming spent with his cousins when he was six, he has never been away from his parents overnight. He is very excited about the prospect, and this is making his mother very, very sad. How can Terry want to be away from me? Even as she thinks it, she feels simultaneously guilty and giddy, the latter because at the young age of thirty-four she has discovered that what drove her nuts about her mother is within *her*. But Rena is trying to put a good face on things. Nevertheless, she picks on Terry over the next twelve days for breaking real and imaginary rules. His glee over going away from his own home ("that we worked so hard to give you," Rena hears in her head) insults her. Terry's dad, Blake, talks about the camp endlessly and excitedly, for he went to the camp himself, was a counselor for four summers, and would go now, were it not that he had to tend to business. This further infuriates Rena, and she has quiet fights in the privacy of the bedroom with Blake ("this man who would rip the baby from its mother's arms," she hears in her head, and can barely contain a giggle as a result). Finally, the day arrives, with everyone smiling, the trunk all packed, and the inventory checked thrice. The bus leaves for the mountains and first-camper's jitters. Everyone survives. Nevertheless, there were a couple of weeks of tension that might have led to real fights had Dad and his son not been good at closing the door on potential conflict that had no sound base. Dad knows that Mom is having a struggle with memories of her mother's behavior. He knows that she "never wants to be like my mother." He agrees, quietly, but knowing that there is ambivalence built on the child's (Rena's) wish to remain loyal to her mother—"who gave me life"—he does not allow himself the passing pleasure of attacking Rena's mother, nor does he point out their similarities. He also knows that the issue is too emotionally charged just now for them to have a full and rational discussion about it. He talks with his son and explains, saying that it is not a good idea to take much of this too seriously right now, because Mom is having a hard time seeing Terry gone for a whole summer. While they may be a simplification, for the issues are important, it suffices to cool things down through not overreacting to Mom's temporary picking on him. (The situations could be reversed as to parental gender and could be exactly the same.)

Henry wanted not to go to camp in the worst way. He hated the smell of the trunk, he hated having to have labels in his underwear, he hated the dumb name of the camp, everything. He wanted to stay home in the warm bosom of his family. But there he was in the bus station along with a grab bag of other campers in their Nikes and blue jeans, and there was no turning back. As he had predicted, he was miserable. Here he was in the woods with a hundred boys he didn't even know. He loved to swim, so that part was okay, but the baseball diamond was another thing altogether. Thank god, he thought, for right field. But there was light: At the end of the first two weeks, there would be a visit from his parents.

The day arrived, and so did Mom and Dad. Henry carried out his plan, throwing himself on their mercy ("Please, oh, please," he pleaded, "take me home. Please take me home, do not abandon this city boy to the woods.") The discussion became somewhat voluble, so Mom and Dad and Henry retired to the car to continue. Oh, the car, it smelled like home—sweet, familiar, comfortable, and safe; "Oh please take me home," Henry pleaded. Mom and Dad argued. "Why should he not come home," said Mom, "if he is miserable here? Would you want to be miserable someplace if you had the ability to leave?" "Yes, dear, I know," said Dad, "but this is his first time away from home, and, well, let's not close things off quite yet, all right? How's this, Henry," he said. "Stay another five days, and then, if you are still unhappy, we will come and get you and that will be the end of it. We don't want you to be miserable, but we think maybe you have not given it quite enough time."

Henry's little palms were wet with anxiety, but Dad was a good guy, and the suggestion seemed okay. "I will stay another week," Henry declared. After his parents left, he returned to his cabin, relieved. Predictably, he was so engrossed for the rest of the summer that he had no memory of ever having not loved camp.

Henry's parents supported his wishes, promising to bring him home if he would only give it one final try. Henry felt secure. He had not been abandoned, he could return to his parents' home, he was not going to have to live in dormitories with strangers the rest of his life. Knowing that he was still connected to home, he could let himself make peace with that which had threatened him.

When we give somebody more than one way of looking at a situation that is discomforting, we decrease the emotional intensity involved. The situation that is yes/no becomes yes/no/maybe. While in certain instances this ambiguity might increase some people's anxiety, the *maybe* acts as a kind of safety valve, and the panic that a person (Henry) might feel is lessened. This is another way of increasing the options, the perfect negotiation tool in this situation. Offering support, love, and the awareness that "you can go home again" without losing face diffuses a situation that could have been quite different. Other possible responses to Henry's plight:

"Well, you are quite a disappointment to us."

"What's wrong with you? Any boy would . . ."

"Shh. Don't be such a big baby/sissy!"

"Of course, dear, but don't ever expect . . ."

"Get your things. Let's go. I don't want to hear a word from you all the way home, you hear, young man?"

Any of these responses could cause a two- or three-way fight that could escalate. Dad versus Mom or the opposite, parents versus child, alliances made between one parent and the child versus the parent who has a different view; any of these could be the match put to the emotional tinder. By making the right choices, by taking into consideration the way kids feel—identifying—we depressurize the situation and thus make dealing with the feelings of aloneness, strangeness, and not-homeness easier for the child. A strong response in the other direction can bring with it the beginning or continuance of a sense of failure, which in turn will bring frustration to everyone in the family, which in turn will result in acting out, which means more fights down the road.

Look for these same issues around camping out with friends and family, pajama parties, a week at the best friend's summer cottage. And remember that the anxieties can be the parents' as readily as the child's, and thus it will be *us*, the parents, who act out to restrain the child. Separation is hard for everybody.

"Beth, how come you spend so much time with the Jerrold girl? I wouldn't have thought she was our—your kind of girl."

"What's the matter with her, Mom, huh? Don't you like her family car?"

"Young lady, I don't think family cars are the point, and you don't have to be so cutting. No, she just seems sort of . . ."

"Well, I'd love to stay and talk, Mom, but I have to get going. I have soccer practice, and I barely have time to get there. See you later," Beth, says, heading out to the garage for her bicycle.

"Beth, I'll drive you if you like. Beth, *Beth*?"

Beth has ignored the offered ride, playing the deaf lady. Mom really would have liked to have driven her. They could have talked more about this problem of that Nancy Jerrold.

The problem of friends chosen is a tough one for families, particularly on the upper end of this age bracket, when kids have so much mobility. They are out of our houses for long periods of time. Anything could happen, and whom they have chosen to be with, to an extent, determines the quality and kind of things that may hap-

pen. We feel at a loss, out of control. We have not only
put them into schools that have great control and influence, but now they are under the influence of others,
some of whom we may not approve or about whom we
may not know enough to feel comfortable. It is both real
and imaginary, this problem, much of it dependent on
our perceptions of what is important, real, possible. Despite the varied nature of situations, and the utter subjec-
tivity of many of our reactions to the suitability of others,
there are things we can do.

Are we objectively evaluating our kids' friends? We
may be projecting onto them the experiences of our
childhood, our own yearnings, or our own blind spots
when it comes to judging others. If we do see a real
problem with our children's friends, a problem that will
result in our children being harmed in some way, then
we must act. In acting, we should be as low key as possible. Otherwise, a child will see this dispute as a major
testing ground of control. If our children are in no danger, but we insist they choose companions of whom we
approve, we should be prepared for frustrated kids who
are either extremely rebellious or painfully tractable.

Let's go back to Beth, her mother, and Nancy Jerrold.
Beth's mother doesn't like Nancy because she is gawky,
unathletic, her father is in a line of work Beth's mom
doesn't approve of, and the Jerrolds' oldest has been
busted for pot smoking. The fact of the matter is that
Nancy is a very funny girl who is a good storyteller. She
reads a lot. Beth reads a lot, too, likes someone to be
with who is just as goofily imaginative as she is, and is
amazed at Nancy's storytelling skills. She can make them
up on the spot, and everything seems in place. Beth also
likes sports and spends about half of her free time swim-
ming, playing soccer, and taking some tennis instruction
at the town courts. That time she does not spend with
Nancy, but Beth's mother fixes on what she doesn't like.
When Beth's mother brings up the subject of Nancy, Beth
dips her brush in the ''my mother is a snob'' paint box,
and is generous in brushing it on.

Mom has made some tactical errors. She brought the
subject up out of context, did it when her daughter was
about to go out, and then did not have a fully articulated

view of why the association between Nancy and her daughter was not ideal.

If Mom had a reason to suspect Nancy was adversely affecting Beth's behavior, she might have proceeded first by putting aside some time to just talk with Beth about "things." In the process, she might have discovered what her daughter found so interesting about Nancy. She might have encouraged Beth to invite Nancy over and gotten to know her. The fear of drugs and related problems is normal, and the fact that one member of a family becomes drug-involved may suggest family problems—which may be true in this instance, but the result might also be that Nancy has had to become a more creative and resilient person. Instead of seeing Nancy as a threat to her child, Mom should take a closer look and see if perhaps Nancy is not a special person *because* her child chose her.

By challenging a child about something as personal as a choice of friends, we do not give him/her breathing space and credit for judgment. We cause our children to lose face. We need to learn to trust them as we have taught them through our actions that we can be trusted. If we find that a friendship *is* having a negative impact, we need to do a little negotiating. Do a little exchange of favors: You spend less time with *X* and I will do *Y* with you as you would like me to (or provide more *Z*, or whatever.) The more independent the child, the harder it may be to succeed in this manner—that is one of the problems associated with being a good parent who has fostered independence. If real harm is possible, then a parent has the responsibility to make decrees, but the reasons must be fully explained to the child. If the child sees the judgment made of a friend as a judgment of self, it may hurt, but the parent can compensate for that through showing love and caring in any number of other ways. Not in delivering goods and services or bribes, but in supplying love and caring.

"This is not a restaurant!"

This is one of the classic remarks of Mom or Dad to the endless demands for food at the most peculiar hours by children, whether it be an only child or one of a passel of kids. Add to this the friends who are brought home, and the opportunities for mayhem revolving around the kitchen are considerable.

Mom's upstairs doing the laundry, Dad's vacuuming the dining room, and Dan and his friends, Tom and Gregory, come storming into the house. They've been playing baseball all morning, and it's around one o'clock.

"Hey, guys, let's see what's to eat. I could eat a horse." They pass Stephanie, and Dan makes one of his twelve-year-old sexist remarks about "playing with dollies, I suppose." He pulls her hair on the way by and she lets out a scream, but Dad can't hear it because of the vacuum. The juggernaut continues on its way to the refrigerator. They decide on the thin reddish "fish stuff" and milk, and then there are these great-looking little miniature pies with fruit all over the top. "Hey, we lucked out today," Dan says. "I've never seen the refrigerator so stuffed before." Gregory asks if it's okay to have a second fruit-pie thing, and Dan says sure. They sprawl, more than sit, around a table, talking excitedly about how great they did this morning in their pickup game at the field, and are higher than kites on being twelve and full of energy and having done well. They finish, put their dishes on the kitchen counter, and rush back out, ready to take on anything in their way.

The scene has a certain charm. It is ebullient, life-embracing. But to Dad, who had cleaned the kitchen after breakfast, the dishes on the side of the sink don't look life-embracing at all. They just look like more work. And to Mom, who arrives downstairs ten minutes later, after folding the laundry and putting fresh sheets on the beds, an inventory of the refrigerator indicates that half of the smoked salmon for Sunday brunch, at which they will entertain, something they rarely do, is missing. The pear tarts are pretty well depleted, as well. Dan's return in the evening is going to be interesting.

This story is just one of the many that revolve around eating. It is not unlike that which revolves around bed making, helping to tidy up, being nice to older people and aunts and uncles rarely seen. The stories are really about taking the necessary responsibility that comes from living in a mutually dependent group, the family. Approaches to solutions can be varied. First, let's look at some bad ways.

"Dan, what you did today was monstrous. Do you know how much that cost? Do you know who these people are that we are entertaining? Do you know that you have put us in a terrible situation? Well, you're grounded for the rest of your life." While clearly an exaggeration, this approach, wherein it is maintained that the child has dismembered the Western world and all that it represents through piggish and boorish behavior, is not uncommon. We all know this approach, for it is the guilt trip we have all grown up with. Often it doesn't work; and when it does, the results are hardly what we want. We do not really want a compliant, guilty child, do we?

We could use reason, as in, "Well, Dan, that was a very selfish act that you committed, you know. It isn't nice to be selfish. That kind of selfishness can only lead to self-centeredness later on in life. Now I really want to bring you through this from beginning to end, Dan, so that you understand the interrelationships . . ." Probably not the tack that would bring a child back for more instruction.

We could psychologize. "Why do you think you ate all the lox, Daniel? Can we talk about that now? Is there some anger against your Mom and me, Daniel? Feelings, Dan, not just words—let your feelings come out." Probably not that either.

Let's look at it. Dan is twelve, he is full of energy, he is in some ways out of control, out of control in twelve-year-old ways that sometimes exhibit themselves in voracious eating, often standing up and just about to run off. It is to be expected, but the fact that it is to be expected is neither here nor there, for we do have as a mission the civilizing of our kids. What do we do with Dan?

There could be a very straightforward recapitulation of the mutual responsibilities within the family, quick and to the point. Then, as to the specific: "Dan, if you want to bring friends in and eat, fine. First, however, there are rules. (We are setting limits.) You don't grab anything out of the refrigerator that is clearly not everyday food. If you had stopped for a minute to think about the lox— the reddish fish stuff—you would have known that it was not everyday eats. If you are bringing friends in to eat, please talk to one of us about what's fair game and what is not. If we are not here, please stick to the regular stuff. You know what we eat. If there is going to be something special going on here and we have special food, I think we should take the responsibility to mark it, so in the future, read the label if there is a label, or just use your good sense. You're a smart guy. In the future, if there is this kind of invasion and we get eaten out of thirty dollars' worth of company food because you don't use your good brains, it's going to cost you. Right out of allowance and newspaper-route money. Me adult, you child: end of story. Now let's go shoot some bumper pool.''

By declaring the parameters of behavior, we have done something constructive. By not attacking Dan, we have made clear the rules that will be in effect from now on. In this instance, there are responsibilities involved on both sides—not a bad notion. If there is an infraction of the rules, the offender knows what the rules are. No guilt, no psychologizing, no bad feelings from attacks. Straight adult talk.

The same tack can be taken with all of the discipline problems relating to tidiness, shared responsibility, etc. The price exacted for breaking the rules would change— no movie if certain chores are not done, promised yard work not done, etc., but the effect should be the same. Once again, it is important to point out that *there must be consistency,* AND paradoxically, *flexibility.* Just as we know it is important to keep a promise made to our children—say, a trip to the north country for apple picking— so it is important that extenuating circumstances—a sudden call to work, the blahs, a cold—be honored as a valid excuse for canceling that particular date. It shouldn't invalidate the commitment for the future or ruin your reputation as a mother or father, but should result in rescheduling. We ought to allow the same flexibility with our kids. While we should work toward consistency, we should not put ourselves or our children in a straitjacket in the process.

There is a passage in the novel *Mr. Bridge* by Evan Connell in which Mr. Bridge, a good, responsible, righteous husband and father, passes his daughter's room and sees her, in her new young adulthood, naked. The sight shocks him, for in some ways he has been unaware of her as a female. She has been only "daughter," but now she is also becoming "woman." He sits on the edge of his bed and finds, to his chagrin, that the image of his daughter does not readily leave him. All of us, male and female, are Mr. Bridge. Whether we wish to recognize it or not, we are, as well as all else that we are, sexual animals. The very fact of the differences between the sexes, and what it conjures up in us, can result in what is called sexual antagonism. Given the increasingly early physical development of children, the fights that cluster around the recognition of sexual development and sexual differences begin to become most apparent near the end of this period, just before the onset—or is it *onslaught*?—of adolescence.

Jeb and Jann have been married since college. They have two really good kids, according to definition, Mark and Thea. Mark is fifteen and Thea is twelve. Mark is a sophomore in high school, and Thea is in junior high. They have gotten along pretty well for twelve years. Thea's arrival when Mark was three didn't seem to put him at all off stride, and his parents are delighted that they have had a pretty harmonious household for so long. Lately, however, there have been some big scenes between the kids, scenes that have spilled over onto Jeb and Jann.

Thea is watching a movie on television on Friday night, and Mark has a couple of friends in to play some Ping-Pong. Mom and Dad are in the kitchen having coffee, talking over the week past and planning for the weekend. The ping and pong of the ball coming from the small basement room is music to the parents' ears, as are the "all right's" of the trio; they could be out doing who knows what at this age. Ten minutes later, engrossed in their conversation, they are unaware that the boys have stopped playing and are in the small study watching television with Thea.

Mark says, "Hey, do we have to watch this drivel?"

"Nobody invited you, Mark. Shhh. Be quiet," says Thea.

During the commercial break, Bruce, who has been

giving sidelong glances at the new, improved Thea, says, "That's one of my favorites, Thea. I love that scene in the rain when Gene Kelly winds up hanging off a lamp-post. God, that guy makes it look so easy. What an athlete!"

"Grooaan! Barf, barf!" These are the primitive sounds of Mark and Art, his other pal, putting down the remarks of Bruce. They continue. "How Brucian of you. Enchantée, I'm sure," says Art. He and Mark laugh. Bruce reddens a little, but Thea comes to the rescue. "You guys are such grunts! You don't appreciate the muscle control, the timing, the strength." Bruce knows from gymnastics, and Thea knows from ballet classes. Mark wants to get the heck out of the house, the whole thing is agitating him.

"Hey, let's go down to Brad's and listen to some music. Coming, Brucie?" he asks derisively.

Mark is aware of the beauty of his kid sister. There has been some talk among the boys about her figure, and Mark is both fascinated and embarrassed at the same time. He feels some guilt about allowing the talk and some guilt about the fascination/attraction, as in, "If she weren't my sister, I could go for her." What happens, however, is that the feeling makes him anxious and he winds up having fights with her over nothing much at all. He swears that Mom and Dad, particularly Dad, play favorites with her. He makes fun of her bookishness and what he calls her ballerina "posing." He also calls her a baby because she is younger than he is, which gets further fights going.

Jeb is, in fact, favoring Thea, although he doesn't see it that way. She is lovely and reminds him of Jann when they were in college together. Jann is now thirty-nine and a very attractive and composed woman, but having this nearly duplicate Jann in the house brings back memories of an earlier and simpler time. Jann and Jeb are very much in love, but there is some antagonism between Jann and Thea, although Jann doesn't see that either. It amounts to Jann picking on her daughter, putting more emphasis on any small thing that Thea does not do that she should than on more significant infractions on Mark's part. There is an alliance now between Mom and her son. He confides in her and avoids anything more than the most superficial talks with Dad—baseball scores, how long the grass is.

This is a classical and totally normal situation. We usually are not aware of the component parts in our own lives, but if we will think back to our own childhoods, we may find similar behavior: the times when you, a girl, were called Daddy's girl by your mother or, more acidly, perhaps, by your brothers and sisters; or for a boy, Mommy's pet. Try thinking back to those times when we thought that one parent or the other was picking on us endlessly and for "no reason at all." We may recognize the similarities in situations, we may recognize the role model for our own behavior in that look back, as well.

Usually the antagonism that revolves around sex differences, attraction/repulsion, fascination/guilt, plays out in harmless fights. But if there are intense but groundless fights between siblings at this time of life, when there is obvious growth and development—or between parent and child or husband and wife related to an alliance between a parent and a child from the cusp of adolescence on—it is useful to explore further. Note that further exploration is not recommended because the situation is to be considered abnormal (which it is not), but rather because tracing to the roots of such special relationships can be relieving and revealing. It is reasonable to prepare for such alliances as part of the norm, to compensate for them by setting aside time to talk with our spouses, to promise each other that when the other becomes aware of such alliances they will be spoken of, not swallowed where they will come out in anger, indifference, hurt.

Let's imagine a slightly different situation with Jann and Jeb. "Jann, I have to tell you something. I feel a little frozen out recently. You are great and I'm really happy that we met and that we had these wonderful kids, but whenever Mark and his friends are around, you drop me and gravitate toward them. Mark is a good friend and son to you, I know. It's his time to have a woman friend to confide in and he couldn't have picked a better woman, but sometimes when you two are together, I feel like an interloper."

"I think you're exaggerating things. He's a great kid, Jeb, I could squeeze him to death with love sometimes.

He's wonderful, but you're going overboard on this, don't you think?''

"Could be, but I can only tell you what I feel about it lately, and I'm telling you that I feel like an outsider."

"What about you and Thea? She hangs on your every word, and Daddy this and Daddy that—sometimes it drives me nuts!"

This is a good beginning of an exchange over a very common occurrence. But it is only the recognition of the problem. If Jann and Jeb play a game of word association, they may discover interesting underlying attitudes related to "the favorite child." Jeb takes the initiative.

"Jann, what's the first word that comes into your mind when you think of Mark?"

"Oh, I suppose *gentle*. And you?"

"*Strong*. He's like my brother Ralph: square-jawed, large-boned, strong, not a tough-guy strong, but strong and self-contained for a boy his age."

"Handsome."

"Responsible."

"He reminds me a lot of you when we met at freshman orientation, to tell you the truth."

"That's interesting, you know. I think of my brother, you think of me. That's nice. Let's do Thea. What's the first word?"

"Lovely, self-confident, maybe too much so."

"Lovely, confident, reminds me of you in college."

"Now that's a switch. I wouldn't have thought that. Have I changed that much?"

"What do you mean, have you changed? Why, you are just as you have always been. Oh, a little older around the eyes . . ."

"She's a little too aloof to be me, I think. A little icy, at least with me."

"Oh, she is not. You're just a little jealous, I guess, exactly the way I am of you and Mark."

"Damned right I am."

It's not unusual that people will look back nostalgically at their courtship, early marriage, and find in their children, with whom they can go through much of it again, the renewed excitement of discovery. Here the partners find themselves yearning in a perfectly harmless way for their old selves. The kids put an edge on things, they help renew them. Each of the parents in his or her own way is smitten with the other's image. It is a tribute to the past and at the same time a small threat in the present. In this situation, coming to the realization that the newly forged alliances are repetitions of the old ones helps to take the edge off of the threat. The next step is to promote a better balance in the relationship between the adults in light of this new knowledge, while at the same time not removing the bonds of intimate connection between parents and children.

On an unconscious if not conscious level, the antagonism may be being transmitted and received loud and clear, resulting in an even more seductive or confidential attitude toward Dad/Mom on the part of the kids. Having enough power at your fingertips at twelve and fifteen to make adults react as they do is pretty heady, and it is not at all unreasonable that a child would use it. While standing firm on keeping up the relationship with the child, we should discreetly discourage its intensification, perhaps by making less time available for valid reasons.

If son spends too much time with Mom, perhaps Mom has to put some evening work into her schedule that will then allow her to say no sometimes, without seeming to reject her son. If daughter cuddles too much with Dad in front of the television set, then Dad might find that he wants to read more often in the evening. We should make a special effort to reconnect with the other child, as well. Dad may have to show some of his own vulnerability in the process, giving his son a view of a slightly less assured self, one who also has moments of doubt, which is very likely the aspect of Mom—nonjudgmental and noncompetitive (besides the nascent sexual aspect)—that attracts son to her. Not only will it be reassuring for son to know a man who is not afraid to speak of emotional issues, but it may be equally useful for Dad to see aspects of himself on the surface rather than submerged and unshared. Carving out times for renewal between the parents is also essential. Given the complexities of family life and the necessity of the two-salary family, time is not so easily set aside, but it *must* be, even if only a commitment of a half hour before bedtime for being alone together. No kids, no business, just talk about each other, in this instance. (This is a modification of the Marriage Preserving Wednesday of Chapter 4).

As for the brother who fights with Sis because of his and/or his friends' awareness of her flowering, or the sister who is overly attached to her brother, who is just "so great," the parents need to help their kids understand their quite natural affection and attraction for each other. Heck, they are only people. At the same time, parents must stress the importance of kids not becoming so attached to each other so as to be meddlesome and nonobjective, as in, "How he could go out with that snake beats me," or "That thug is going out with my sister?" without abandoning the role of friends, protectors, and fans.

Clearly, those parents who have a difficult time comfortably acknowledging their own sexuality may react more strongly to the physical manifestations of maturity in their children, and will not recognize those reactions for what they are: normal. Their guilty discomfort at an unconscious level will drive them in other directions, toward "picking on" issues that are farthest from the center—it's more comfortable that way. Thus the scapegoating of a child between twelve and sixteen can occur. Dad, rather than recognizing the flirtatious closeness of the daughter, or Mom of the same in relation to the son, will fix on chores, behavior, language, tidiness, almost anything, rather than confront the reality and accept it as a two-way street. It certainly is that.

Historically, we have thought of daughters as their fathers' comforts and consolations as time wore on, with sons providing the same comfort for their mothers. The flirtatious and seductive behavior, the intensity of the son revealing thoughts to this older woman that he never could to his friends, or to his dad, most especially; the very clear-cut rivalries—son for Mom's acceptance as very special vis-à-vis Dad, daughter for her temporary overshadowing of that rival, Mom—are not new. Greek theater would have been much less rich without these themes, which later became theories of psychiatrists. The incest tabboo is very old and very strong, and some of us feel so vulnerable that we do not accept the innocent and normal developmental attraction for what it is.

We must again think back to our own childhoods, to

how we felt at twelve, to what the other relationships were like in the family, to what our own struggles were with our parents. We may see connections. The sister who got all of Dad's attention for a while, and who, when she was ready, could scarcely be seen in the house for her sea of outside activities, leaving him bereft, for he had become reliant on that temporary intimate relationship that allowed him to be both wise and knowing while replicating the fond boy-girl flirtations of the past. The brother who stole the affections of Mom by confiding all in her. Or the father who scolded the pretty daughter for no clear reason, which made you wonder if Dad had all his marbles. (In some families there can be so much rage around this issue that intervention is recommended.)

We find that we often imitate the behavior of those whom we have sworn we would never imitate, be it Mom or Dad, a grandparent who had a particularly strong impact on our lives, or another person who had great importance to us in the past. After all, it is in our childhood that we learn behavior, and although we plan to make rational decisions, when we are confronted with emotionally laden situations we sometimes react, not on the intellectual level, but on that level where the old movies are archived. Now is the time to thread them into the machine, sort out the details, sort out our behavior, and make changes when we can, together with our spouses. Just as salespeople have found over time that to ask in some way for the help of the potential customer creates a bond that may lead to satisfaction for both the buyer and the seller, so, too, for spouses. Run those old movies in that half hour set aside before sleep. Do not talk about issues—"He was autocratic and I was independent, thus there was a clash of wills"—but of how you felt *then*, what it was like *then*. The effort is worth it, for the testing continues as we approach the years of the glands, of the child's need to truly find its own way in the world. Adolescence in full bloom is straight ahead.

9

Puberty and Adolescence: Thirteen Through Eighteen

This is not only the period when "sex rears its pretty head," but also a time full of pressures for both parents and kids. The years between the end of "the little kids' school" and high school and the beginning of career or further education, with all of the expectations that ride on performance and decision making that will affect the "rest of your lives," are nothing if not intense.

Parents hope very much for their kids' happiness, but often in their own terms; they want some reflected glory. The intensity of peer pressure is enormous for everybody. Parents are under pressure from their peers in the inevitable comparing of kids. "My daughter is doing very well at high school, and her preliminary SATs are terribly good. Probably a toss-up between Radcliffe and Yale." The same competitive pressures exist within families. Cousin A is doing better than son B, son Randolph is doing better than daughter Patty, etc. On entering high schools, kids are often making course and life selections for the first time. It's confusing, threatening, and new; and since so much seems to ride on what those decisions are, kids are prone to short-circuit from pressure overload.

Physical growth is often marked, the girls becoming fuller in hip and breast, their height increasing. Boy fill out, and their height can be a point of competition with peers and parents. The timbre of male voices becomes fuller, and the individual (and thus different) rates of change can cause problems, as "different" becomes "bad" or at least not as good. Makeup is a factor for females, one that can cause parental intervention over the definition of too much or "too old for you." The maturing body must be clothed, so the choice of clothes becomes very much an area of potential conflict in the family. Kids try to define themselves with their clothing, of course, and the statements they wish to make about themselves with their clothing can cause great outbursts of wrangling, for the parents' definitions of *themselves* are in part affected by the face their children show to the world.

In this period, as much time is spent defining who one is *not* as is spent on who one is. Since much of what one does not want to be is what one's parents are, the rejection of values, styles, and much else that helps the parent to form her or his identity can make the parents feel insecure, and cause a great deal of conflict as a result. The kids' push-pull between closeness to their parents, which they may see as dependency, versus self-definition and the need to belong to another family "out there" is yet another source of anxiety, conflict, and family fights. The aspirations and ideals of kids are usually still intact at this point, and the dissuasive powers of parents are nonexistent, from the children's point of view. "You see, Dad/Mom, you don't understand . . ." Yes, we must reinvent the wheel yet again, if we are adolescents; the experiences of others mean little to us. We are going to go into the world and make it anew.

The subtext and the text are integrated above, just as they are in life. They are inseparable, for the most part, but it is also clear that by far the most important subtext for both parent and child is that of identity: Who am I? We struggle as parents to know who we are, to finally be able to say to ourselves, "This is me, this is what I do, this is what I am, and I am comfortable with that reality. I will continue to search and learn, but I at least am something, a base of identity from which I may make sorties into the world." As our children go and take on their own identities, painfully banging them together little piece by little piece, just as we did before, the process repeating from generation to generation, those identities may be in conflict with ours. "I am not the mother of a fifteen-year-old who wears one black sneaker and one white," says a parent, incredulously, or "That kid with the one earring clearly can't be mine. There's got to be an emotional problem. Got to get him to see somebody." Or conversely, the new "straight" kid who says, "Hey, Dad, you dress like a hippie, you know that? You're out of it!" We adults sometimes feel as if *our* identities, our very reasons for being, are under siege.

The child faces external pressures from peers, internal pressures from biology, and the incorporated messages of parents and society about what is desirable and "right." The adolescent's "job" is to become somebody in these years, despite the stresses. There is an ill-defined holding pen called junior high school, which a child leaves near the beginning of this period, and upon entrance into this other place called high school there is a whole new set of rules and expectations to be faced. "It's about time you grew up," we say, just like that, like magic.

Growing up also means growing away, becoming someone separate from parents in meaningful ways. The conflict between parent and child is often over *which* meaningful ways. It gives truth to the expression, "You can't win for losing." The house as haven begins to lose meaning on one level, for the child is preparing, bit by bit, to leave the nest. On another, the aspect of haven becomes terribly important, for it is the one place where you may go to rest, to go forth again to take up battle for the self. Alas, the house itself becomes a battleground as we parents feel challenged, threatened, not wishing to give up our hold on "our" children. Thus, control becomes the second major subtext issue. Another irony: Children control us with their behavior, while we attempt to control them with our words. Who's in charge here, indeed? Let us look.

"It's my room" could be the title of the life of the child between thirteen and fifteen. It is also the line most often used by Bernie and Stacey when their parents get "on their cases" about their rooms. No matter how many times the issue is raised by their parents, there are threats and escalations.

"Give me a break, will you? I don't ask you to sleep in there, do I, so . . ."

"Watch your mouth, mister, don't let me hear you talking to your mother that way or you'll get . . ."

"Come off it, Dad," says Stacey, coming to her brother's defense. "This is not exactly the end of the world."

"I have had enough of it. You, Stacey, are to butt out, and now. Bernie, get in there and don't come out until that room is just the way that we want it."

Bernie enters, slams door, hollers about how his life is being ruined by this insanity, never will see daylight again. "I'll come out when you people get reasonable," he says, and with that said, the bolt that he put on his door to assure privacy is slammed shut.

Within a few minutes, Stacey has been given some duty that she dislikes for having butted in and for not having picked up after her shower this morning. "What do I look like, a maid?" asks her mother.

Problem: A certain physical slovenliness vis-à-vis parental standards.

Usual response: Holler, accuse, get four people involved, broaden issues to unrelated matters, devise ad hoc punishments, relent after the absurdity of them is clear. Repeat again tomorrow.

Too often we respond to behavior in a knee-jerk manner. Even though these responses are ineffective, we sometimes find them so comfortable we won't let go of them. They are like old shoes we insist on keeping: They're a disaster in even the lightest rain, and sometimes we wind up chilled and sneezing, but "they're so darned comfortable . . ." The health of a family, however, deserves better than an old-shoes approach. What do we do?

For what it is worth, maybe Stacey's grandmother treated Stacey's mother just this way, so this would appear to be imitative behavior come down to haunt yet another generation. It could be that Bernie's Dad is a real anal retentive and the mere sight of disorder gives him a hint of his own as-yet unleashed tendencies toward sloppiness, sensuality, and goodness knows what else that lies inside. The child as a reflection of oneself can be the crux, as well, and we are not messy, are we? If this were

Vienna at the turn of the century and we were rich, we might not only come to some intellectual understanding of all of these depths, but might even work them through, in the psychoanalytic sense, and learn not to project our fears and needs on our children, but by then the kids might be too old to benefit. But we can know something about kids and their needs at this age. That which separates them from us also individuates them, makes them Bernie at thirteen, Stacey at fifteen. One of the ways they differentiate themselves from us is by behaving more like their peers (what we consider "pack" behavior) while almost flagrantly flouting the *rules according to us*. Let's look at some possible approaches to solving the problems of the surface.

Mom and Dad talk about Stacey and Bernie and the rooms that are shambles, the bathrooms left for "the maid" to clean up. This time, instead of the usual clichés that simply fix on the problem—"aren't they terrible, why can't they cooperate, they're unbelievable" (reminiscent of Rex Harrison wondering why a woman can't be more like a man)—they play a game of remembering how *they* behaved as children of thirteen and fifteen years. They discover some commonalities. Dad talks about how important it was to conserve everything in his household, how hard times were, how many kids there were, how cooperation was very important or the tenuous life of a poor black family of seven would become chaotic; and how his dad would take a strap to him if he behaved in a less than perfect manner, for the standards by which a black man was judged were higher than those applied to the white population. Dad has gone on to become a successful high-level employee of a major corporation, and yet there is always that need to be very correct—not even just correct, but perfect. "So I know I go overboard, but gracious, can't they just . . ." As for Mom, order had always been such a part of her life in her family's household, and at the church schools she attended, and even at the college dorm where she was an undergraduate, that her kids' behavior is as foreign to her as is the language to an unexpected tourist in Tibet.

"We're doing this for us, not for them. We don't live in their rooms, so let's see if we can let them alone about this for a while. Maybe the contrary impulse will reign:

If Mom and Dad don't care, then I will. I'm not sure, but what the heck, I didn't think that day care would work out in our factories, either, so let's give it a shot," suggests Dad. Mom agrees, but with some modifications. The bathroom is often shared because the kids like their parents' bathroom better, so the bathroom cleanliness has to be the responsibility of each person who uses it, she says. Pick up towels after a bath, hang them properly on hooks, get rid of the hair around the drain with a tissue, and if they "don't use my hairbrush," the deal is a deal. A few days later, they offer their compromise to the kids, who accept, and the fighting stops. Stacey's room begins to look more civilized now that it is not the issue around which her identity revolves. Bernie is just as sloppy as ever.

The room as private space can also become an issue. ". . . and stay out of here or I'll murder you" is a typical exaggerated threat of one child to another. The transgressor is usually younger, for the younger is still part of the communal life; but for the older kids their rooms are where they live in the metaphoric sense. It is also where they put things that are private and "none of anybody's business." It is where a kid can be alone, an island, one, not just a part of family. On the developmental level, these things are positive, for the child is individuating. On the interpersonal level, it is difficult, for Mom and Dad have had the run of the house up until now.

"What's this, Johnny? That's kind of neat. Where did you get it?" This innocuous question from Dad about a model racing car that Dad had not seen before is met with a nearly vicious response. "Can't I have any privacy? Do I come into your room and go through the drawers, huh? Give it to me." A tugging match ensues, and Dad's victory is a hollow one, which only succeeds in humiliating his fourteen-year-old. Mom comes roaring in. "What's this all about? Don't let me hear you talking like that to your father." "Hey, cut out the hollering, will you?" That's Veronica, Johnny's sister of sixteen. "Hey, it's his room, it's his stuff, and if he doesn't want you coming in, I think it's up to him to set the rules about his own room, don't you?"

Mom and Dad are taken aback by this affront to their authority and tell the kids, in the heat of the moment, that in no uncertain terms the house is *their* house, and until the children are out of their house and on their own, the rules are the parents' to make. "Yeah, well, you can do that, all right, but I'm not going to do anything around here anymore. I don't care, you can punish me, you can do what you want, but I have rights, too, and dammit . . ." Johnny begins to sob in absolute indignation. This sobers the parents, and Dad moves toward Johnny to give him a hug, but then moves away when Johnny looks at him with what could pass as passionate dislike at this loaded moment. The notion that Johnny, even for a moment, could hate him, chills Dad and brings him to the realization that both his son and he have crossed lines. Dad has crossed the privacy zone that Johnny had been slowly erecting, the one that was making him separate from the rest of the family when he wanted to be separate. Dad had invaded his kid's room and had had a physical victory over a fourteen-year-old. For his victory, which became public with the arrival of Mom and Veronica, he has more than a little bit of repair work to do.

This territorial problem is very common, and once fairly resolved, it is over with; but for some families it can become a continuing source of fighting. The real issues are about private versus public, me versus you, about individuation and identity. When a parent or parents cannot relinquish control of a child, the control to which we had been accustomed when our children were in earlier and more dependent developmental stages, these issues become exaggerated. There are a number of things we should consider in situations like this.

First, we must think about territory and how important it is to each of us. "Hey, that's my hammer!" My desk, my office, my book, my everything. If we go into our offices and find others sitting behind our desks, what do we feel? We feel invaded, insecure, annoyed. We define ourselves in a lot of ways, and the exclusivity of territory and goods are two of them. That the secretive, private Johnny of fourteen, who is not to be confused with the open, funny, easy-to-hug fourteen-year-old Johnny that Dad might have seen in the living room a half hour ago, is miffed at Dad will not be surprising if we can think of it in relation to ourselves in our workplaces. Second, we have to remember that kids at this age are trying out the edges of their selves by attempting to exercise control over their environment. That is a sign of health. (If it is excessive and dramatic, it may be other than healthy, and it might be useful to talk with other parents to compare notes and/or consult with a mental-health professional.) We ought to be able to let go of some of our control, to cede it to them. As hard as it may be—and it is hard, for it dredges up thoughts of going away, of loss—the ability to cede that authority is a sign of our own health and maturity. Three, if we wish children to respect our privacy, we cannot invade theirs. No matter how close and smothery we want to be, we have to remember that we cannot trample that other person's sense of territory or privacy without demeaning that person. Here, the toolbox of techniques is useless. We just have to be responsible, reflective, to identify with our kids and see our invasions from their point of view. Will they sometimes overreact and be "off the wall" in their responses? Yes. Yet we must continue to be responsible, loving, and supportive. It is a lousy job, sometimes, but if we don't do it, what then?

If kids are struggling for their identities, we parents are not far behind. As is clear from the sneakers and earrings examples at the beginning of the chapter, looking to one's own child for affirmation of self, completion of self, either through our kids' positive or negative behavior, is not at all uncommon.

Anthony has always been a "middle management kind of guy," according to his brother and himself. It started out as a mild rebuke by the older and more successful Damian, but Anthony turned it into a little "joke." There is nothing really funny about it. When Anthony makes the joke with new acquaintances, his face smiles but he feels horrible. That will soon be behind him, as his son Lawrence, a terrific student with all kinds of potential, is about to make some college and thus career choices. Anthony can hardly wait. Lawrence knows it, and he *can* wait.

For weeks now, while the senior class is hellbent on getting all their applications mailed off, Lawrence has been dragging his feet. Anthony has been indirect in pressuring his son, but the pressure is there nonetheless, which only slows Lawrence down a little more. Despite the fact that he loves his dad a lot, he is beginning to be impatient with him. Finally, after a lot of oblique references to Lawrence's future, Anthony finally asks him point-blank: "What colleges, and when are you going to send the applications?" Lawrence says, "Screw that. I'm not going to college. I'm going to take some time off, get a job, think about things. Gotta go." Anthony is crushed, Lawrence is miserable, still seeing his dad's unbelieving face as he rushes out the door.

Lawrence and Anthony begin to fight over everything. "I haven't been hard enough on you," says Anthony. "You don't know what you're throwing away. You're a fool. How do you expect to amount to anything?" "Off my case!" That's Lawrence's most frequent response. He starts acting up, drinking, staying out late, doing things that he has never done before. His father's ire now has some real targets, but the basic reality is not changed. Anthony has wanted redemption in the form of a son who is more than just a "middle management kind of guy." When his chance at redemption seems to disappear, Anthony attacks his potential redeemer. Lawrence would love to fulfill his father's unfulfilled dreams, give him that something extra special to dote on, but he cannot sacrifice himself for a dream that is not his own. The plight of this father and son is circular. Until one has the good fortune or insight that will allow him to break out of its destructiveness, each will be miserable. Other family relationships will be tainted, the father will see his son's "failure" as the logical result of his own inadequacies, the son will incorporate his father's pain, for which he will feel guilt, and he will be on hold. Neither father nor son will get what he wants, and that is sad to contemplate.

This kind of circular and destructive reality is not uncommon, nor is dealing with it easy, for the substitution of one person for another (son or daughter for parent) is pretty much done with mirrors. It is complicated, and on a conscious level we are not likely to readily see or admit that we have placed that burden on another person, one whom we love. How is it to be faced or even recognized?

We can become more observant and critical of our behavior toward our children. If we train ourselves to identify with the realities and pressures of our children's lives, we at least have a chance of seeing our own behavior and our children's responses to it. If our spouse commits a behavior that we think is problematic, we must communicate our concern. What else are families for but to talk *with* each other, not simply to, or around, or over each other. Let the friction that causes heat and light appear. We must not be timid. We must not avoid ''getting Anthony's dander up.'' There is an obligation to do so, to point out to him his relationship with his son and the accompanying pressures that are militating against that young man's fulfillment of himself.

Dorothy is a slender woman of forty-two. She dresses well and pays a lot of attention to her hair and makeup. Her fourteen-year-old daughter, Sharon, however, is putting on some weight, and Dorothy is not happy with that. She mentions it to Sharon often. She tells Sharon that she has just got to slim down or she won't be popular. This makes Sharon anxious, and Sharon fills up the anxiety hole in her stomach with fries and burgers, the favorite foods of her fourteen-year-old pals. Dorothy also tells Sharon how to dress, but the advice is either not quite on the money or Sharon hasn't got her heart in it. The result is that she often looks overdressed and chunky. Yet it is clear that she wants to please her mom. Alas, what happens is that her mother draws attention to her daughter's weight when with friends, draws comparisons between herself and this child twenty-eight years her junior, and makes Sharon miserable. Sharon cries and yells at her mother when the friends leave the house. ''If you weren't such a pig . . .'' her mother finds herself saying, and Sharon bursts into tears of bitter humiliation. This fight is repeated and repeated until the whole family is divided around the issue of ''porky Sharon.'' Pretty, skinny, little ten-year-old Sarah is definitely in Mom's camp. Fortunately, Sharon's dad has been an ally, along with Len, her almost unbelievably kind brother of twelve. Dad thinks he has a handle on what's going on. He approaches his wife.

"Sharon has a weight problem, as we all know, and I don't think I have been very useful in helping to address it. Let me see if I can pitch in here, do something that might help stop the fighting. Let's make a deal with her that if she loses eight pounds—that's two-thirds of what she needs to lose—in the next three months, we'll pay for those riding lessons she has been crazy to have."

Mom isn't so sure. "That sounds like bribery, Jerry. I don't like it." Jerry persists and finally, if reluctantly, gets Dorothy to agree. Sharon is wild for the idea. She gets all of her nutrients but cuts out the stand-up pb&j's after school, the junk foods and multiple ice creams from the malls, and well before the deadline she is nine pounds lighter and looking great riding English saddle at the stables on Saturday morning. Dorothy, however, is forever telling Jerry that he has set a bad example for the other children, and that she just doesn't like this "bribery" tack at all. Now, rather than picking on Sharon, she ignores her, which makes Sharon sad. As Sharon tries to drown the sadness with milk shakes, she puts on the weight again, and Mom's girl is back! The fights recommence, but at least Mom is recognizing her.

Dad has had a pretty good idea of what was going on. He thought that the essential conflict was not going to disappear, but if he could prove to Sharon that she had control over her appetite, and that such control would lead to something positive, it would make her feel better about herself. That worked, for a time. He also thought that his wife would recognize this and let up, but he was wrong about that. She simply changed the nature of the battle from overinvolvement in "Sharon's weight problem" to "Sharon who?" Now Dad has to get in there with what he thinks he knows of the essence of the problem and expose it without too many fireworks resulting.

That night when the family has finished dinner, Jerry brings the conversation around to his high-school years, remembering the awkwardness that he felt, the real hayseed that he was. "Let's see some pictures, Dad," says Len, as if on cue, "let's see how dorky you were." Dad feigns the inability to produce pictures, but Len points out that Dad's high-school yearbooks are with the photo albums on the top bookshelf in the living room, so the five settle in for a session. "Boy, you really were a dork, weren't you?" says Len, quickly adding, "only kidding." There are all kinds of remarks from "you were kind of cute, Dad, then," from Sarah, to more "dork" remarks from "Only Kidding Len." Dorothy is silent. Then the cry goes up for Mom's yearbooks, pictures of her adolescence. Dorothy tries to break things up with instructions for bed and bath, but she does not succeed. Dad is calling for fairness. "Hey, I've taken my lumps here from these little savages. Now it's your turn." There it is in black and white: chunky Dorothy. "Gee, Mom, you were real different," says diplomatic Len. Sarah pokes some fun at the "little fireplug" that was her mom all through high school. "Yup, I was a bit of a chunk," Dorothy says. "I was not very popular, needless to say," she adds. Sharon is silent. When the kids go off to bed, Dorothy gives an extra hard hug to her fourteen-year-old girl, that mirror of the self that had made her so unhappy.

Mom clearly had a hang-up. Dad knew it was there and acted to make it public without a direct challenge and without attacking her. Instead, he created a situation where a truth about Mom's childhood could be revealed, and shared with the kids. It gave Sharon the opportunity to see Dorothy as a person who had been unhappy being fat. Mom probably found Sharon's fat comforting, now that Mom was thin and could make rude remarks about that old fat self of the sixties; problem was that the old fat self was her daughter.

The guidance toward resolution in this instance was superb. Dad did not psychologize, attack, threaten. The natural surfacing of feelings surrounding the way that Dorothy felt as a young woman was made possible by the pictures. Dad had exposed himself to rude remarks and could not be seen as setting up his wife for the knockout punch. There is a very good reason to be optimistic about the future of the relationship between Sharon and her mother.

One of the more popular fights during this period is that which relates to dress fads. As we know, some of us see our kids as extensions of ourselves, extensions that, if judged negatively, reflect negatively on us. If we subscribe to a segment of society that is strict in its conformity, then the judgments of others will seem important to us; therefore, we will want our kids' dress reflecting positively. Some wisdom:

1. This is not the fight to pick. It is not important. What is important is the individuation of the child, and dressing differently from one's parents is a normal way of symbolizing that. You did it—or wanted to—and survived long enough and with enough self-respect to go out and buy this book in a bookstore. (Clearly, this does not apply to people who by religious belief and prescription must dress a specific way.)

2. It is not a fight that can be won. While there are adults who are glad that their parents made them take piano lessons, we do not know of any adults who are glad that their parents did not let them wear pegged pants (the fifties) or bell-bottoms (the sixties).

3. A lot worse things could happen, believe us. This is not meant to minimize the importance of dress as symbolic of an attitude and of other problems, as the following example will indicate.

Claudia Trent is sixteen and really quite striking. She is 5'9" like her mother, is very well and somewhat generously proportioned, and attracts a lot of glances from older men. She is a mediocre student in a family that prizes studiousness, so she is not getting a lot of stroking. In fact, she is rather the "odd man out" among the kids (of whom she is the second oldest), the other three being whizzes in both the sciences and the humanities. She is looking for her niche in life, and since she got this rather womanly body at an early age, she has recently decided to make the most of it.

"I need to get some things for school, Mom, some clothes. Katie and her mom are going to the mall, and I thought . . ."

"Sure, dear, take my credit card. Don't be too long. I've got to go critique Graham's paper on Wilson and American idealism for history class. Bye."

"Tell Dad I went, okay?"

Two hours later, Claudia has returned. Mom would love to see her things, but she doesn't have the time now because Bud has to have a little help with his trig.

"Hey, Dad, want to see what I got? Went to the mall with Katie, and . . ."

"Shhh. Sorry. Wait a second. There. Sorry. Had to figure out Jerry's last move. I'm down a knight. Katie, huh? How is Katie?"

"Good night."

Silence.

Next morning. The usual craziness of four kids and two working parents is on, and hardly anybody has a minute to do more than grunt and avoid collisions. Claudia arrives last, makes it to the door without much notice, but at the last moment, just as the "See you tonight" begins to fade, Mom gets a good look at Claudia's new dress and says, "You're not going anywhere in that, young lady. Upstairs, now. If I'm late for the office I'll . . . be late for the office, that's that. Let's go upstairs." All heads are turned toward Claudia, eight eyes follow a very tightly sheathed derriere as she follows Mom upstairs. Well, Claudia thinks, now that I have your attention . . .

This dress behavior could grow into a "thing." Her parents could use it to push her further away than she already is: "Not only is she not going to perform academically, but she is also going to bring us disgrace." She could become the Designated Scapegoat. There could be a lot of psychologizing, there could be any number of negative approaches to Claudia's dress. But despite the "heads in the clouds" appearance, the Trents are pretty good at problem solving.

"Okay, Claudia. I know we had it coming," Mom begins. "We are a rather narrowly focused group, I know. More damn books and journals than a person can stand around here. Sometimes I think we're a little nuts, and we forget that all this academic stuff is only good if it relates to people, but there you have it. Just because you haven't been the Einstein of the school, you have been ignored, and I think that stinks. I'd erase all of that past if I could but I can't, so all I can do is tell you that I'm sorry, that I love you, and that I am going to pay a hell of a lot more attention. I want you to know how really creepy I know we have been. You had to go waving that pretty fanny at us in order for us to realize what the hell we've been doing, but at least we are recognizing that. Maybe all this emphasis on the academic is paying off in that respect.

"As far as the dress is concerned, I think it's pretty outrageous. Looks like something from an old Rita Hayworth movie, or whatever. *Sadie Thompson*, maybe? Anyhow, I take back what I said. If you want to wear that dress to school—how dare you have more cleavage than your mother, by the way—then I think you should. It is definitely inappropriate and a bit much for almost any setting, but it's your body, my dear. I love you. I want to see more of you—no pun intended—and let's talk tonight when we're both home. Now with head out of sand and a little wet of eye, I'm going downstairs and then to work."

Claudia thinks it over. She is touched by her mother's honesty and genuine concern. That her mother has retreated from the hard line does not make her see her mother as weak but as fair, something Claudia values highly. She changes into skirt and sweater and goes to school a little later, missing English literature but glad to have had the time to reflect.

Mom and Dad *do* make amends, talking more with Claudia about what she wants for herself and the future. Her love of the theater, something they had completely forgotten about because it was not an interest of theirs, is very strong, they discover, and they decide to support her interest with the gift of tickets to the local repertory theater. Yes, if she is still terribly interested in her senior year, they will talk further about a theater school with a two-year program. Mom and Dad alternate in going to the theater with Claudia, and they discover that they are enthralled with it themselves, and thank their daughter for broadening "our narrow little heads."

These parents have shown real interest in their kids, and when made aware of their own shortcomings, have been able to make changes that satisfy the "odd man out," while not short-shrifting anybody else. They are good at listening. Fortunately, they are also good at reading the surface of behavior as having more meaning than what's apparent. They have been responsive, intelligent, and responsible. They aren't perfect, obviously. They are inveterate intellectual snobs, and are difficult to live with because they focus so hard on a narrowly defined sense of what matters. But they are not purposely cruel. They are smart, and when they figure things out, they act with as much fairness and love as they can muster. They can muster quite a bit, clearly enough to make Claudia love them in return.

Others might have taken a very hard line, made unjustifiable assumptions about Claudia based on her provocative behavior, have hardened up the kid's response in the process, and begun an unhealthy cycle of provocative behavior/hard response/temporary reform, *ad nauseum*. If a child discovers that she needs to poke you in the nose to get your attention, you may wind up with a pretty sore nose, as well as a child who comes to see negative behavior as the only way to get any strokes at all. That usually causes great difficulty in relationships in adulthood.

There are many problems that have no deep psychological foundations, but are really the stuff of everyday life that arises when there are adolescents in the house.

That music! Kids play their music too loud and too late. Why? Most of the time because they like it, sometimes because it says they are not you in a loud and clear way. In short, it is another piece in the puzzle of becoming. Their growth is to be permitted, yes, but not at the expense of our eardrums or privacy. So how do we deal with this aural catastrophe?

1. We might shout "Shut that damned thing off. How can you listen to that garbage anyhow? I'm sick of that junk booming all day long!"

This simply reaffirms for the child that you are a fogy or a Philistine. You have made an attack not on the kid's music but on the kid, in her or his mind. That is the kid's music, and your lack of tolerance for its qualities is an attack on his or her qualities. The noise, however, is another thing.

2. Or perhaps we could dispassionately say, "That's too loud, Perry. We're trying to talk out here. Could you please either lower it or use your earphones? Thanks."

This is a reasonable way of settling the disparate needs of the members of the family. If Perry objects, there is a pretty good chance that Perry wants to be unreasonable for a purpose, perhaps to annoy because he is fifteen and we are thirty-eight, and he has found a way to control us with *U2* and his stereo equipment.

3. Then there is the possibility of setting expectations and limits on behavior before the fact, at the appropriate time. The stereo equipment in the house has always been Mom's and Dad's, but now the kids are old enough to use it carefully themselves. "The stereo equipment is there for you, and I know you will want to play it louder than I like, so let's make a deal now, okay? Play it as loud as you want (consistent with where the family lives, obviously) until Mom and I get home, but I would really appreciate it if you would use the earphones when we're downstairs and talking, or watching the tube, or cooking. If we're upstairs working or something, fine, use the speakers, but please keep the bass down. It really breaks concentration. Okay? You guys are sensible, use your judgment."

If the kids have their own stereo equipment, or if there is a common room where such stuff is kept, there may have to be negotiations as to who gets to use what, when, and at how many decibels. The important thing to remember, however, is that the prearranged sharing and setting of limits, if reciprocated—we can't play *Turandot* at full volume at will while the kids are studying or entertaining, either—and consistently held to, can make whatever conflicts occur more easily adjudicated. It is also much fairer to everyone if each of us is dealing with the known parameters of acceptable behavior in what is a pretty complex social organization. By extension, this method of dealing with the infringement of others' rights—taking over the entire kitchen table with homework, hogging the television set, sloppiness in common rooms with the expectations that someone else will clean up, etc.—can be usefully applied. The sharing of limited resources can be particularly difficult during this time, because much of the time the teenager wants it and wants it now, especially if "everyone else has one, gets one, doesn't have to."

Carol comes rolling through the house in the early evening and announces that she will not be very late and she will drive carefully. "Bye, Mom and Dad, see you later." Barely having had the time to assimilate the rapid-fire recitation, Mom runs to the door and gets there just in time to tell Carol that Mom and Dad need the car tonight to get to a dinner party at the Crowley's house. "What?" Accompanying this response is a look of incredulity. It looks as if Carol's life has just ended. "Why didn't you tell me?" Carol asks. "I could have made other plans. Now I'm really in a bind." "You might have told us of your plans," says Mom, but not in an argumentative way. "Come on back in and let's see what we can work out." What might have been an opportunity to attack the teenager's irresponsibility, which would have made everyone miserable over the long haul but might have brought an "It's our property" victory, is going to turn into a lesson in cooperation.

Mom and Dad explain their needs, Carol explains hers. They work out a schedule that will allow Carol to get to Maureen's house in plenty of time before the other people arrive—she had promised Maureen that she would help prepare some food for a little get-together party—and only the strategy for getting home remains. Carol bridles at the suggestion that her parents pick her up. It isn't practical, either, because it would mean their not having the flexibility they think they should have on their rare nights out with friends. "Do you think it would be convenient for Maureen to let you stay at her house tonight?" The very notion that Dad would make that suggestion fills Carol with some pride in her own maturity. Dad is not being lazy but is responding to a daughter he has always been able to trust. She is a trustworthy and responsible seventeen-year-old woman. "Well, I'll ask, but I don't know. You guys may have to come for me." While her parents would just as soon not have to make a special trip or leave a dinner party early—it could be awkward—they decide that if arrangements cannot be made with Maureen, then they will do what needs to be done. "One final thing, though. In the future, please let's coordinate things a little more carefully, okay? If we had a second car, it wouldn't be a problem, perhaps, but we don't, so we really do need to have a schedule of auto use."

Others might have handled this differently. For example: "No way. We need the car and that's that. If you don't let us know in advance, then it's too bad.'' While that attitude might be justified by the lack of notification, it is a very hard and uncompromising line to take with anyone other than a person who has not been reliable in the past and has not responded to pleas and opportunities for reform. Even at that, it is not likely to do anything but reinforce the attitudes of the miscreant. There is no room for compromise or face-saving. ''I'm the boss and you are wrong, and there's no discussion'' is the way the message would be read. That stance probably makes sense only with one who has a long history of noncooperation.

Then there is: ''Why were you so thoughtless last night? You know, your mother and I had plans to go out and have dinner with the Reids, but we couldn't go because you, young lady, took the car. Oh, yes, I'm sure you didn't know. You *never* know. Yes, I could have run to get you, could have screamed in the driveway, but if a person is thoughtless, what's the point? Some day . . .'' This slow trip of torture and character assassination is demeaning and is designed to drive everyone to the edge of sanity. It is the old guilt trip that breeds nothing positive and fails to address the problem in a soluble way. It is intended to make people feel bad, not to reform their behavior. Another passive-aggressive technique of similar efficacy and repute is psychologizing, wherein the first sentence is slightly modified to ''Why do you think you were so thoughtless last night? There has been a pattern like this, hasn't there, dear? Why do you think that is?'' While the tone is sweeter and positive, as in speaking to a mentally deficient person who has a knife in his hand, it's just another ''parent as martyr to the child's horrible ways,'' as above, and a nonconstructive approach to problem solving.

There may be times when the only answer is ''No.'' When that time arrives, the response needs to be justified and in the context of a household where *no* is a reasonable and expectable answer.

Jack has the family's second car, an old clunker, but he is delighted. He had made a bargain with his parents that he will be out until midnight, and not a minute later on a Friday night. Generally, he is good about it, but tonight he comes in at twelve-thirty. Mom and Dad are up watching television, and as soon as Jack's key is in the door, they are both up out of their chairs. They could go berserk, or they could say nothing. Saying nothing would be dumb, because they would not have held someone to a bargain made. Going berserk could elicit a similar response from their son, or might result in his sheepish acceptance of their rebuke, not a good result in itself. Let's look.

"Hey, you have a good evening?" asks Dad.

"Yeah, real great. We went to see that new Scorcese movie. Pretty good."

"We read a while and then put on the tube about twenty minutes ago. The Connell novel is not as good as his earlier ones, but it's good," says Mom. "As for the tube," she continues, "it's never going to get better, is it? I hope your ability to tell time gets better, however. You are thirty minutes into our worry time, you know that?"

"Yeah, I know. I'm sorry. That parking lot at the movie house was really jammed, and it must have cost us another twenty minutes, and then I was dropping Cathy and Gene, and they talked forever. I'm sorry. Hope you weren't worried." In the classic parental retort, Dad says, "You will never take that privilege from us, young man. Now get into bed, will you? And don't let these crowded parking lots get to be a steady thing, all right?" Jack goes to bed after giving a squeeze to his dad and kissing his mother's cheek.

Here is a commonplace situation regarding time that is appropriately handled. Nobody is attacked, nobody overreacts, everybody is left with dignity. The lines have been reaffirmed and yet there is enough flexibility so as to allow for traffic jams, gabby friends, and a tiny bit of shaving the facts to prove that the kid is not an automaton. Too often, however, we react differently, nonconstructively, and in a manner that inflames everybody rather than lights the fire of reason.

Thomas has been seeing one particular girl for months. Tonight he announces in a throwaway line to his sister, Fran, that he and Caron are going steady. The next day after she gets home from school, Fran tells Mom, and

Mom goes berserk. "Steady? What does he want to do that for? He's only sixteen. My God, there's a whole life before him. Going steady! Who is this Caron? I've seen her. Cute, but Thomas?" There is more, but more of the same. Fran rolls her eyes, sorry she brought up the subject. She thought it was kind of nice.

This is a nonproblem. If Mom makes a problem out of it, then she will have created the crisis, not Thomas.

Steady and not steady, to the extent that it exists at any given time, is dictated by Thomas's peers, not by us or Thomas's mother. It is either cool or uncool. In November of 1988, in and around Boston, it is mostly uncool. The less parents say about the mores of the tribe of adolescents, the better.

"If you don't do your homework, how are you ever going to _____ (fill in the blank)?"

"Don't worry, okay? It's my neck. Have I flunked anything to date? No. If I want to throw my life away, I think I'm old enough to make that decision. That's not what I'm doing, but, listen, I'm a big girl now, Dad, and I won't listen to this stuff anymore, really."

This fight could go on and on and on. The parents could try to apply some leverage, such as access to money (often not as major a factor as it once was, since kids can work for four hours at a fast-food place and come home with twenty-four dollars), access to the family car, etc., but the number of cards in the parental deck have dwindled. It is clear that there has been a shift in the balance of power.

Just as Harry Truman fooled himself into thinking that having the "exclusive" on the atom bomb made the United States the "keeper of the peace" for the indefinite future, so do we sometimes fool ourselves into thinking that we are in charge; we are not. A sharing has come, year by year, and now we can no longer get agreement because of our indomitability. Our kids have learned that we put our pants on one leg at a time, too, and while that makes us more real and human to them it also means that they know our limits. So forget the ultimata. If we get agreement, it will be won at the loss of something else, in all probability. It *is* his/her life.

* * *

''That's the last time, believe me. I can't trust you. Three times this year you have been at least a half hour late and that's it. No more car for you. Give me those keys.'' That's Mom's reaction to the same problem above.

Dad comes in and takes the son's side. ''Don't be so hard on him. You'd think he had committed murder, or something.'' Now he turns to their son. ''And you, you dope. Can't you get it straight that twelve o'clock is twelve o'clock? Get into bed. We'll talk tomorrow.''

In the bedroom, Mom and Dad have a row. Dad says Mom has really screwed up again. ''That's no way to handle a problem. You're always flying off the handle. Let me handle it.''

''Like hell, you'll handle it.'' The fight goes on. There is a lot of heat but no light.

In the morning, after Mom has left for work, Dad tells their son that he'll fix things up. ''Just lie low for a while. Agree with your mother. I'll take care of her. Here's some extra spending money, by the way. Don't tell her.''

This destructive response is part of a problem family therapists call ''triangulation.'' The parents are at war, often over serious dissatisfactions that are not spoken to. An alliance is made between one parent and a child against the other parent. The alliance is their secret, for on the surface the parent does some agreeing with the other, but in a more ''mature and moderating fashion'' than the other. In fact, the child is used as a weapon, as a tool to undermine and weaken the position of the other parent. It is important to be able to recognize this deceptive and divisive behavior, although once under way it is not easily dealt with except in some formal therapeutic setting. But if we find ourselves beginning to contemplate such an alliance, we can stop and reflect, and perhaps dig around a bit to find what the submerged problem is. What is it that is making us so angry as to want to denigrate our spouse?

Disappointment in career, affection, sexuality; lack of communication, listening, caring; having married the mirror image of the dreaded parent of the past so as to try and work out the problems of that relationship the second time around—all of these and more might be the underlying reasons. The important thing to remember, however, is that *our* problem, that of the two adults, is being visited on the head of the child. It is unfair, of course, and we have a responsibility to be aware of what is going on and to take steps to repair the relationship between parents; without that, the child is at a terrible disadvantage in a very stressful period of growth.

Sometimes kids get out of control. What the causes are in a given situation is less important at this stage than the fact of out-of-controlness. There could be an unconscious encouragement of wildness on the part of a parent who had a very strict and straight life as a child and regrets it to this day—just like the "I was never a cheerleader/quarterback" syndrome that is so familiar to us, and that puts pressure on our kids to fulfill our dreams. There could be a wave of out-of-controlness sweeping a town or school, one that can only be explained by the occasional lemminglike behavior of groups. All that we know for sure, however, is that there is a kid seemingly out of control.

Our reactions are often panicky. We are all very busy. We may both work, we may have very little leisure time, time to think things through; so we react when we should be responding. Reacting is very different from responding, the latter connoting some knowledge of the meaning of that which demands a response. Sad to say, in this new world, thinking things through has become a luxury. (Perhaps that accounts for the widespread use of therapy, that definite, set-aside time when one must think and, we hope, feel, things through.) We thrash about, setting limits, resetting limits, re-resetting limits, threatening, cajoling, appealing to reason, bribing, negotiating (or trying to) with somebody who may not have any real wish to give on anything. We fight over cars, alcohol, grades, the future, and our fights fall on deaf ears. We are tired, and sometimes we give up. We rationalize that we did our best (which is often true), and lick our wounds while promising to concentrate on those remaining kids whose characters are still malleable, who are still responsive to our love and affection, who may "turn out just fine." It is good to be hopeful, it is sometimes sensible to cut our losses and regroup, but it may be premature to count somebody out of the family.

We must take the time to sit down with our spouse and

quietly and methodically discover what we can about the patterns and possible causes of behavior. Other members of the family can be brought in, not as "squealers" or as people with whom we can *share* our complaints, but as members of a family who might have insights that we don't have. The kid with the problematic behavior must be brought in, as well, but not in a threatening or face-losing way as would occur in a family convention. That might appear too much like "them against me" to be effective; it is more likely to be counterproductive. Friends, teachers, and guidance counselors should all be used in searching for clues. If after all best efforts the child whose behavior is in question shows no signs of cooperating, then it is reasonable to seek professional help.

If the behavior is particularly destructive or points in that direction—hanging out with a really tough group of kids, recklessness with an automobile, drinking, doping—then it is reasonable to explore the problem with a therapist, as a couple, at first, and then with the child. Don't forget that the family is a system, and one glitch within it can have repercussions in other parts of the system. We may discover that the behavior is a reaction to some other dynamic, or we may not, but the exploration with a person who regularly works with families and their concerns can be very valuable. (Note: not a panacea, but valuable.)

At sixteen, Ernest is a big, slender, intense, olive-skinned boy of some native charm and courtliness. He and his mother, Melanie, have been very close for the last couple of years. Lately, however, there has been some distance developing between them, simultaneous with some very long telephone conversations he has been having in the late evening after homework. Ernest sits on the floor, half in and half out of his bedroom—that's as far as the cord will stretch—speaking just softly enough that no one can hear the words, but the *tone* makes it clear that he's talking to a girl.

"Come on, Ernest, will you get off of that phone? Enough is enough," says Mom. Sister Leslie is twelve and ready to go to bed, but she gets her digs in on the way. "Bet it's old fat cheeks, Julia, huh?" This is the first time Mom has heard the name. Now it is clear: another woman. "Come on, get off of that phone now. Suppose somebody wants to get in touch with us," she says. "You're not the only one in this house, you know." In a purposely louder voice, Ernest says, "Sorry, some of the old folks here have to phone in their prescriptions, get their warm milk, and toddle off to bed. Okay, see you tomorrow." With that, he returns the telephone to its place, walks with Cheshire-cat grin to his bedroom, turns, says good night, and closes his door.

Over the next several weeks, the agitation of the telephone continues, with Mom escalating her nagging to such an extent that Dad gets involved, putting down his "homework" or leaving the television set to intervene, and complaining loudly about this tying up of the telephone. Soon the arguments over the telephone become the evening fare. Move over, *Dallas*. The telephone begets a litany of transgressions new to Ernest's ears. It goes on and words get angrier and louder, and before long everybody is pretty unhappy. What's going on here?

There are at least two things going on, but at the center is the fact that Mom is losing her son to another woman. She carried this kid for nine months, a virtual stranger, fed and diapered him, helped him to learn and to walk and to run and all the rest, and now some Julia—who looks like a chipmunk, according to kid sister—is taking over. Mom is not a good loser.

Her husband spends a lot of time doing work at home in the evening and watching television, so she has become too dependent on Ernest for male companionship, but now he is ready to fly away. While the end result of good parenting is a child ready and able to become independent, Melanie does not want to reap that reward. She wants her son. The telephone is an excuse over which to fight, as well as a device that can connect him with "them out there."

The other issue is less compelling in this particular instance, because the family is not as telephone crazy as some, but the overuse of the telephone by one or more family members limits other members' access to the outside world. Ernest is the guilty party here. Conscious or not, his behavior is provocative.

Ernest should be confronted over the practical matter of telephone use during an appropriately quiet time when he is not on the telephone. Very few discussions that take place in the presence of the behavior that is being spoken to are fruitful, but rather tend to broaden the issues and make people defensive and offensive rather than rational and conciliatory. Every family member should be present, and the parents should have decided on a strategy. It should not be accusatory but rather address the question of equity. Do we all have equal access to the telephone in the face of Ernest's excessive use of it during the school week? Is the question on the table? Note that the issue is not Ernest's personality, his abilities in sports, or his scholarship, nor is the neatness of his room. The right of every member of the family to have access to the outside world via the telephone is the issue, and Ernest stands accused of overuse, period.

Options:

1. As a result of discussion, there will be a voluntary limiting of time in the context of the needs of other family members. In the best of all possible worlds, this is what we hope for.

2. Limit time by decree of parents. In the most simplistic of worlds, this is often the solution. This kind is usually no solution at all, for there is no agreement involved.

3. Negotiate a reasonable amount of time in the evening for kids' use of phone and parents' use of phone. This begins to make some sense. Give some, take some, figure out what is *fair*.

4. Expand the pie by addition of another phone, thus sidestepping the problem; and if there is an economic consideration, negotiate the cost sharing, or if appropriate, let the kid or kids pick up the whole expense of a second telephone. This is a good solution, but it can be a trap, as well, by suggesting we can buy our way out of this problem by getting the kids a telephone of their own, which implies that problems revolving around cooperation and equity can be solved by the checkbook. Having the kids pay for their own telephone service might be a great solution, as long as it is not applied in such a situation as to put a significant crimp in a kid's ability to do other things with his or her friends; that would be

"negotiating," an essentially punitive solution. Perhaps there is yet another way of skinning this cat.

5. After discussion of equity and fairness, get agreement on what is reasonable use of the telephone, and add the proviso that after a specific negotiated period of time there may be the need for a second telephone, which will be financed in another negotiated manner. This last solution requires everybody to give thought to the consequences of their phone use. It does away with unknowns and threats, and rationalizes the tackling of the problem of the telephone.

The other problem is more complex. Melanie's jealousy, from which the initial complaint derived, her fear of the impending loss of "her" son, and the resultant picking on Ernest (much like that of Lucy and her son in Chapter 2) requires some exploration on the part of Melanie on her own or with her husband, or an insight on the part of her husband, Derek. How might she come to some understanding about what is going on? The first step would be to have made a promise not to allow the same argument to occur more than three times within a relatively short period of time (the Rule of Three) without taking some time out to think about the dynamic and what might underlie it. "What is it that made me angry enough to make such a fuss over the telephone behavior, particularly when I did not need to make a call? Did my reaction fit the 'crime'?" These questions might lead to interesting answers, answers that may speak of sadness, loneliness, lack of stimulation, need to reconnect with a husband who has tuned out and lost himself in work and television. "Is my normal need for male attention putting an unfair burden on someone who cannot give it to me, and thus making me angry at him because he won't fulfill me? Where is that man I married eighteen years ago? What changed in that relationship to make me dependent on a teenage son and turned my husband into a couch potato?" Melanie might also talk with other mothers about their kids and perhaps discover in the process that she is not alone (This is very common. Fortunately for women, discussion of intimate matters—love, family, conflict, fears, sex—are not taboo. The burden of the peculiarity of problems that we feel when we are estranged from others, when we are operating solo, is lifted, as we discover the commonality of experiences and as we learn from others how they have dealt with those problems. Men do not often benefit from the same open social processes.)

If Derek were more involved in the family, he might see the dependency and wonder about what he has done to cause his wife to lean on their son for sympathetic company. Perhaps he can be guided by his wife's insights gained from her friends' experiences, and that may help Derek look inward, reassess his priorities, and make some needed reconnection with his wife. Such reconnection is important not only in the short term, to deal with the problem of the couple and to alleviate the resulting pressure on the son, but in the long term as well. The kids are growing, and they will not be there to provide the focus, the glue of what there is of family life. These two will soon enough find themselves dependent on each other, and if the lines are down, they may be very lonely together.

Denise has just finished crying furiously after a row with Phyllis, her mom. She is lying facedown on her bed, fully dressed, and although the crying has ceased, the fury has not. Through clenched teeth, she mumbles into her pillow, "I hate her, I hate her, I hate her . . ." Until this year, Phyllis and Denise had been very close. But ever since late September, Phyllis has found fault with Denise's table manners, her dressing, her bedroom, her eye shadow (which Mom calls very overdone), and just about anything else. It is making Denise nervous. Thank goodness, she thinks, for Ms. Hepburn.

This was the year that Denise really caught her stride in Ms. Hepburn's gymnastics class. Denise has always been a good competitive gymnast, but Ms. Hepburn was able to show Denise her true body balance, which in turn relaxed and centered Denise, and now she is a superb competitive gymnast. Like a lot of athletic and poised young women, she had aspired to ballet, but at about fifteen she became a realist and knew that she was not of the quality for a good ballet corps, so she is delighted with this marked improvement, and grateful to Ms. Hepburn. Ms. Hepburn is twenty-seven, and it is easy for Denise to identify with her. It could be said that she has a crush on her, as well, not at all unusual for a young woman her age.

Mom never mentions Ms. Hepburn's name when arguments come up about everything else except the amount of time Denise puts into gymnastics and the amount of time she spends confiding in her new mentor. She did not react to Denise's new haircut, a lot like Ms. Hepburn's, actually, but ignored it, treated it with indifference when asked, further infuriating Denise. Yet Mom would gladly add fuel to the fire under this "Joan of Arc Hepburn dame," as Phyllis thinks of her daughter's instructor. Clearly, Mom is in a jealous rage as strong as any experienced by young lovers; but nobody is talking about it.

This situation can only get worse if the depths are not plumbed. The surface is not treatable because the surface is only a symptom of the real problem, which might be: "I am angry at you because you have 'left me' for another. I will not admit it, so I will find every occasion to criticize and find fault with your behavior." Somebody has to get hold of this situation, and it does not appear that the somebody will be Phyllis, who is too enraged and invested in her vendetta to make the necessary admission to herself, no less to her daughter. The insight or the opportunity for the insight has got to come from Dad or from Denise herself, but Denise is probably too much against the wall to be able to sort things out well. It is probably up to Dad. The way that insight comes into play becomes paramount in turning things around.

Dad has become sick and tired of the stony silences, the sniping, the occasional yelling and the too-often tears from "his little princess," as he has called Denise from birth. His wife's general irritability has gotten to him, and although he is Not Mr. Introspective himself, he has spoken to Phyllis about "taking a hard look at things, at whatever it is that's bothering you." Phyllis has been unresponsive, only stiffening up over the mixture of guilt and embarrassment resulting from her nearly uncontrolled rage. So Dad takes the opportunity to spend more leisure time with Phyllis, and after a few evenings out to movies, a little meal, and quiet walks along the river, Jim finds Phyllis relaxing, gaining some of her old self-deprecating wit and gentleness. The stiffness can almost be seen to leave her body.

''You look great, Phyl. Really great. This is such a treat getting out together. Feels like old times.''

''Yep, there's some romance left in these forty-four-year-old bones yet.''

They talk about their courting during college, and *that* river, the walks, and the so-serious talks until the sun began to cast a rosy glow. Dad does not lose sight of the ball, however, and goes on to say, ''Yeah, you look great, more relaxed than I have seen you in a long time.''

This repetition and the fact that the oblique reference is to the stiffness and unhappiness that Phyllis has been recently experiencing do their work. Phyllis's lightness darkens a bit, and she admits that she has been having a hard time the last several months. Jim does not pounce but says that he thought that Phyllis was probably having a hard time. ''I'm only sorry that I was not more sensitive to what was going on. Can I help?''

Phyllis talks about the dependence that she has had on their daughter, that she came to rely on and identify with her ''too damned much. I know that Denise has to grow away, to grow up, but why all at once?'' With that, Phyllis begins to cry, the cry that before was repressed and turned into a weapon to hurt her daughter, who was causing her pain. Jim continues to comfort her, and by guiding his wife toward talking more about what's on her mind during this period, the extreme jealousy of Ms. Hepburn comes to the surface. Instead of attacking his wife ''for causing all this ruction because of immature jealousy—you ought to know how girls are at that age,'' Jim gives plenty of room for self-revelation while providing comfort and understanding. Jim also notes that if he had been more observant, he would have seen things coming, and if so much of Phyllis's identity was wrapped up in their daughter, maybe Jim had been less good a husband than he thought. He promises to make that up to Phyllis, to make possible more times like these—the walks and movies—to renew their connection, to live their lives together, and not vicariously through other people or things.

It is once again clear that the insight of one person is often required through the tender and oblique addressing of the problem, by providing a nonconfrontational context for getting it on the table. The revelation must be treated respectfully. This is no time for one-upmanship or placing blame. If things are handled in the best face-saving manner, the other may talk about the unspoken problem without feeling the fool. The one who has the insight might also take some of the responsibility for the problem without fear of being wrong. As a result, the opportunity may be created to talk about feelings with the victim. (In this instance, Phyllis can tell Denise that she feels abandoned, lonely, already bereaved while her daughter is still at home.) Chances are that in a situation like this the response from the victim (Denise) will be positive and relieved. New lines of expectations can be drawn. (Mom can have part of her girl back—she did the rejecting, after all—while letting go a little bit more each day. Denise can be more sensitive to her mother's feelings of competition and loss.) The opportunity for bettering the situation can be assured by creating some positive momentum. (Here Dad vows to pay more attention, to find opportunities with Phyllis to be together and to hang their lives on more than identification with their daughter.) Together, a couple must work at maintaining the lines of communication, and most of all, they must follow through and not allow their promises to become small buckets of water used to douse little fires, but real commitments to act in positive ways to build a better life together.

No question is more loaded than that of drugs and alcohol among kids. Sexuality is a concern, but is more narrowly focused on females. Substance habituation and abuse, however, does not recognize gender.

Seventeen-year-old Gloria has just come in on a bone-chilling midwestern winter Saturday. She is a real motor mouth these days, which pleases her mother, Mary. Gloria used to be very shy, but now she's full of life and gab. "Hi, Mom, hi, Dad, just came from the football game. Boy, were we terrific. You should have seen . . ." She continues her recitation all the way to the stairs. As she passes her father, who is reading the newspaper, a familiar scent comes off her cold coat to reach his nostrils: marijuana. Bill doesn't say anything but decides that he and Mary will talk about it tonight and decide how to deal with this little piece of news. He thinks about it on and off all afternoon. With two younger kids in the family, Bill wants to get this squared away as soon as possible.

In his straightforward but calm fashion, Bill tells Mary after everyone else is in bed and they are having coffee in the kitchen. Mary turns pale.

"What are we going to do? Is there anything we can say to her that will make a difference? Oh, my God! Now its clear. This new sociable Gloria, so full of words. That's just how it was with me in college. Couldn't shut me up, couldn't feed me enough. Why didn't I recognize it? And she had always been such a good student until this year. I figured for one year let her do less well, at least she has come out of her shell."

"Well, that's all true, but we have to talk about a way of approaching this. It troubles me but I think we need to have a sense of the scale of things, don't you? Maybe we should see the guidance department on Monday. I can talk with Steve Finn next week; I'm going to have lunch with him. His boy was pretty much of a head, you know; he's fine now."

This has all the appearances of a rational start to tackling a legitimate parental concern. Marijuana, like any product burned and inhaled into the lungs, is not good for health. It also impairs time sense, and when combined with alcohol can be particularly troublesome. Kids have impaired motor responses as a result of marijuana smoking, and smoking and driving is dangerous. The longer-range effects of smoking marijuana are also not what we might order for our kids. Any habituation, of course, is to be discouraged, whether it be to alcohol, marijuana, or Seconal, for what seems at first to *allow* us to do things—be sociable, calm, or ebullient—can become a prerequisite for doing things.

Consulting with those experienced in the problem of substance abuse, in confidence, is a great first step. The second step is talking with Gloria frankly and nonhysterically and ascertaining the extent and length of her "smoking." "For all we know," Bill says, "Gloria may have smoked her first and last joint this afternoon, and the marks and sociability are coincidental. I'm not making bets, Mary, but I think we need to keep our minds open."

As it turned out, Gloria admitted to have done some smoking during the last months, but not a real lot. Her parents did not accuse her of anything, but simply indicated that they knew she had smoked some marijuana on Saturday and that they had a legitimate interest in her experience and point of view about the weed. Everyone was calm, but Gloria a little less so. She felt guilty, she said, because she was not good at sneaking or lying, but it was awfully hard not to do a little experimenting. The marks and sociability preceded her first marijuana experience, she pointed out. Now that she was less closed off from people by overcoming her shyness, she found herself being offered all kinds of things to ingest, all of which she had said no to except for a few "joints" in a few months. She talked about how she devoured four bags of potato chips the second time she smoked, and she could barely stop herself from laughing in between swallows!

"Listen, guys, I don't want you worrying. I'm sorry that you had to worry from last Saturday until today—five days of worry. I'm really sorry. But don't worry anymore. Your little 'dopehead' is not going to give you any more worries like that. Honest."

(Kids can, and often do, start experimenting with drugs and other such substances at an earlier age than did Gloria, of course. It is more frightening and threatening to parents when they discover that a younger child is smoking the weed or cigarettes, drinking with pals, or experimenting with other substances. The hardly useful "what have I done wrong?" question can quickly turn outward to the "you'll stop or else" threat, which usually has even less utility. The best policy is to take a deep breath, be rational, and proceed calmly in the manner of Gloria's parents. Do not polarize the issue, but be firm in your beliefs. Support your beliefs with facts and leave room for the kids to save face.

In those instances where kids have a serious underlying problem and develop substance dependencies, we can only repeat that outside help should be, no, *must* be sought.)

It is not difficult to think of the potential this situation had for becoming a major family battlefield. Dad could have stopped Gloria with accusatory remarks before she got to the staircase. Mom could have become hysterical and self-accusatory, the younger kids could have been dragged in, the confidentiality of the concern could have been thrown out, Gloria could have been psychologized to death, been made to feel guilty of sacrificing her parents' peace of mind and good name on the altar of a cheap pleasure. But the situation was sensibly handled, and what could have been an opportunity for mayhem became an opportunity for the parents to learn more about the values of their daughter, the daughter to learn about the deep and careful consideration and love her parents have for her.

One of the obvious keys in starting to deal with a situation such as a potential dependency, where a fair amount of social stigma is perceived to be attached, is knowing that you are not alone. There are great numbers of drug- and alcohol-dependent kids spread across the social classes. The kinds of drugs in use are often socially dictated, or were until the democratization of addicting substances through the development of relatively cheap chemical expanders or substitutes, but there is little reason to think of a potential drug problem as unique. It is not. Nor should it matter if it is, for what is at stake is a kid. If a kid sees our fears of social stigma in the guise of secrecy and hypocrisy, there has to be a negative effect. ("What are you afraid of, that your friends will find out?") We must let our values be clear and on the table, or they could take over the center, with us under attack. Opening up, talking about any drug experimentation that we may have gone through, talking about our own alcohol consumption, if any—these are proper subjects for discussion. To attack and make it "us against them" is entirely inappropriate.

Indeed, all stories of alcohol and drugs will not have such happy endings as Gloria's, but the approach should be the same: careful, nonaccusatory, informed by love and concern.

Any number of problems revolve around the fact of gender, and never are they more pronounced than during adolescence. Parents worry about their daughters' sexuality. Although we think that we are terribly liberated, the fact remains that there is a double standard for judging sexual activity. "Boys will be boys" remains a common view, and their "conquests" a rite of social passage. (In the wake of AIDS, that view may be changing, however.) The female, on the other hand, is still thought of in terms of vulnerability, and thus subject to more supervision, protection, and fretting. Let's look at two seventeen-year-old kids announcing the night's plans to their parents.

Patrick: "Hey, Dad, Mom, I'm going to stay at Fred's brother's place tonight after the concert. It'll be late and all those druggies on the road, no way do I want to be out in that at midnight. Safer to stay in town. Okay?"

Mom and Dad say, "Sure, makes good sense," both knowing in their heart of hearts that it is not at all unlikely that Fred's brother is not the ideal chaperon, if he's going to be in his apartment at all, and that the boys' dates for the evening may go for more than a peck on the cheek after the music is over. Well, they'll have to learn to accept this aspect of their son's life, they think; boys will be boys.

Patricia. "Hey, Mom, Dad, I'm going to stay at Grace's sister's tonight after the concert, okay? You know, there'll be a lot of guys out of their minds driving home and I'd like to be alive in the morning. Grace's sister's only five minutes from the stadium, and those twenty miles could be hellish. Okay?"

"Now wait a minute," says Dad. "What about Fred and Patrick?" Fred and Patrick are the boys who have invited them to the concert.

"I don't know, I guess they'll go to Fred's brother's place. You know them, they're pretty straight and . . . hey, there's nothing to worry about, if that's what you're thinking."

"I don't think this is a very good idea at all, Patricia. I don't like it. No, I think you ought to come home. Just drive carefully, that's all. Stay in the travel lane and to heck with the time, you'll just have to plan on being here a little later, that's all. I don't know why you want to throw these things at us at the last minute when we don't have proper time to think. No, come home. That's it.''

Dad agrees.

''When are you going to stop treating me like a baby? Don't you trust me? What the hell do I have to do to prove myself to you guys, anyhow? Saint Patricia, I suppose. It's unfair. You never let me do anything. It kills me to see that you don't trust me. Have I ever lied to you about things before? What do you think, anyhow? Do you think I'm some kind of sleaze or something, huh?'' Patricia begins to get louder during this recital, and now come the tears. ''Don't you think I have any judgment? Don't you think I have any self-respect? If I don't, then it's certainly a reflection on the examples at home, don't you think? What about George, huh? He can go and do whatever he wants. . . . ?''

''Now just shut up. That's different. The issue is closed. You are coming home, and that's all there is to it. If I have to meet you in town and drive you home myself, I will. I won't hear any more of it,'' says Dad.

The argument escalates, there are accusations, recriminations, slammed doors, and when the youngest kid in the family comes in for a quick pb&j, she gets involved by saying something about those ''gropers'' who are taking Patricia and Grace to the concert. Mom and Dad feel all the more justified based on this ''solid evidence'' of an eighth grader.

Clearly, there are differences in the approach to dealing with the question of ''staying over.'' These markedly similar parents with identically aged children are responding based on the sex of their offspring. We could change the sexes, and the responses would probably be reversed in each instance above. The questions are two: Where do these views come from, and how do we deal fairly with these issues, and deal with or defuse fights built around this double standard?

The first obvious answer is the double standard as mentioned above. There are a number of long-term social notions that have been historically held. Females are to be protected. They can cause great shame and pain because their ''transgressions'' can have physical substance, to wit, a child. ''Looseness'' among females is sinful and wrong, the same among boys is a rite of passage. (Nobody ever figured out where those available girls came from, but so it is with thoughts that have passed into the common wisdom.)

A second answer may be that the father, having been a young man, knows the thoughts of young men, and would prefer that his daughter not be victimized by them. The mother's experience with boys during her own adolescence may have been less than ideal; she felt the pressures of sexual experimentation as premature and does not want her daughter to have the same experience.

We must also think of our own attitudes toward sexuality as informing our protectionism. By nature, an adolescent is going to be attracted to some experimentation if only because of the glands. With the loss of the physical contact experienced as a younger child—the hugging, cuddling, "in Mom and Dad's bed" of a Saturday morning—the need for physical contact is no less present. If we have negative views of sexuality, if we are censorious as a result, we may overreact to problems like that of "sleeping over," even making the prospect more alluring to the teenager who is fighting against us to become himself or herself. Yet balanced against this is our experience and our sense of obligation to inform and protect based on that experience. It is a problem fraught with emotional conflict for everyone involved. How do we deal with it?

Although it is not comforting at all, in all honesty there is often less to be done than we would wish. By the time a child has reached late adolescence, the children are no longer children but young men and women. They have developed under our guidance, have observed our behavior and values; have chosen what they want, for the moment, from the world of peers, the world of cinema and television, fantasy and sport, and have created a picture of themselves, no matter how unsteady or temporary. All of this has been achieved at considerable expense in battle with us and the world. It should not be surprising, then, if there is some resistance to our attempts to control their social behavior. How do you control an eighteen-year-old person? The answer is often that you try, but you do not often succeed. Yet there are ways of approaching the "problem."

1. "I think that's a great idea, Patricia, but over my dead body. As long as you are living in our house, you live by our rules." Probably not a great or effective idea. The implication is that children cannot be trusted and that once they are on their own that's their problem, but for now "you reflect on us," which suggests to the kid that you're only worried about "appearances."

2. "Oh, no. You remember the time that . . ." Anything that can be dredged up from the past is, and although there is nothing in kind to be discussed, the excuse of any transgression keeps us from having to deal with the real question, which involves trust.

3. "Why don't we speak to your mother when she gets home?" Dad then talks with Mom and suggests that the answer should be negative. Then Mom takes the blame for what Dad did not have the courage to say. Sometimes this develops into the "if it were up to me" routine (the old good cop versus bad cop) that allows the miscreant to identify with the "kinder" of the two parents. (This alliance is often formed because one parent wants to inflict damage on the other as a weapon in a longer-term and more deeply rooted battle that has nothing to do with the child's concerns. Sometimes it is the result of a parent's inability to take control.) If ever there was an unhealthy alliance, it is here, for it erodes the confidence of the child in the family as a group of people holding similar goals and aspirations. Short term, it causes problems for the parent who must "take the weight"; long term, it makes the "weaker" and conspiratorial parent look deservedly foolish.

4. Then there is honesty. "We care very much about your vulnerability. You cannot blame us for that. There are pressures, and quite honestly I don't know how strong you are in resisting them. Sometimes I wonder if we have given you enough love, have held you in high-enough esteem so that you will resist that short-term bit of appreciation that a nice and amorous boy might give. No one would be at fault, of course, but it seems too soon. We think you need some breathing space, some time to know more about yourself and to make decisions about intimacy from strength, not from weakness. With all that said, we have talked it through, and if you want to stay out, for goodness' sake it is your decision. You are not

a baby. You are old enough to be making a lot of decisions about your life every day; I guess it's the subject, sex—that really intimate thing that should be shared so carefully—that gives us pause. We both know that is what we are really talking about, that possibility that the staying over is really about that intimacy. You decide. We love you, we trust you." If her parents are justified in their trust, Denise cannot be less than sobered by her parents' candor about their feelings and their fears regarding sex. What was a hidden agenda in other situations is now on the table.

What of the sexist attitude that still seems pervasive, giving the male a silent blessing to celebrate his maleness in the face of the vulnerability of females? We would hope that attitude would change, but thirty years of the sexual revolution, and the resulting awareness that has come to men, is a pale mark on the page of history. Nevertheless, Patrick's parents should take the same tack with him as Patricia's parents did with her, reversing things, indicating the vulnerability of the receiver of a male's ministrations, of the seriousness of it all, yet acknowledging again its attraction.

There are many other possibilities for dealing, or not dealing, with a situation like the night away from home. When all is said and done, the fourth is the most straightforward one, the one that takes the game-playing out of the question, that really puts an adult situation on an adult basis. It is only appropriate, for our sphere of influence shrinks. Soon they will be their own masters, beyond us, making their own lives on their own terms, perhaps left with the good marks we could make on these once "clean slates," our children.

10
Letting Go

The events leading up to a young person's departure from home can be traumatic. Although there will have been any number of movements in that direction—the growing apart of parent and child through individuation, an ongoing process not without its own attenuated pain—the fact that a child we have nurtured is leaving our daily lives is difficult to accept. We begin to mourn the foreseen physical separation, feeling the sense of loss before the fact; while our intellects tell us that the kid has to be free to go, our emotions tell us that we are being rejected, that we are of no real importance anymore in the life of the child, that we, like some male spiders, once having spent our passion and fertilized the female, are of no value. Only death awaits. Kids going away also make us feel older, and since some of us don't deal well with aging, we just might put roadblocks in the way of our kids. All the complex feelings that arise in us often result in fights. This applies to our children as well as to ourselves.

That same thing that we feel when we love someone and in our exuberance hug that person too tightly and say, "I could hug you to death," can be in operation. The loose translation is: "I love you so much I can't ever imagine being without you, and right now I am symbolically merging you into myself by hugging you very hard." But when kids are leaving home, sometimes we do the same thing by pushing them away. The pain of departure is too much to take, so we complain, we pick, we tell them how imperfect and insignificant they are. They may do the same to us for the same reasons. Sometimes, too, we try to tie them to us with guilt, with dependency, with criticisms or subtle hints that they are not yet ready for that, "out there." And sometimes they behave in ways that suggest that they don't feel fit to go, either, blaming us for the necessity. Yet pain or no, the time comes. How we handle that inevitability matters very much, for in that critical and emotionally confused moment of "leaving home," we can set the tone for our continuing relationship with our kids. Letting go, proud of having been an essential part of the shaping of a child from cradle to the moment when he or she is ready to leave us, is not easy, only necessary.

"I remember standing there on the balcony of a fancy hotel near Phoenix, my father next to me, looking out into that desert and thinking how far it went, how free it would feel to just walk out there, to where it didn't matter. It was just the idea of it, the illusion of endless space before me, and with all the energy of my seventeen years it hardly seemed impossible."

Len had come from the East with his mother, father, and sister. It was a major vacation, a real trek to "the Coast," by plane to Phoenix, then bus and car to the Grand Canyon, Las Vegas, San Francisco, Yosemite, Los Angeles; the postwar American Grand Tour. At Grand Canyon, Len fancied descending that great vacancy alone, by mule and foot, but it was only when the mountains outside of Las Vegas captured him that he succumbed, only to find himself hot and thirsty and still thirty-nine miles from the mountains that had looked so near. Yet even as he made tracks for the air-conditioned hotel and the security of everything in its place, he could not resist the occasional glance over his shoulder at what had suggested solitude, peace, freedom, self-sufficiency. Finally, at the Beverly Hilton, he put it to them. "I want to go back to New York. Give me bus fare, let me hitch, I don't care. I want to do some traveling on my own."

Dad blew his cork immediately. "You little creep, we have done all this planning—and all for you and your sister, by the way—and you want to screw things up. Not on your life." Mom said, "You're going to stick it out with us or we will all go home, and that's that. You're just getting a little too big for your britches."

"Things cooled down a little bit after all my adolescent posturing, my James Dean/Marlon Brando takes were over, and then we struck a deal. 'Okay,' said Dad. 'Your mother and I have talked it over, and you can take the bus to San Francisco by yourself and have a few days alone. Here's some money for a cheap hotel, here's some eating money. Pack your bag and we'll meet you at our rooms at the Mark Hopkins next Thursday. For cripe's sake, be careful. Your mother's going to be worried as hell for six days.' He was probably going to worry, too, but he wasn't about to tell me that.''

"It was incredible. I stayed at the YMCA, walked my legs off, higher and higher each day until finally I found myself at Twin Peaks, my own private perch, looking at this fabulous city twinkling before me in the late evening light. Bicycling through Golden Gate Park, through the Presidio, below the bridge to a bizarre animal cemetery. I was *alone*, I was traveling *alone*! I was thrilled."

At the Mark Hopkins on the appointed day, there was both jubilation and coolness, a sense of hurt from Mom and Dad—happy to see their oldest child safely there, to touch him, but beginning to know that they would never touch him in quite the same way again, because he was nearly ready to let go.

Here was an experiment in independence, in letting go, the son of his parents, the parents of their eldest child. It succeeded, but not without the parents' awareness that this rehearsal was not very far from the real event, when they would become peripheral to his everyday reality. For the boy, it was a discovery, too, that he could navigate without the advice and care of his parents. It was also an adventure, a lark. He could go home again, in just six days, to Mom and Dad and Sis at the Mark Hopkins, the realities of rent and food and laundry and all those other "things" of independent adult consideration not yet part of his daily world.

These sorties into the world to test skills are essential for our children. The assurance that they can go without fear of retribution, that they can return without having to file a report, gives them the confidence that is required to do the testing.

Sometimes the signals and the communications are mixed. "I wish he'd be more independent," parents say in one breath, while in another is heard, "Why did you do it that way? It's all wrong. Here, let me show you." We actually set our kids up for just that kind of reaction, knowing darn well that they will not perform a task in the way we would, thus giving us an opportunity to show our "supremacy," although there often is no clear-cut right or wrong involved.

"Gregory, will you do me a big favor this weekend? I have to go to a meeting, and I have to get the rest of the fence stained before the rains start on Monday. Stain and brushes are in the garage, there's a tarp to cover the grass. Thanks a million."

Greg does the staining. He does some on Saturday before his baseball game, a little more in the early evening, finishes up on Sunday morning. Monday, when he sees his father at dinner, it goes like this:

"Thanks a *lot*, Greg! Now I'm going to have to do the whole damned thing over. Don't you read the cans, for crying out loud? You know you're supposed to overlap the staining and not stop in the middle of a run. Now it's all splotchy. It looks ridiculous. Can't I get any adult cooperation around here? Blah . . . blah . . . blah . . ." Greg's father is on a streak.

"What the hell do you expect? I never stained before. I was happy to do it and . . ." Overriden by his father's endless litany of almost direct insults, Greg finally gets up from the table and exits the house, slamming the door behind him.

"What the hell's with him?" his father asks rhetorically of the rest of the family, who are doing their best to digest dinner and avoid comment so as not to get directly involved in the brawl.

Fourteen-year-old Trudy, four years her brother's junior, is later heard to say to her mother that Dad sure is a dope sometimes. Mom puts her fingers to her lips, calling for silence, but it is clear that Mom agrees.

* * *

The young man on the hill, alone, sniffing the air and the sense of independence in the moment, and Greg, set up, dumped on, brought to task in front of the whole family at what should be a time for quiet pleasure or family reconnecting, are bound to have different views of their own outer edges if the qualities of their experiences are at all consistent over time. Len, no matter how reluctant his parents, was being empowered to be independent, to experience that independence for a definite period of time, and to learn from it. Greg, on the other hand, was being told that he just wasn't very good or clever, hardly an empowering message, nor one to make the heart glow at the sight of the parent who carries it.

During this period, there is less direct problem solving to be done and more call for learning to recognize those situations that engender a great deal of emotion on both sides and becoming aware of the kinds of behavior that can result. If we can prepare for our kids' leavetaking in the same way that we hope they will for their careers, or we for our retirement, then perhaps we can turn those potential conflicts into times when the expression of our real and underlying feelings can enrich our understanding of ourselves and the family as a very special unit.

A lot of what goes on at this time is not about our kids' abilities, but about ours. Are we mature enough to let the leash loose? Do we think that together we have helped to create an environment, an ethic, in which our kids can come to be equals over time, the all-important individual decision-making passing from parent to child? Are we challenged by our kids' grace, intelligence, size, independence, skills? Are our own marital relationships strong enough so that the absence of a child, companion, friend, and ally will not leave us depressed and impoverished in some vital ways? Are our own needs for control of others so strong that we would limit the freedom of our kids to satisfy it?

Len's parents are certainly not enormously enthusiastic about his solo practice flights. They know they are going to miss him when he is no longer right there, but they feel confident enough of their parenting to take the very big step of letting him go off on his own. Greg's dad, however, is acting quite immaturely, blaming his son in a situation that does not involve the security of the Western world but one that does give Dad an opportunity to embarrass his son, who does not have a record of "screwing up," at the dinner table! That boggles the mind, if you think about it in a clinical way, yet many of us have behaved in the same manner in similar situations.

What we may feel when our kids are ready to go: Lonely, abandoned, afraid, insufficient.

Our children tell us that they are going to be away on Thanksgiving Day to see the Football Game. They will miss dinner. "Oh, that's all right," they say, "you guys go ahead. We'll have dessert with you. Oh, yeah; and save us some stuffing." And they are gone. It is the first time. There is just husband, wife, and the "baby," the twelve-year-old who is too young to be out in "that frigid stadium for three hours." Thanksgiving, humbug!

There is an awareness at that moment of how much our children mean in our daily lives and rituals, and how much their absence affects us. We feel lonely, and that feeling which we may not have experienced for a long time threatens us; and as we know, when something or someone threatens our lives or upsets our equilibrium, we are candidates for reaction. Sometimes those reactions are the stuff of fights.

After the thankless Thanksgiving caper, Dad starts getting on the older kids' cases. "I want you around here this weekend, John. Your mother was very hurt by your not being here for Thanksgiving dinner. That was thoughtless. I've already talked to your sister." In fact, Mom didn't say a word. In this instance, Dad is projecting his own feelings. If John is attuned to his father's way of communicating, perhaps he knows that the message really is that Dad's nose is out of joint. This "wise" John then takes some steps to make amends, to give Dad his strokes, to let Dad know how much *he* is loved. But just as parents' lives are busy, so too are kids', so it is just as likely that John is going to struggle with his father over independence, unaware that the surface text of Dad being a "pain in the butt" is only the surface, and that the subtext of "Gosh, how I'm already missing my kids," is the one that is driving behavior.

What might the father do instead of fighting, or presenting issues in a manner that may precipitate conflict? He might be aware of his true feelings (which is not at all unlikely a proposition), and express them to his eldest son and daughter. "Whew, it really winded me, Sally, you and your brother not being around for Thanksgiving dinner. I wasn't ready for that. It was weird without you guys, really weird. It wasn't as much fun, you know? You guys are both off to college over the next two years, and I know that we'll be close and that both of you will probably be home for one or two of the big holidays— the more the merrier, by me—but I wasn't ready. Your mother didn't say much, but when she gets that quiet, I know something's cooking besides pumpkin pie. Anyhow, how about a little more notice in the future, huh? We love you guys, and we would like to see as much of you as we can before you're off."

"No, you can't take the car, I may need it." Here is one father's withholding in response to the feeling of loneliness and abandonment. Dad does not need the car, but he *may* need it. He may also get bitten by a rabid night owl, but he does not carry vaccine with him at all times. "Aw, come off it, Dad; you're going to watch that play on cable with Mom and be in bed by ten-thirty. Why can't I have the car?" Bud has said this nicely, not contentiously, which only aggravates the situation, since Dad is already in a hastily built logic-tight compartment. Under those circumstances, his only appropriate defense is a dumb one: attack. "Listen, Bud, you're getting a little too big for your britches. When I say no, it's no. When you're out of this house and on your own, then you can make all the decisions about things. You want a car? Buy one. Now get out of my face." Bud knits brow, stalks off wondering if his father has had a small episode in his skull since breakfast. While we, sitting comfortably outside of Bud's family's life, can see what's going on and wonder, how is Bud supposed to fit the puzzle together, connecting Thanksgiving dinner with a Toyota Corolla?

Once more what is required is insight into the subtext and a willingness to take the risk of showing the raw emotion that sometimes drives us.

It is not at all unusual for a child who is getting ready to leave home within the year, let's say, to begin to find fault, to break rules, to belittle, to stretch the binding tissue of the family's understanding. Why? Because the child is trying to build a case for separation that otherwise does not come easily. If everything went well, would it not be difficult to leave home?

Greg is nineteen and fully employed. He has had two years of college and has taken an Associate's degree in accounting. He also has a girlfriend who lives in Albany, and would like to move out of his family's house in Saratoga and into her apartment. Lately Greg seems to be correcting everything his father says or does. "The grass is too damned long. Here, let me adjust that. It should be one and a half inches. This blade is lousy. You kidding me? You sharpened this? I'll bring it to Tim's. He'll do it right." There are few subjects in which Greg is inexpert after nineteen years on earth, it seems.

Greg's father is a pretty even-tempered man, but recently he has gone after Greg with his tongue, calling him a know-it-all, threatening to turn the screws down on Greg's life if Greg is going to "continue to live in my house." "You've had your last favor from me, mister," Dad is heard to say one evening after having taken more abuse from his son. This seems to make Greg even more belligerent. He forms a kind of pact with his mother, indicating that the father has become impossible, that he can't see staying home much longer. "I just can't get along with the guy, Mom, I'm sorry."

Mom gets on Dad's case, heaping blame on him for Greg's wanting to leave home. "You have to have more tact with the boy. He's quite a nice boy, and he's doing well. I would hate to see him leaving home over your pigheadedness." Dad blows up at Mom. "Whose pigheadedness? That son of yours . . ." You can fill in the rest.

Greg is unsure of his ability to leave home with some promise of success. He is trying to prise himself from the family and into the world of adulthood with all of the independent decisions that are required to make it work. If he essentially begs the decision by making everyone's life miserable, including his own, he can walk out righteously as the wounded one driven from his home, victim of his father's intransigence. This makes a nondecision of what should be a decision, taking some of the worry out of it, because "there was nothing else I could do." If there was no other recourse, then how can the "decision" be faulted?

What might have been different? It would have been good if the parents were aware of the ambivalence that is inherent in this kind of provocative behavior. "I want to go, I'm afraid to go, so I'll force myself to go by being an obnoxious pain in the rump." In this instance, the setup is for the boy to leave on his own but "without any real choice." In another situation, the behavior might be so disruptive as to result in the parents asking the child to leave.

Once we are aware of the ambivalence in such behavior, instead of fighting we can try to see what it is that creates that ambivalence. Do our children feel confident enough in the face of a complex world, and is there something we might do to help them gain the necessary confidence in their decision? Do we indicate so much dependence on them that it becomes difficult for them to leave in a straightforward and positive way? We can talk with our kids about the decision in rational terms. Leaving home is a task—a highly emotional one, but a task nonetheless, one in which our experience might be useful to our kids.

Even if we resolve these questions for ourselves, we must accept the possibility that there will be conflict, *despite* our best intentions. No matter what moves we make toward peace, it seems that some kids require a great deal of distancing, the preparation of a menu of conflict and fault that will justify leaving home in a peculiar way, thus making it easier for the parents who might think, "Thank goodness, that pain in the ass has finally left. He was making us all miserable." The kid has done her or his work well, setting up a rationale for separation on both sides.

It is also very important for our children to know that their decisions in early adulthood are not unalterable. Although we would not want to encourage their making decisions foolishly, knowing that they can always go home again, it is important for them to know that going home is a possibility, that there is still that place where one can return after sorties out into the world to test possibilities and wings.

Kevin had had a great deal at home. No room or board, a suite on the third floor, all kinds of emotional support, and the deep and genuine admiration of his younger sister and both parents. He was finally ready to fly at twenty-one.

He knew his mother's dependency pretty well, but was shocked to discover the depth of his father's. There were not two days that passed without his father calling cross-country to see how his Kevin was doing. There was such an unfamiliar and plaintive sound in his father's voice that he decided to pay a surprise visit, thanks to a promotional plane fare, on the weekend. Maybe that would cheer old Dad. It did, a great deal, but Kevin was struck by his mother's coolness, her being out of the house during most of his visit, either shopping or seeing friends. What was most shocking was that the first night, when he said he was ready to turn in, he was directed by his mother to a very small guest room on the second floor. He stopped by his old rooms on the third floor to find that everything that had been his had been removed, the walls repainted, new carpets put on the floor, and evidence that the rooms were now his sister's domain. The next day, he found three rooms' worth of his past jammed into a corner of the basement.

While Kevin's father made his sense of loss clear through his frequent phone calls, Kevin's mother could not be so direct. She felt too hurt and too vulnerable in her hurt to be gracious, so she transformed what had been his domain for seventeen of his twenty-one years, denying his presence through a redecorating scheme, and banishing the remnants of his presence to the damp basement. Kevin felt cut off, denied, an outsider. He had only been gone two months, but he had been written out of the family history, in a way, much as Khrushchev had been from the official histories of the Soviet Union. Kevin was cut off too quickly.

If Kevin's mother was hurt by the "sudden" departure of her son, Kevin was hurt by his apparent nonperson-hood. He might have said, "To hell with you guys. Nice visit. Cripes. I'm just out of here a couple of months, and you dump all my stuff in the cellar! It'll be a while before I see you guys again. Say good-bye to Laura for me, I'm going to head back.'' Or Kevin's response might have been to be as brusque and businesslike as his mother was toward him. This could result in growing distancing, alienation as a by-product of a highly charged symbolic change. Again we see the need for the combatants in this silent fight to be open and frank about how they feel.

''Mom, Dad, I was shocked last night when I went upstairs and saw the third floor. It was as if I had never been there. It felt very strange, really strange. And then this morning when I went down to the basement and saw all my stuff jammed into the corner . . . I can't tell you how that made me feel.''

''What nonsense. Your sister is home. Why shouldn't she have your rooms? You're making a mountain out of nothing,'' says Mom.

''Tell you the truth, Kevin, I never gave it a thought,'' says Dad. ''Now that you mention it, it must seem strange that after only two months there's almost no evidence that you ever lived here. We didn't think, I guess.''

''Don't exaggerate. You still have a place to sleep if you care to visit,'' says Mom. ''We'll be eating at eight o'clock this evening.'' With that, Mom begins to leave the room.

Kevin's mother is hurting but not communicating it directly. Kevin's father is now aware of what things look like from Kevin's vantage point, but he has not been a good communicator in the past himself. Somebody has to keep the pressure up to get all of the cards on the table, or attitudes will harden and alienation may follow. Kevin rises to the challenge and asks his mother to wait. He then tells her how he feels, how scared he was for the first time really going on his own, yet how he felt that he was still very much connected to family and to the house in which he had done much of his growing up. He gives testament of his love and concern for his family, embraces both his parents, and says that he hopes that they don't think that he has abandoned them. This may be useful in healing what is clearly a situation in which his mother feels no longer a significant part of his life, a realization so exaggerated as to require her purging his presence.

If unresolved, such situations often result in widening differences among family members and the lines of communication being cut. When that happens, the affected party is not only the departed and denied, but the whole family. Thinking again of the family as a system, as a balloon that when squeezed at point A becomes distended at point B, it becomes clear that the absence of one person who is written out of the family story in this way will put extra pressures on the rest of the family. Other kids may be asked to take up the slack, something that no one should have to do, of course, but which someone might see as a way of winning approval. Alas, given the kind of active depression that is suggested by the mother's coolness and the premature redecorating, it is not terribly likely that a kid can be a winner trying to fill the shoes of the idealized absent one.

We should be aware of the potential for a reaction depression like that described here and should prepare for it. The best preparation, of course, is not in reaction to, but in anticipation of, the inevitable. We should be able to subscribe to some verities about the roles of children and parents.

1. We have kids not as ornaments but as people. While we hope that they will follow certain pathways that are often no more than wish lists, fantasies in our heads, we must remember the operative word, *people*, which should prepare us for the most striking characteristic of that genus: individuality.
2. Individuals are not made to fulfill others, whether husbands, kids, cousins, or parents, but themselves.
3. If we do our job well, if there is enough love, if there are not overriding social problems, if, if, if, we will have a shot at helping a bit of tissue grow up to be interested, interesting, productive, useful, and good. When that tissue becomes adult (somewhere around eighteen years and upward), it will want to go away to make its own nest. That may be permanent or part of a testing process. Eventually, however, it will be permanent. It is a natural for kids to do this. It is not to be taken as a personal rejection.

If, despite this knowledge, we continue to feel desperate, lonely, alienated, picky, and sad, we ought to talk about it with our friends, our spouses, and maybe a therapist. All major transitional stages carry emotional weight, the "loss" of a child through moving out among them, so a strong (although distressing) reaction should not be considered out of the ordinary. What is most important, of course, is to come to grips with the reality and to keep the lines open so that the family members are not harmed.

It is also important to examine other family relationships, particularly that key one between husband and wife. If the reaction to the leaving home of a grown child is like that of Kevin's mother, we should be curious about just how much emotional support and rapport there is between this couple. Kevin was probably providing more than his fair share of support—thus Mom's reaction, and thus our impulse to see what goes on inside the primary relationship. If it is lacking, then that ought to be discussed. Maybe Kevin's mother had too much responsibility for the house—note her husband's nonparticipation in the redecorating scheme, or at least his nonthinking in regard to the same—and Kevin provided solace. That solace now gone, there is a reaction.

Once we have determined that the relationship between husband and wife is lacking, we have to do something about it. Make the time to reconnect. After raising children, those old skills are in need of sharpening. This is a time for courtly behavior as well as honesty. Negotiating skills are very useful here. With one less person in the household, there will be more time for other things, not proportional to the percentage of change in family size, alas, but some more time, nonetheless. Manage it to make those reconnections.

A sensitive wife in a Chicago suburb saw what the loss of a daughter to a job in a New York publishing house did to her husband's outlook. The other kids were too young to be taking up the slack, and he had become snappy and churlish, and could turn almost any small disagreement into a night of silence "reading in my study." She wasn't happy to conclude that the daughter had been providing a great deal of intellectual stimula-

tion to her husband, stimulation that had formerly come
from herself. Without making a whole lot of excuses for
herself, she decided that rather than fret about history
she would change the present. Her responsibilities as a
medical-center administrator didn't leave her much leisure time, but she made the time in the evening to read
in areas that were of interest to her husband, and in which
the daughter had been fluent. She was able to pique his
interest after a while, and a real dialogue got started, one
that had stopped at the birth of child number two, she
now realized. She also made some demands on him to
become engaged in *her* interests, something he initially
did with reluctance, but in the end with enthusiasm.

Once again, one partner has had to become the en-
forcer, the motivator. Whether it is a he or a she does
not matter. What does matter is that a very important
relationship has not been left to falter, to limp along toward the inevitable end out of habit.

It cannot be stressed enough that it is often the one
brave and insightful person taking the risk who creates
the opportunity for change and growth where there was
before only the potential for disaster or the dullness of
lives lived in the same spaces, but unconnected, unen-
gaged.

There is an old expression, "Up to me but no higher
than me." It speaks to a parent's wishes not to be ex-
ceeded by a child. It may have come out of the country,
where a parent would not only feel left out by a child's
worldly success, but where the loss of a laborer on the
farm would be sorely felt, as well as resented. Though
the farmhand aspect may be absent, it continues to be an
issue between parents and children.

"I suppose Mr. Smartypants can give you the answer
when he gets home, Esther. He seems to have all the
answers. He'll never get to Yale on my checkbook, I'll
tell you."

"Now just a minute, George, that's our only son you
are taking the hard line with. Just because you're pump-
ing gas and tending store doesn't mean that Henry has
to."

"You've made the damndest dreamer out of that kid, Esther . . ."

This kind of unsubtle "no higher than me" attitude can develop over time and escalate in hurtful ways. The parents can become enemies in the process, the child alienated or turned upon by both parents if the pain of the defending parent's conflict is too much for that parent to bear. At best a child is stifled, submerged in the limited views of the parents; at worst, completely estranged. The kid's ambivalent leaving is made even more difficult.

"You will really like the business, Ralph. It's steady as a rock, and you get to meet a lot of people. Granted, it is not genetic research, and it is not Berkeley, but I think you'll like insurance."

The fact that Ralph really ought to be going to the best possible university for his interest and aptitude does not make a dent on his dad. The fact that Ralph would rather sell pencils from a cup downtown than enter the family business also eludes Dad. But one day real soon Ralph is going to tell his father that his applications to the two prime universities in his area of interest have been approved. The reaction, not in so many words, will be that Ralph has betrayed him. The coolness will become purest dry ice, and the connections between father and son will be badly damaged.

Of course, the opposite circumstances, where a parent or parents want their children to fulfill their wishes by going to MIT, becoming a lawyer, entering the Foreign Service, can have the same results as those described above when the kids fly away to become their own selves.

How do you deal with these great life changes, these departures, these disappointments? It would be lovely to say that there are solutions that can be applied at the time of departure, like Band-Aids to a skinned knee, but there don't seem to be. Just as in cooking, a lot is in the preparation.

When we find ourselves in a position like this—no higher than me, or why aren't you going into medicine like I always dreamed—before we say a word, we should look back at a little checklist:

1. Is this something like what went on in my family? Is this the way Mom or Dad reacted to my wanting to _____ (fill in the blank)?
2. I am me, and my daughter/son is not me.
3. Do I feel bad about what I am doing, and can't feel good about my own kids' opportunities? How do I begin to deal with my bad feelings about my work/ life? Maybe a little therapy will help.

OR

4. Am I so wrapped up in images that I can't accept the fact that my kids don't want to be kings of the mountain? If so, why?
5. Maybe there is a special question that only I can pose.

It is hard, so hard, letting go. Most other animals, it seems, take this inevitability in stride. Maybe it is because they are smarter, or simpler. Whatever the case, from this vantage point it looks much less complicated than we make it. It is hard for us. It is complicated. Feelings are oddly entangled, the wishes for the independence of our kids contradicting our wish for their dependency. It is no different for the kids. Yet when we can let go without bitterness at what we are losing—those good companions whom we have helped become independent—it makes us free, too. They are gone now, and we remain, alone together. That is a whole other story.

11

The Empty Nest and Return to the Nest

In any marriage, there is an accumulation of scars, injuries, and hurts undealt with because of the necessity of "getting on with things." Raising a family while both parents are working (as is the case with the majority of American households) does not leave as much time as we would want to work problems through. While kids are at home, it is necessary to cooperate or fight creatively (we trust) around a number of practical, moral, and ethical issues: who gets shoes this week; how do we get everybody at least a little of what they want and as much of what they need as possible; how do we possibly find the money for three kids' college tuitions; what do we do when the one car has a mechanical problem; what about staying over; drinking, and smoking; all the rest. When they are absent, we are left with *us*. It becomes two-for-teatime once more.

Under idealized circumstances, as played by Henry Fonda and Katharine Hepburn, there is an understanding called wisdom, an acceptance that goes by the same name, a few familiar and comfortable fights, and a great deal of affection and respect. One would hope, of course, that when our children have first left us, we will not quite be ready to hear the cry of the loon for the very last time. If, like most of the universe, we lead less than idealized lives with suitable background music, then we may have to work just a little harder at our present and future lives together.

In addition to the fight menu accumulated during marriage, there is still baggage from the further past, unresolved conflicts from the second date (how long and skewed our memories can be), new demands on our emotional and financial resources from aging parents, the apportioning of resources to our kids out there in the world, and often most acute loneliness in the face of the kids who are gone. As a result of the lack of common focus—the kids—and in the face of loneliness and an awareness that we may not really know each other, this can be a most trying time for a marriage. We should know it, but we don't. When our friends of twenty or more years decide that they will divorce after twenty-four years of marriage, we are shocked. "Gee, they seemed so good together," and other narrow perceptions are brought forth. But when we examine the relationship, it is often that they were not connecting well during the child-rearing years, took no steps to improve the connections there already were or to build new ones, and when left alone without the binding children, did not know what to do. The accumulated baggage may have broken their backs. Sometimes divorcing is the only reasonable resolution; often it is not.

Here are some of the fights in this period, together with some suggestions for resolving them.

"What the hell are you doing that for, Donald? I don't like my eggs/shirts/socks/the dishes/almost anything that way. Haven't you been paying any attention the last twenty-two years?"

Fact of the matter is that this is probably the way he/she has been doing things all along, but now we have the time to notice. We are bored, we are sad that the house is empty, we don't know what else to do but to nag, to kvetch, to noodle things until the very life is out of them. Chances are that neither partner has been paying enough attention the last twenty-two years. It's about time that changed.

This is a new game. In some ways, this is a new person we are dealing with. We are new, as well. Twenty-two years of building a home, rearing kids, doing what needs to be done, and now it is pulled out from under us. In the absence of those commonalities, we are no longer the same people at all.

Address the text. "Oh, how do you like the dishes stacked? Show me and I'll do it that way."

If the response is, "Oh, never mind, I'd rather do it myself," do not accept it, but gently force a resolution of the particular. If the particular cannot be resolved, then the subtext has got to be found, which may well be the text of our second fight.

"I don't know, Gladys, but I think you have consistently let me down. You've undercut me with the kids, you haven't supported my efforts to do community projects, you've . . ." Bill's point of view may be correct, and it may not be. He could be blaming Gladys for his own feelings of inadequacy as a father, husband, citizen; he could be absolutely right and more than justified; or he could be somewhere in between, with the partners having played off of each other over the years in ways that allowed each of them to escape from responsibilities they did not want to undertake by getting the other to collude in subverting action in an indirect way.

While the first impulse may be to become defensive in the face of such accusations, the appropriate response should be more thoughtful. "I didn't realize that I was doing that or that you felt this way. I wish you had told me before. Tell me some more about this. God knows, you're important to me and I would never want to do anything to hinder you. Let's go to that little café you like for some coffee after work tonight. Maybe we can begin, okay?"

Follow-through is essential, of course. One of the most common results of these beginnings is to put a Band-Aid on and call the member in full health. That was a reasonable solution to the sporadic fights of kids over transient issues, but this is for the rest of our lives, so we have to really keep at it. As the old Henny Youngman joke goes, "How do you get to Carnegie Hall?" "Practice, practice." Reconnecting, getting attuned to the emotional lives of each other, understanding each other's needs, desires, disappointments, and the history of our interactions is essential. In order to do this, we need to make time to talk (the excuse of kids is no longer valid) and to talk honestly. It is just as essential to listen honestly. Too often we listen with one ear and do not really get involved, thinking that this, too, shall pass. Remember that the effort is not to please somebody else, although we get to think that way in a confrontational society, but it is just as much for ourselves! Even if only symbolic, Reagan and Gorbachev making their agreement to pare down nuclear arsenals without suspicion that the other was going to benefit more (as if there was such a thing as being more dead from a nuclear error) accomplished something beneficial for the entire world population by suggesting that two confrontational societies could agree on a major confrontational issue.

"We never go anywhere," or "You never take me anyplace." It is very easy to respond, "What the hell do you mean; last month we went to the damned flower show. You know how I hate flower shows," or "I went to the basketball game with you, and you know how much I hate basketball." It is easy to respond in an aggressive or semiaggressive way if we think we are being attacked. That response, however, is a prideful one. If our false pride can be set aside for a moment, we could say, "Gee, let's see. Well, we did go to the _____ three weeks ago, but I guess that's been about it for a while. What would you like to do?"

This could become an "I don't know, what do you want to do?" round, but it is more likely to focus the initiator on particulars to replace the general. If there are no particulars to present at the moment, such as, "I would like us to go to the movies every Wednesday, two concerts next month," or whatever the case may be, it may then force the complainant to face the real underlying issues, which may be boredom or a loss of a sense of being needed. In some instances, it may only be a gambit to get talk going even if the premise is not a sound one, this arising out of the assumption that it is better to be alive and fighting than alive and alone.

Joan's complaint that Bertrand never wants to do anything is not far from the mark. Since the last kid has gone, his interests have reverted to the tax code and a basketball team that is a contender for the NBA championship. He's pleasant, he's polite, but it is a little like living with a slightly animated rock right now. Joan tries to get his attention, but the results are not great. When she gets home from her office at around six-thirty, Bertrand is already immersed in the new tax code supplements and is very businesslike and pleasant with her, but not engaging or engaged. Joan thinks about things to do but waits for Bertrand to propose them. When he does not, she gets annoyed and withdraws from him. He barely notices, which makes her fume and withdraw more. This goes on for several months. It might go on for the rest of their lives, if they are not careful.

Bertrand feels very lonely since his eldest child left home. He loves Joan, but she does not make up for the great loss that was his irreplaceable Gerard. Gerard made him feel young, involved. They played touch football for the last time just four months ago, and now . . . Joan never suggests anything to do. He thinks he would be happy to go out and do things, to see friends, but he thinks that is Joan's role to play out. "I was not born to be a social director" has always been his first and last thought on the subject. But when he gets lost in the complexities of the tax code, or when he gets the old blood flowing watching his team running that ball back from their end of the court, well, he feels really turned on, feels younger and engaged. When he switches off the tube, he seems to change, go blank, just like all twenty inches of the Trinitron.

Here are two people who have some of the same goals, but they are not talking about them. It appears that Bertrand is less well off because of the relative insularity of his job, which does not require a great deal of human contact, and because of the dependence he had had on his son for companionship. Sure, some of it was an immature *Rabbit Run* need, but at least he was doing something, was more animated. If he was an old Chevy, it isn't clear if he would start on a cold day without a jump-start.

Joan has a lot on the ball, but she just gets annoyed and withdraws when her needs are not being met. She does her job, she comes home to an uncommunicative husband, gets her reading done, and wonders how this is all going to end. "Well, at least the kids will be home for the holiday," she reminds herself. Stalemate. Impasse. Nothing. *Nada. Nyet. Rien.* What this couple needs in the face of a nonfight is a controlled blowout.

Since Joan and Bertrand do not dislike each other and aren't fighters, they have to find a way to get the unspoken problem on the table. "Joan, I am lonely as hell since Gerard left. It's no reflection on you, but that doesn't make it any easier. I bore myself and I probably bore you, but I don't seem to be in control. I seem so damned unnecessary. What the hell can I do?" That's one possibility, but considering Bertrand's relative passivity and his ability to concentrate on the code for endless hours, it does not seem that this scenario is very likely. Besides, it is dependent on the notion that this man can come forward and reveal inner feelings. Sadly, it is not in the tradition of Bertrand's family to behave in such a straightforward manner if you are a male. His dad would sooner immolate himself than seem needy, and his brothers are just like that, as well. The kind and compassionate—and passionate—Bertrand is another thing, but right now the compassion and passion are submerged in low and negative feelings. Thank goodness his kindness is still intact. He is like a becalmed sailboat with a jerry-built sail, which, were it to fill with a freshening breeze, would be of relatively little use, since he doesn't know where the shore is.

Joan is engaged on a lot of levels, but they are all outside of the house. Her job is satisfying, she enjoys reading contemporary fiction and has the time to do it (although she would be happy to trade some of that for engagement with her husband), she sees women friends at lunch during the business week, but this man she has lived with and had kids with, to whom she has been married for so long, is becoming a stranger, and she does not like it a damned bit. She does not like confrontations, but on the other hand she does not quite fit the profile of "wifey" or wallflower. Knowing that there are risks involved in challenging Bertrand, yet thinking that in his depressed state he might actually welcome some engagement in battle, she steels herself and after dinner one night just puts it to him.

"I'm sick and tired of this sulky, private, uncommunicative husband, Bertrand, and if you don't snap out of it, I am going to really raise hell around here. This is ridiculous! I hit the ball to your side of the net and it sits there, unreturned. That's enough to drive a person crazy. Look, I miss Gerard as well. He was a great friend and I miss his noise, his wit, and even some of his ridiculous demands on us, but I am not folding up my tent and creeping away from our marriage. That is not something that I will do, nor will I tolerate it in you, dammit. I'm insulted! You have been acting as if you have been sentenced to be here in this house with me. Well, I think that stinks. I've given you your privacy and your time to heal after this big event we have both been through. *Both*, remember, *both*. Now it's time to get on with things or not. I vote yes. You can vote yes by rediscovering me as more than Gerard's mother. I want to have some attention paid to me. I want to be courted, I want to be talked to, I want to be challenged, I want to be made love to. We can have one hell of a good time as husband and wife, or we can grow apart and dissolve in our separateness. I don't want that to happen to me—or to you. What do you say?''

Fortunately, Joan has been right in her perceptions of her husband. He does not go to the attic to get his bags, but rather feels a little sheepish, and stumbles toward a kind of apology for his "funkiness."

"Yeah, I've been mired in my little tax-law rut and sad over Gerard's going away, but it's got nothing to do with how I feel about you, Joan. To tell you the truth, I haven't thought about you much since he left, only about me and my loss. That's selfish and myopic. Too much close tax-law reading, perhaps. Look, let's put that behind us. By the way, old girl, you are not exactly the vivacious girl at our first Grateful Dead concert, you know. You've been dragging some, too.''

The battle has been engaged. What more could we ask for? Touching those earlier days of courtship, using photograph albums as guides through courtship, marriage, and children—these are reasonable means of starting to connect in important ways that have been unused over the family growing years. These are not simply exercises in nostalgia, but ways of bringing back feelings that have been lost or dulled by mortgage payments, car repairs, orthodontia, new shoes, and washing dishes. It is important that the exercise not stop there but proceed to engagement in the present.

One woman discovered in the process of a similar purposely initiated fight that her husband, David, did not feel as loved as he needed to be. The moving away of their only son, who had been a constant admirer of his father, cut the legs out from under David, and he went into a funk like Bertrand's. His wife decided that she would have a special day for him, not a birthday or anything connected to a holiday, but a special "David Day." All of their friends were contacted and told that X-Day was going to be special for David to be appreciated for being David. Almost everyone responded with little gifts, telephone calls, flowers. A small dinner party was held by one couple to celebrate David. It was a great success, for David was quite touched by the affection of his friends, and if they could care for him so much to go to this trouble, he must be a pretty good guy, he reasoned.

It is extremely important, of course, to build on the moment. This is the time to agree on one or two events that can reoccur. Bertrand and Joan must follow through, they must become reengaged. They should meet for a movie at a less than usual time and in a less than usual place. Seeing each other in different settings, having to experience things and times out of the ordinary, is healthy and helps to give us new perspectives on each other. (Dick tells of how exciting it is to see his wife in a different setting, simply walking in the street, for the moment oblivious to him, to see her differently, and to admire her composure, strength, beauty, to see her in a way others may see her.) Each such step gives an opportunity to both renew and to gain new perspectives on each other and on a relationship. Building positive momentum is essential to gaining control of our lives together when there has been the drift that often occurs while raising a family.

We must see our being back in each other's company— our *raison d'être* as parents, providers, disciplinarians, teachers, now apparently passed—like the Chinese character that has two meanings, disaster or opportunity, not as a problem to be solved as a result of unfamiliarity, but as an opportunity to be exploited for mutual benefit and delight.

There is more than the rediscovery of the other, however. With children gone, there is the opportunity for discovery of the self, and it is there that another conflict arises.

Lorne has built a nice business over the years that employs three hundred people in four small manufacturing facilities and is looking forward to reaping some of the fruits, now that the kids are gone. He wants to devote six months to traveling and six months to his business affairs. His executive staff can oversee things very nicely, so he has no concern during his absence, but he doesn't want to feel retired, either; thus the six months of work. Dale, his wife, is not enthusiastic over this plan at all. Since their marriage was a traditional one for most of its duration, Dale stayed home and raised the children, this despite the fact that she had been trained in nursing and would have enjoyed at least part-time work outside of the home. Four years ago, she took a business degree at the local university in a part-time program and now wants to apply her two areas of expertise to the delivery of medical services in the private sector. When Lorne told her of his plans, Dale was crushed.

"This is absurd! I feel like a fool. Did I go to school for nothing? I want to use my degree. I spent all that time at home raising our kids. You could devote your time to business and get some satisfaction from that while the kids were well cared for. I'm glad to have had the experience, but I am not just a little homemaker, Lorne, and I want very much to put my skills to work. No. I can't see this plan at all, not at all."

"You can't see it, you can't see it? I have worked hard, Dale. Our kids have been to good colleges because of my hard work. I'm proud of them. They are a credit to us. I made this house possible with my hard work, I made the private schools possible with my hard work, and, dammit, I am going to enjoy the fruits of my labor. You can do some volunteer work in the hospital. That ought to satisfy your urges to serve."

"My urges? You fathead! If I hadn't . . ."

"Listen, my dear, if I had been like your father . . ."
"Over my dead body . . ."

This brief but acrimonious exchange is about life plans
in conflict. It is also about people not understanding each
other's needs and not knowing how to compromise. Dale
has certainly made a major contribution to her children's
educational and life success and to her husband's business success. It is fair to say that Lorne is more than
somewhat out of sync with contemporary life, and sees
Dale as a "helpmate to a hardworking and dutiful husband" who goes out into the world to do "man's work."
There's something in his wanting to travel and enjoy the
fruits of his labor, as he said, but while he was having
the joys of building a business, watching his kids grow
up under the thoughtful and intelligent guidance of a more
than full-time mother/wife (he was never home much in
the first ten years of building his business), Dale was
sacrificing her career desires.

What do they do now?

On one level, it seems reasonable to say Lorne is a
fathead and that he should just plain have to put his
agenda aside until Dale has had her innings as a professional in the medical field. In fact, short term, at least,
he should come to see the lack of wisdom in asking his
wife to sacrifice her career to his wishes to be free half
the year. Since he is a businessman, it would be reasonable to do a balance sheet on who gave what and when,
as well as who sacrificed career wishes so that others
might prosper. The point of this would not be to make
points for martyr-of-the-month club, but to quantify the
parenting roles.

"Would you tell your secretary to stay in her job for
the rest of her life, despite the fact that she might have
superb skills as a general manager, so you can go tarpon
fishing for the rest of your life?" Dale asks.

"Of course I wouldn't, Dale. That's ridiculous. You're
my wife!"

"There it is. It's clear. Because I am your wife, you
can ask me to make sacrifices that are unreasonable, that
you would not dare ask of an ordinary employee—"

Before Dale gets too far with this developing argument, which might turn into a tirade on day four of this continuing saga, Lorne interrupts.

"You're right. You're right, and that's all there is to it. Let's talk about this some more in a few days, please, if you don't mind. I need to think this through. Maybe we can get some plan together that will work for both of us."

As it turned out, Dale and Lorne were able to tailor a plan that satisfied the underlying needs of both of them. Dale was aware that Lorne got a lot of his identity from his business success, his wife's success as a mother, his kids' success as students and in their careers. So she turned her *potential* success into something that would further help Lorne feel good about himself. Essentially, it went like this: "If I succeed—and I will—you will look good *and* enlightened. I will be happier if I get to do what I want to do and will be a better companion, friend, wife." On Lorne's side, there was acquiescence and a proposal that if it was possible in the near future for Dale to take at least five weeks of vacation to travel, it would be ideal. A few years later, Dale formed a consulting firm with seven other people in her profession and was able to create a more flexible schedule that accommodated Lorne's desire for travel and her own professional needs. Just as Dale had at an earlier time, Lorne had to wait to realize his dream.

What could have been an ugly confrontation turned into a creative one. A man who was not used to treating his wife as quite an equal was forced to bend as a result of her maintaining a reasoned position. He had to abandon his position and rethink it in light of a household of two. He discovered the two were equals, and accepted that as fact. This result could not occur if there were not a substantial bond of love and respect.

We can make our lives good or we can make them bad when the kids are gone. We can reacquaint ourselves with who we are besides Mommy and Daddy, or we can feel empty as our roles of twenty-odd years are lost and our identities with them. We can blame our being at sea on each other, or we can come together to form a new team with a new agenda. We can experiment with our new relative freedom or we can go lock step together toward whatever it is we think we see at the end of the road.

* * *

It is rare that a parent is not perceived as having a favorite child. While some parents *do* favor one child over another, the fact is that different children mean different things to us. It is just that way in our adult relationships, as well, of course. We enjoy friend A but not to the exclusion of friend B or C or D. Each of us is different in some subtle way, and we tend to respond differently to different aspects of others, including our kids. We should be prepared to be perceived as playing favorites, nonetheless. What parent has not been accused by a child of having favored another when the accuser is not getting what he or she wants? Parents may accuse each other of favoritism, as well, sometimes because it is real, more often because one parent sees the other as neglecting one of the kids. Yet during the growing of a family, for some reason, this real or perceived favoritism does not come into quite so strong a focus until the parents are alone.

Thomas Johnston has just had a letter from his eldest daughter. Since it was sent to his office, there is an immediate aspect of confidentiality about it. Had Lonna wanted the letter to be considered otherwise, she would have sent it home where Lonna's mother, Beth, would have known of its existence. Lonna would like a loan from her father, and asks that he not "bother Mom" with this fact, because "she'll only worry." Thomas keeps a small checking account for gift surprises and such, so he makes a check on that account and sends it to Lonna with a nice warm note. He loves his daughter a lot, and has been accused of favoring her above the other kids. They do have a special relationship, to be sure, one he is a little embarrassed to recognize, since she reminds him most of himself when he was her age.

Beth has a call from Roberta Johnston-Burbank. Married and living in semi- if temporary poverty, the result of her husband being in graduate school in one of the most expensive cities on the mainland and her being paid university wages, Roberta would be most grateful, she tells Mom, if she could just have the loan of a "couple of hundred bucks" until "God know when." It's extremely cold this February, and the barn of a house she and her husband are living in is eating up oil the way a slot machine eats quarters in Las Vegas. Beth hesitates but sends a check on the common account of Beth and Thomas. She hasn't had an account in her own name since marriage.

Thomas, master of precision, loves balancing the family checkbook each month. It works out fine again in March, but he is more than a bit quizzical about this check to Roberta for three hundred dollars. He brings it up with his wife. She explains, but he goes off on a little rampage about Roberta having a husband of her own, "and if he can't provide, if he can't get help from his family, if he can't get a better-paying fellowship, if he and Roberta don't know how to budget, then they should take another look at their lives. What the hell's a guy his age doing in graduate school, anyhow?" he asks rhetorically.

The donnybrook of donnybrooks ensues. Thomas doesn't like Roberta for marrying this "perennial graduate student." He really doesn't like his son-in-law a lot. "Thirty-two, a wife, two kids, and counting angels on heads of pins at that theology school. And then what? A fifth-tier church with a run-down parsonage and twenty-six thousand dollars per year?" This can go on, and it does, for several days. Your favorite, Daddy's special girl, your little sweetheart—these become epithets in the war of favorites.

The same conflicts can occur among children who have left home and who feel that now or in the past they have been less well treated, less well loved, less well supported in either or both emotional and financial ways. They can rip families apart, they can truly estrange people from each other over long periods of time, perhaps even to the end of their lives. What can be done?

The best thing of course, is to *have* done the best thing in the first instance, to wit, your damnedest to love and protect and to be equitable from day one. Perhaps there are two things of some concreteness that can be said here, however, the first relating to the process of growing with a family and the second addressing the question after the fact.

1. We all have one shot at growing up with our children and with each other as husband and wife. Take a moment each day to examine how we behave toward each

other, a moment away from the emotion of normal daily activity. If we discover that we are, in fact, at the moment, favoring A over B, admit it to ourselves, try to recognize its roots, and do not flagellate ourselves over the human failing inherent in the different way we relate to each child. But also try to spend each day in a way that will make clear to every member of our family that he or she is loved by us.

2. If all best intentions—or no intentions at all—result in there being breaches among family members, make it a rule that you will confront the breach straight on, and with care and affection. If there is a breach between Lonna and Roberta as a result of the latter's perception (unfortunately correct) that Lonna is "Dad's special girl," one or the other of the parents should put aside prejudice and let the children know that they are loved equally well. If there are differences in *identification* with one child over others, be honest but not cruel, and state it truthfully. Finally, however, one must be able to give the love and approval that is usually the bottom line of human relationships. In order to do that, we must recognize our own shortcomings, our own weaknesses, our own unthinking prejudices.

No matter how good our intentions, breaches will occur, some of them irreparable. Even in those instances, however, we must communicate our love and maintain a connectedness with the estranged child, for the relationship is a fundamental one that, no matter how much we might otherwise wish, has great impact on our lives.

Full circle, a round tripper, home again, home again, jiggity jig. As baseball commissioner Bart Giammatti wrote in his former incarnation as professor at and then president of Yale, a whole literature is built on the theme of going home. It is where the heart lies, where the head rests easy, it is that to which Odysseus returned after his wondrous journey as well as what impelled that Ted Williams swing. It is where we feel safe, accepted, at home. Though it may not have been in the script we wrote for our lives, in these changing times we may be called upon again to make it the safe harbor for those whom we have sent out into the world. Whether it is divorce or a non-marital breakup, a blip on the career screen, a retreat from the world, or an economic necessity, many "kids" have been coming home in the last decade. For some couples, the return of a child to the nest may be quite welcome, providing new focus for lives that never quite adjusted to the return of two-for-tea time. For others, it might be the very straw that, while not breaking the camel's back, makes each footfall a little heavier. For the latter among us, we need to set some guidelines.

Liana called her mom on a Sunday morning and told her the news. She and Geoffrey were not going to be able to stick it out together. Their marriage had been great through college, but once he started his career, they started to drift apart. Marriage counseling, a little therapy, time apart, intensive time together at Geoffrey's parents' summer house—none of it worked.

"Oh, I'm so sorry, Liana. No matter how much of it you see, no matter how much you prepare yourself for it, it is a wrenching moment—for me, as well. I'm so sorry, dear. What can your father and I do to help?"

By now the dam had broken on the other end of the line, and between sobs Mom heard "my room" and "so grateful to you, Mom," and what else could Mom say, what else would a mom say but, "Of course, dear, come home."

Yes, kids should be able to come home again. This "again" does not connote again and again and again. Building that place we know archetypically as Home is not simple. We will have helped our offspring build a concept of family and acquire the appropriate tools and enough room in which to use them; but even with all that, they may not be able to build Home the first time out. So we should be prepared to let them come home again. (The parental home will for some always be "Home," these kids never reconstituting something in the world that becomes "Home" for them.)

Coming home should not be conditional; *staying* home should be.

Liana's parents should most of all be welcoming and comforting, not prying or judgmental. If Liana wants to discuss the breakup, fine, but it is not up to the parents to force that issue. It is Liana's life. On the other hand, the parents also have their life, which is being "interrupted" by their returned child, so Liana's plans are important to them, and thus fair game for discussion. Before such discussion takes place, however, the parents should agree on how to proceed, setting parameters for Liana's stay. These can be very loose and informal or quite formal, depending on the parents' needs. No matter what, they should be honest reflections of how the couple feel about this child's return. (Make no promises or pronouncements until there is agreement. Unilateral agreements are the very soil in which conflict grows.)

Do not rush this phase, for the return itself is a charged event, one that could be perceived as resulting in the loss of face by the parents or Liana. There could be enough emotion surrounding the event to dredge up earlier and negative experiences and responses connected with the past, some of which were not useful then, and which will be even less useful now. In all of this, it is important that Liana's parents try to put themselves in their daughter's shoes.

"She was always so damned impetuous. I never thought much of that damned Geoffrey with his ascots and watery eyes. She has such lousy judgment about men. Anyone could see that guy was a loser. She's always been . . ."

Here is Dad dredging up negative experiences and impressions, hardly walking in his daughter's mocassins; in fact, the tack being taken here is not likely to result in a positive and useful discussion of how to handle life with the return of Liana.

A more sympathetic and understanding approach might be:

"Dammit, she really has thrown a wrench in things. We've just gotten used to our being alone together, and now we have to go through *this* again. Well, we all do our share of screwing up, and some of what Liana is results from having us as parents, with all the problems *that* must have presented to her! Well, she's home and she needs our help. Let's see what we can do to help her feel better about herself. She's bound to feel 'failed.' I know what that's like from having been passed over at work, and from not always having been the greatest husband or father. We're going to have to give her a little room to maneuver.''

Once parents have reached some unanimity about their needs and desires vis-à-vis the returned child, there might be a family meeting to discuss whatever needs discussing. This could be a little or a lot, depending on the particulars of the household. Old issues may wind up back on the table: smoking, access to cars, meal schedules, music/sound interference, privacy, telephone, the whole kit and caboodle. Above all, any active and unresolved anger should be discussed, so that the sitting-on-a-powder-keg feeling, which might be mutual or experienced by only one party, can be set aside. It is better to have a free and even confrontational but honest talk than to have the hurtful silences and general sense of mere tolerance or active *un*welcome that can make the return to the nest more a sentence than a shelter in a storm.

In such situations, there may be a great deal of self-consciousness for a time, an overawareness of each other's presence. If a kid is coming home with tail between legs, somewhat whipped by the world, there may be an oversensitivity to criticism or anything that could be interpreted as such. Likewise might parents be overly sensitive to the ''interest'' of their friends and relatives, as in, ''How come Liana's home? Things didn't work out, huh?'' But this will pass. Any impulse to act precipitously during the resettling period is to be avoided. If we act quickly, we are very likely to act wrongly, and in response to emotion rather than to thought.

If we can identify with our kids who need to come home for whatever reason, if we are honest with ourselves and with them about our feelings about our privacy, their dependency, and whatever other issues may be on the table, we can establish new and often better relationships with our kids than we otherwise might. Sure, it would be great if they left home and did nothing but send back messages of victory from the front, if they'd married lovely women and great men, given life to perfect children while we were showered with the reflected light of these young gods and goddesses. But that's another movie.

Part Three:

FAMILIES IN CRISIS

12

When Fights Get Physical

Home is not only where the heart is, but also the center of intense emotional interaction, some of it negative. For the very same reasons stated at the beginning of this book—that there is so much at stake, so much interdependence and mingling of identities, and so much intimacy—experiences within the family can become physically as well as emotionally destructive. Some facts:

The home is the place where we are most likely to experience violence. The most anger and violence that adults experience in their lives is from or toward a blood relative, and that anger is more intense than that experienced in any other relationship. Responsible research tells us that 3.3 million wives and more than a quarter of a million husbands have experienced *severe* beatings from their spouses. The incidence of physical abuse of the elderly and of children in the home is alarming and a national scandal. You don't need to be in the social sciences to know that, but only to read a daily paper. All of this is irrespective of class, religion, color, ethnicity, which does not quite fit the clichéd image of "that kind of behavior" belonging to "those people"—the undereducated, the deprived, the "not quite up to snuff."

Clearly, it is possible, perhaps even statistically likely, on one level or another, in greater or lesser intensity, that we will experience some violence in our own homes. So what do we do?

253

Let us start with this. We *strongly* believe that there is one rule that should underlie our behavior toward our children and each other, one that, if maintained, will provide a positive model for our children's behavior and may have a salutary ripple effect in our own and other lives we touch:

Never use physical punishment. It is never justified.

Obviously, many will take exception to our point of view, but we remain firm in our belief. There are often short-term gains from the use of physical force, whether it is a slap on the arm, a strapping, a rattan, or a cuff on the ear, but the short-term gains are not worth the long-term message, which is: It is all right to use force to gain your point of view. Physical punishment does not teach anything but that one can get one's way by hitting, at least in certain situations. It also suggests that "when I am big enough, I, too, can gain supremacy through the use of force." While we do not wish to overstate our view of the ultimate ramifications of the free use of force, we do think that what is sanctioned at home is carried into the world. Is the world a safe and friendly place? The answer to that question should help to inform your view of the use of physical punishment within the family.

With that said, we do not want to suggest that a contrary view makes the holder of that view a bad person, or that any physical response to conflict will destroy a child, a spouse, a relationship. There are many people who think that the moderate use of simple and not truly physically harmful punishment is necessary and sound. We do not agree, but we do not believe those people to be pariahs. Yet, one of us as a clinician, the other as a social psychologist and teacher of negotiation techniques in the broader world, and both of us as parents and observers of the world around us, are convinced that the use of force comes back to haunt us. Even when people have said, "I am grateful for the whippings I took as a child, I would not have responded otherwise," we have generally found that the anxiety and fear associated with that time has been suppressed, while the message of the legitimacy of violence has been incorporated into that person's life.

Are there alternatives to violence? Of course. Just as there are alternatives to psychological hurt through fighting, there are alternatives to physicality as a response to conflict. There is reason, negotiation, the power of the mind to analyze and discover variant ways of reading the map of a situation and getting from point *a* to point *b*. It is not easy, and there are probably not many among us, including the writers, who have not at one moment or another resorted to the easier, graphic, and certainly attention-getting method of the almost reflexive cuffing or spanking of a child; still, our view remains.

Roger, fifteen, Phil, twelve, and Sallie, ten, were all at the Sunday breakfast table waiting for Dad to serve breakfast. As was the Sunday tradition, Mom had gone out for the newspapers, and by now everybody's timing was such that breakfast hit the table just as Mom got her coat off, and before the kids got too antsy. This was no different from any other Sunday morning in that respect, but in another it certainly was. When Dad put the platter of French toast on the table, Roger, who had been insufferably fifteen for months now, his glands and moods swinging this way and that, said, "Yecch! This crap again!" With a great display of something intended to show macho displeasure with the boring predictability of breakfast at the Hill house, he pushed the table and his chair, got up abruptly, and in so doing, sent juice, coffee, plates, and a mountain of French toast to the floor. In response to everyone's shocked response, Roger covered his own shock at what was an unintended effect with more loud, rude remarks, and thundered off toward the front door.

Here is the moment of truth. Possibilities for mayhem abound. Mom hollers, "Who the hell does he think he is? My favorite sugar bowl, you remember, George, when you brought that back from Greece. That creep!" while Phil and Sallie are goading Dad with "Do something with that idiot, will you? Look at my pants/skirt. Get him and nail him to the wall, Dad, will ya? He's out of control." Dad isn't all that pleased himself. He sees a kid out of control, who knows how many dollars of broken crockery and glass on the floor, the necessity of cleaning it up, the possibility that he will lose face or an edge if he doesn't act decisively, a lap of warm coffee, and thirty-five dollars' worth of dry-cleaning bills!

This situation can go any number of ways, but let's simplify. Mom can run after Roger and give him a good hard slap in the face, or Dad can jump on the case quickly, go after Roger, whose behavior we already know is pretty erratic and who is in a very physical mood, and maybe use some physical force with Roger, who is as embarrassed and shocked as he is scrappy. Remember, Roger is fifteen and well developed. He is strong, and while the moment is one of shock, yes, it also is one in which there is an adrenaline surplus and the fear of looking weak; and that could mean reflexive blows. It is clearly a moment when a situation that is unpleasant and has had negative consequences in the social sense could turn into one that could have negative physical results, as in split lips, slapped faces, and a dangerous escalation—to what end? Or . . .

Mom or Dad could firmly stride after Roger and make it clear that she/he wants to talk about this incident, realizing that the effect was unintended but that there comes a time when people have to sit down and talk about behavior and what is acceptable and what is not. This could be delivered in a serious but nonthreatening voice, and she/he would not further excite what is clearly already a pretty excited young man. This would not be a personal attack that would make him further lose face; the act itself has done a pretty good job of that. If Roger is too excited/embarrassed to talk now, and instead feels the need to storm off in the role of the one wronged, Dad or Mom could wait until Roger returned and then have a head-to-head talk about what the heck is going on. Dad or Mom would also not worry about losing face, because each is sure enough of his own sense of solidity not to have to worry about temporary surfaces. If I have to win the "respect" of some of the family members by nailing a fifteen-year-old boy against the wall, then I have screwed up somewhere, he or she thinks.

Which way would you choose? Assert supremacy in the heat of the moment and risk the physicality that might be involved? What might be the short-term and long-term results of such a strategy? What about the second option?

What is to be lost by staying calm but being firm? What might be the short-term gains or losses of that second strategy which leaves room for the transgressor to save face but may leave the onlookers somewhat unsatisfied?

Clearly, we would suggest the second strategy. It requires more self-control, it requires us to be somewhat less good-old-human reactive, it means taking deep breaths while the adrenaline swirls. It also requires our having a strong sense of who we are and that we can cope with our lives in a rational way most of the time. It means not letting our glands rule our lives.

In the above illustration, which actually occurred as told up to the moment of the spilling of breakfast to the floor, everyone involved, including Roger, was shocked by the results of whatever it was that had made Roger act out so dramatically. It scared everybody. The kids and parents were shocked by Roger's behavior, Roger was himself shocked and made fearful in seeing the destructive results of his anger. Everyone froze for a moment, and then Roger, near to tears, apologized, bent down, and began to clean up the fruits of his angry behavior. Nobody panicked. Dad did not remonstrate, brother and sister did not demand punishment, Mom did not insist on groveling. Instead, everyone became quiet, and one by one each bent down to help, to clean up this aberrant mess.

Everybody felt frightened by this chaos, by this physicality that threatened the family's peace, but unlike many of us, their response to threat was not to attack but to stop and to try to make right again something that had gone wrong. After the tension of the moment dissipated, one of the kids said, "Boy, Rog, that was pretty dumb." Roger laughed a heroically false laugh and said, "Tell me about it. I'm going to be paying for dishes for the rest of the year!" After the mess was cleared up and Roger had had the opportunity to apologize to the family without being pressured to do so in what must have been a very embarrassed state, Mom and Dad went off for a walk together to talk about what the heck that had all been about. Before leaving, Mom held Roger by the shoulder and said that maybe they would talk later. Roger went to his room and was quietly concerned, read a little, and then just sat staring out the window wondering what

the heck had been going on. Phil and Sallie played a
halfheartedly earnest game of Scrabble and at one point
Sallie said, "What the heck was that all about?" The
point is, of course, that rather than seek immediate resolution by responding to unexpected behavior with demands that are not likely to be fulfilled, and that corner
the person and cause him or her to lose face, which may
heat up the conflict and perhaps lead to physical responses that solve nothing, we should try to find out what
is going on. Knowledge is power, fists are for the weak.

Roger and his parents sat down together to try to answer that question. Everyone acknowledged having been
surprised by the outburst, but it became clear that Roger
had hardly intended to upset the table and send everything spilling to the floor; his chair had gotten stuck in
his Rambo imitation and his knees were already in motion, so that the table incident had been a mistake. After
some talking and exploring, it became clear that Roger
was being very fifteen, very "you guys are boring, this
food is lousy, boy, you dress like a clown, Dad." He
was putting distance between "them" and "us," an expected part of the separation process. Roger allowed that
he was particularly obnoxious that morning and that he
was rude to complain about breakfast when he was being
waited on and hadn't really contributed a damned thing
to the morning except criticism. Paying for the broken
dishes got worked out, Roger making a down payment
on the spot.

Without overpsychologizing, Roger's parents again and
again gave opportunities for Roger to express anything in
particular that might be bothering him, but nothing specific came out of that. While Roger was sorry about the
specific episode, it was clear to his parents that no miracle
had been worked, as Roger still got in some fifteen-year-
old digs at his mother's "dumb-looking hairdo—what are
you, scared of looking your age?" and at his father's
"funny clothes" before the day was over. At his parents'
request, however, Roger again apologized to his brother
and sister for the morning's ruckus and, on his own, went
so far as to use his paper route and allowance money to
buy breakfast for them the following Saturday at the little
"greasy spoon" downtown. The younger kids took Ro-

ger's apology well and were relieved that their brother was not going to be "off the wall" in his relations within the family. The incident turned out to be just that, an incident, not the beginning of a pattern of outrageous and physical behavior. Had it been treated differently, the result might have been quite different.

A physical response would first of all implicitly sanction violence being met with violence. It would make a dumb episode, half of which was unintended—remember that Roger really just wanted to put down his "boring" family's Sunday ritual and go off feeling superior—into a major life event. The trust that a kid should be able to feel—that a parent will protect and not harm—would be seriously brought into question. The already frightened Sallie and Phil would have to reassess family relationships if the physicality escalated beyond a minor slap and "Into your room, young man." Parent A could incite Parent B to do violence in the name of justice, the kids could further aggravate the situation by baiting their parents, and the result could be a protracted fight that could escalate to do more than damage trust; it could damage bodies.

Unfortunately, there are numerous examples of the use of force in families. While it is not pleasant to dwell on that dark side of the family and the way conflict is handled within it, it may be useful to look at individual situations so that we might understand their dynamics and apply what we discover to our own families' lives.

Mrs. S. keeps a strap hanging on a peg in the kitchen. If one of her kids raises his or her voice, doesn't obey her orders, or mouths off in any way, the strap is used on the kid's rump. The strap is a legacy from her father, one that he inherited from his father and that had been made for stropping a straight razor. When it strikes a bare rump, it sounds like a rifle crack, but to Mrs. S. it is a connection to the past, where it was a given that children have a tendency to wildness, and they must be stopped in that tendency. What better means than a strap?

Mrs. S's kids "love" her dutifully, for that, too, is as much a given as the need to curb the young and to make them "respect us." Underneath the "love," however, is fear and anxiety. The older kids who have gone beyond the age of strapping are outwardly quite straight in their behavior, never "crossing" Mom in her house, but their private behavior, now that they have mobility because of their ages, is something else. Some of that behavior is hardly unusual, but the kids practice it with a great deal of guilt at their inability to "curb their wildness," while also feeling anger at their mother for making them feel bad about what appears to be the norm—like sneaking a smoke or masturbating. The kids also feel free to settle disputes with fists, when necessary, except for Donald, who has reacted to Mom's use of physical punishment in the opposite direction. He would rather be called a sissy and just walk away than do what he thinks is wrong; he's known the humiliation of the strapping before his brothers and sisters, and he will not do the same to another.

It is through Daniel, Donald's sixteen-year-old brother, being sent to the school counselor and then to the school system's psychologist, that we discover Mrs. S. and her strap, and the theory of the inherent wildness of children. Three girls that Daniel has been dating have made complaints to their friends that Daniel has been more than a little "rough" with them in some petting sessions. Two of the friends spoke to the counselor, and after she talked with Daniel, who saw the "little rough play" as another kind of norm for boy-girl behavior, she recommended that the school psychologist have a look. After a few visits with the psychologist, it became clear that Daniel had his most intimate moments with his mother over her knee as a younger boy, smelling her sweet woman scents while she applied the strap to his behind. Those moments suggested that intimacy and a little "rough play" were inseparable. Moments of intimacy were confused with aggression. The very good intentions of Mom were coming back to haunt her son.

Love and violence can be very easily confused under circumstances like this. We make many connections on an unconscious level, of course, and that seemed to be what was operating for Daniel. The mildly sadistic behavior of Daniel was a problem, to be sure, but not one that could not be dealt with. He needed some reorientation, just as Mom needed to have another look at her premise. She could think that she had not whipped Daniel enough or she could come to see that maybe the sanctioned violence was mixed up in a curious way with his affection for her. After some discussions with the school psychologist and a referral to a local clinic, Daniel's mother, and finally the whole family, had some fruitful group therapy sessions with other parents who had been dependent on force to maintain family discipline. (See Chapter 13: When to Seek Help.)

This is not a mother-bashing story. It could just as reasonably have been Dad and the strap. It *is* a violence-bashing story, however, because the confusion of affection and some aggression in this particular child's mind was the result of family-sanctioned violence. The other kids in the family came to see physical aggression as a reasonable response to conflicts. Note, however, that the pacific Donald had reacted in the opposite way. Nevertheless, this does reinforce our first dictum: *Physical punishment is never justified.*

"Dad, Ronny just hit me."

"Ronny, don't let me see you hitting Darlene, you big dope. If I catch you I'll show you what a hit is like."

Minutes pass.

"Dad, he just did it again! Will you cut it out? Hey, Dad, do something, will you?"

"If I have to get up and come in that room, Ronny, you are going to be a very sorry boy."

After incident number four, Dad is pretty angry, so he gets up and goes into the room where the six-year-old Darlene and the eight-year-old Ronny are supposed to be quietly playing. Ronny defensively rolls himself in a ball to protect himself from Dad's slaps.

"Don't you ever hit your sister, you hear? When I say no, I mean no." With that said, Dad gives some stinging slaps to Ronny's legs and fanny. "You hear me? Huh?" Each time Ronny does not respond, Dad smacks him again.

Finally, Ronny says, "Okay, I promise, I won't hit her again."

Dad returns to his book in the other room.

This story is repeated again and again with different players in millions of households every day. It is called using force to prove that force should not be used. We do not offer it smugly, for to repeat ourselves, who among us has not been in the same situation and reacted or nearly reacted this way? Kids can make you nuts, but there are other ways of dealing with the problem of kids hitting each other.

1. Hitting is learned, so let's figure out where the learning is taking place. If it is being learned at home from us, then we are in a position to change the familial model. We must not use force to settle conflicts if we expect our kids to honor our wishes that they not use force.
2. There are other punishments for hitting. Depriving a kid of some expected pleasure is obvious. You hit, you get no television/movie/dessert/whatever the kid expects as a matter of course. Or try a reward system for changed behavior.
3. We can talk about hitting being rotten and stupid and not too smart a response to whatever it is a response to. We can also not expect much in the way of results with most kids. Pleas for rationality can be tried, but be surprised only if they work.
4. Look at the repeated hitting situations analytically: what kids under what circumstances, widespread or particular, times of day, availability of parents, fair sharing of resources, etc. Take the time (you *must* take the time) to observe and to discover patterns, particulars of fights, rivalries, inherent unfairness in the family structure. Use what you discover to create appropriate changes.

In the above situation, Dad discovers that when his wife is home alone with the kids, Ronny never lays a finger on Darlene. On days like the Saturday depicted above, when his wife is working and he is alone with the children and reading, Ronny goes after his kid sister. Dad also becomes aware that his son asked him a lot of questions at breakfast after Mom left for work, but that he did not answer most of them, rather spending his breakfast time reading the newspaper. Then he did the vacuuming upstairs, made the beds, put on the wash, and the minute he sat down to read a book, in came Ronny looking for attention—and Dad said, "Go play." Assuming that Ronny's sister-hitting was a way of getting Dad into some interaction with himself, even if it was hitting,

Dad decided to restructure the Saturdays when his wife worked so that the kids would get more of his time. It wasn't easy. It meant leaving his bed undone until the end of the day and doing the laundry at night—or maybe involving the kids in doing the laundry with him—and giving up a couple of hours of reading time, but it would be worth the effort. As it turned out, Dad's experiment was fruitful. He found a new balance between chores, reading, and being with his kids. Ronny was weaned of hitting his sister to get attention as a result of getting attention without having to get hit himself!

There are a number of dos and don'ts that are generally useful with minor squabbles, in keeping the heated-up fight from turning into a serious and hurtful one.

- Reinforce positive behavior and discourage negative behavior seems like a pretty obvious thing to say, but when you realize that negative behavior is sometimes rewarded, as in, "I'll give it to the little lout so he'll shut up," it bears repeating. If a kid feels neglected, we reinforce bad behavior by paying a lot more attention to it than we normally do to the child when behavior is neutral or positive.
- Don't use your mouth or your hands before your mind.
- Don't jump into the middle of arguments that are heading toward fisticuffs unless you are going to be able to smooth the rippled water. Do be calm and evenhanded so that no one in a conflict feels wronged or that you favor the other.
- Whenever possible, physically separate children who are heading toward combat. Be firm, do not match violence with violence. Provide a cooling-off period and then talk it out.
- If you are part of the problem, remove yourself from the danger zone.
- Do not demand justice summarily done, as in, "Aren't you going to do something about your daughter? What kind of a mother are you anyway?" or the loaded "Do you know what *your* son just did?" Similarly, do not bring up problems of discipline with a spouse the minute that person appears on the scene after shopping, working, whatever. The same rule applies at mealtimes.

- If a fight occurs more than once, look hard at it and figure out the variables and commonalities. You may find a way of preventing another occurrence.
- Be consistent in all of this. Be fair.

Norman is forty-seven and lost his job six months ago. He has had a very hard time being "let go" for the first time in his adult life and is having just as hard a time getting interviews. Much to his shame, he has lost his temper a lot during this period of time and has even hit his wife in small disagreements. One day he got so over-wrought by the mildest of provocations that he knocked the coffee table over and stomped out of the living room. Sitting in the dining room alone, the blood pulsing through his head so that he can hear it like an internal drum, he feels lost, not knowing what to do in what he sees as a downward spiral over which he has no control.

Unfortunately, male identity is often so tightly wrapped up in work, with a place in a larger structure, that when that wrapping is undone, severe feelings of worthlessness and shame can follow. (Historically, motherhood and the ability to raise a family and maintain a good and orderly household have been parts of the cornerstone of female identity. While that is in the process of changing, it still holds for the majority of women, although women are less likely to use physical aggression for reasons that parallel the historic role differences between men and women.) Norman is in that horrible position and may need some third-party intervention lest his bad feelings, now turned outward in irrational violence that is atypical of him, destroy his family. (See Chapter 13.) Yet there are some steps that might be taken within the family to help Norman begin to cope constructively with the reality of his situation.

Bernice, Norman's wife, might make special efforts to define the important role he has in the life of the family, not in traditional terms of the hunter bringing home the kill (which would not be the case here, anyhow, for he and Bernice have shared the working and financial responsibilities equally, she as a full-time nurse). Given the apparent damage to Norman's sense of self, even this may be considered intrusive and interpreted as a jab at his identity rather than as a sincere and supportive gesture. What may be more helpful, then, would be an opportunity to look back at what these people have meant to each other. It might be very good to reminisce about the early days of building a family, trying to build careers, having some hard financial times but never really allowing those early pinches to impinge on their relationship or their lack of money define them as any lesser beings than others with more. Reaffirming the positive aspects of personality, of the essence of Norman the man as opposed to Norman the guy who works at Benificent Associates and earns XX thousand dollars a year, is what might help. Counseling from close friends, particularly those who have been through similar situations, can be of enormous help; if such counsel can occur without Norman feeling that he has been trapped in such situations, all the better. That kind of emotional support plus any opportunity to get something positive going, something that will allow his competence to become apparent to him, even if it is a home project that he has wanted to do for years but has not been able to because of the time constraints, can help Norman to begin to build a new sense of his self.

Yet there might not be a darn thing that Bernice can do to help in this situation. If Norman does not respond to attempts in this direction, and if his behavior continues to be erratic and include atypically violent moments, then the necessity for third party intervention may exist. (See Chapter 13.)

Mack is a sweet guy much of the time. He works very hard in the advertising business and enjoys its challenges enormously, but there is a lot of pressure. Mack's response to that pressure is to stop off with his cronies in the business two or three times a week for a few drinks before going home. The problem is that Mack is a different guy after four martinis than he is after his second coffee in the morning. Mack gets abusive, and Janet and the kids avoid being in the same room with him because he might just take a slug at one of them.

While there can be all kinds of superficial advice about understanding husband/father and looking into the past for reasons supporting this behavior, there are two serious problems here that demand hard steps toward resolution: Mack has a drinking problem and something underlying it that results in his potentially doing physical harm to his wife and kids. We humans can be extraordinarily tolerant and partially amnesiac when we do not want to face problems that are really so threatening that they hurt us too much. Alas, those problems do not fly away. Instead, they often grow quietly in size and seriousness by our not dealing with them until they are ready to swallow us. Janet and the children have to be able to admit that 30-40 percent of the time Mack is not a good person to be around, that, in fact, he can be a dangerous person to be within reach of. Janet has to insist on total and immediate reform (the results of such ultimatums are not often very good), or, more realistically, help Mack to see the problem and to seek outside help.

To do otherwise is to be less than responsible. There are no trade-offs here, no negotiating stances to be struck, no promises or bribes to be offered or accepted. No matter how essentially decent and loving a man he may be, it is whistle-blowing time. Get help or get out is the message. We should continue to be loving and supportive, of course, while attempts at resolution are being made, but we cannot risk our children or ourselves to an abusive mate.

Human beings are nothing if not adaptable creatures. It is extraordinary the extent to which we can fool ourselves, make ourselves forget. In one sense that skill is positive, what keeps us level and sane. If all of the dangers of the world were to press in on us, we would be overwhelmed. In another sense, it is a weakness, because it can keep us trapped in dangerous situations like the one above. He'll change, she says, thirteen years after the first beating, the evidence of which is always blamed on accidents, she now having the reputation as the most accident-prone woman in the state. She'll stop drinking and abusing the kids, he says, eight years after the birth of their first child who now goes to school with black-and-blue marks on her arms. That kind of self-deception is not only absurd, it is morally irresponsible. Never is it more plainly both than when a child is being abused.

* * *

It has been going on for a long time, but Diana is unable or unwilling to acknowledge it in a conscious way. She thought fleetingly that something might have been amiss when her seven-year-old daughter was able to get anything she wanted from Frank. Frank was not a very warm and giving person, actually, but any little request from Anna was immediately attended to, while the other kids went ignored by their father. In Anna's face, there was a slyness at those moments, but she actually was more often withdrawn and pensive, when not seeming anxious—so anxious that her sleep was intermittent. Diana would enter Anna's room sometimes in the middle of the night and there would lie Anna, stiff as a board, eyes open, face taut. Her answer to her mother's question was always the same: "I'm just thinking." Diana knew but would not admit that Frank had been sexually using Anna for five years.

In her second-grade class, Ms. Langley has a little boy named Chris, who comes to school two or three times a month with noticeable bruises on his arm and legs. He says he doesn't know what happened, and his parents say he "falls a lot. His skin bruises easily." Ms. Langley doesn't quite buy the explanation, and suspects that there might be some family problems here. But it is so touchy to deal with, and, of course, I could be wrong, she thinks. Ms. Langley decides to stay out of it.

The battering and sexual abuse of children is far more frequent than we as a society wish to acknowledge. It is a hidden and secret crime against humanity that is very painful to think about, but once we think we know it to be true, we have an absolute responsibility to confront the problem head-on and seek help. Diana *must* do something. There are national and regional organizations that will help in such matters (see Appendix B). Ms. Langley *must* deal with her suspicions. In all likelihood, there is a mechanism within her school district or agency in her state that can act on her complaint. No matter what the risk or pain there is for an adult in acknowledging abuse, it is nothing compared to the pain that children who grow up abused will feel for most of their lives.

* * *

The physical side of fighting goes from the common-place sibling slapping to the very dark and ugly and more-common-than-we-want-to-think physical and sexual abuse of children. On one end of the spectrum, there is the simple attempt to modify behavior by rewards or non-physical punishment; on the other, the necessity to reach out for help, to take the risks implicit in acknowledgment, and to blow whistles to protect lives.

13

When to Seek Help

Since the family is a highly charged institution, and since the problems within it are often not "simple" one-person problems as much as family problems, third-party intervention can be very useful. But when do you know that you need help? There are a number of signals that should indicate it is time to go outside of the family for the necessary help.

- When fights are regularly "settled" by physical combat.
- When the boundaries of intimacy are violated. Sexual abuse MUST be dealt with at once and without fear.
- When fights revolve around substance abuse, whether too much fine French wine, hard or soft drugs, or two six-packs after dinner. The repeated belligerence and bruises are all the same. (See Appendix B for helpful organizations.)
- When there is eternal squabbling within the family. Constant family conflict is not funny, and life has no laugh track. This much conflict suggests that the family system is sick, and an outsider can help identify the problems and help guide us in finding solutions.
- When there is an absence of any open conflict but an indication that all is not well in Denmark or the living room. This does not mean that you should go looking for trouble, but the lack of *any* conflict is often the

sign of avoidance of conflict, which, according to our premise, is necessary for growth and change.
- When there is "that troublemaker" always in the center of any disputes in the family. This is often a signal that the system is out whack and one person is silently selected to embody the problems.
- When one member of the family continuously uses psychological abuse against another.
- When no matter how strong the good-faith efforts, the same old fights recur.

What is required in any of these circumstances is the heroism to act, to set things in motion toward the resolution of our problems. To whom do we turn for help? Who is this dispassionate and wise third party we have heard so much about all of our lives?

It may be a clergyman, a psychotherapist, a social worker, a friend, possibly even a relative, although the availability of a wise friend or relative who would not be perceived as favoring one or another party to a conflict is often problematic. Whoever the third party, the role played will be the same.

The ideal helper should bring new perspective to our conflicts. We have been inside of a system, and we are often trapped by it and its recurring patterns, so much so that we don't even know what the dynamic is anymore. The third party will see things anew, will be more able to identify patterns *because* they are new to him or her, and thus will be able to bring new ideas to bear on our tired old ways of doing business within the family.

The ideal helping third party should be able to hear *how* we talk to each other when all we hear anymore are the words. And in helping to point out to us that we may be talking but not listening, we may be receiving but not hearing, the third party may help to reorient us in our communications within the family.

Someone trained in psychology and its therapeutic uses should be able to help us focus on the feelings that underlie behavior. We know that in conflict we tend to get hung up on behavior and positions, leaving the underlying feelings undealt with. The therapeutic setting should also provide a safe place for the exposition of those feelings, which might lead to blows in a different setting.

Too, this third party should help us to stay focused on the problems that underlie our conflicts rather than become mired in the *ad hominem* arguments of personality that do little but whittle away at self- and mutual respect.

Somebody with a successful background in seeing the family as a system can help to identify the glitches where the system falls down, where the scapegoat has been chosen, where the system is dedicated to the continuance of conflict rather than to its resolution. This ideal person will also provide a nonjudgmental environment in which we can yield without feeling the loss of face.

So where lies this solution to our family problems? *Nowhere*, for a third party intervening in any therapeutic sense is only a facilitator, a new pair of eyes and ears on our conflicts. We are the ones who have to solve the problems by the application of our own commitment, intellect, and energy, as informed by the new insights that we hope will come from the therapy itself.

As a side-effect of any therapy, we may become aware of far greater differences of attitude and values within the family than we were ever aware of. Sometimes that begs some major questions, such as ''Are we, husband and wife, essentially antagonistic to each other to such an extent that the marriage's continuance is called into question?'' While we often would prefer not to grapple with questions of that gravity, it is sometimes necessary to do so, lest the basic underlying differences drive the family to more and greater conflict over time.

Once the decision has been made to seek help, we need to know how to find the right kind of help for *us*. We can start by asking our friends, clergy, school counselors, or family doctor, who may know from experience or reputation the names of therapists who are used to dealing with family problems. States and regions also have referral services that might be useful resources in gaining access to the right kind of therapist for ourselves. (See Appendix B.)

There is a pecking order in the therapy world just as there is in any other profession. The psychiatrist is at the top, having achieved an M.D. as well as specialized training as a therapist. Next comes the clinical psychologist, with a doctorate in the field, then psychiatric and certified social workers, and finally, psychiatric nurses.

Fees tend to reflect status. The appropriateness of a given therapist, however, is what really matters, not the number of letters after the name or how large a fee is charged. The fit between therapist and client is obviously a very important aspect of that appropriateness, so we should know something about what we are looking for in the first interview visit.

Therapeutic styles are as varied as human beings, starting at the very passive listener who brings you the old Freudian "talking cure," and arriving at the other extreme of the highly interactive and aggressive participant. There is no truly objective way to determine what is "right" for us, so we must use our good sense and instincts in evaluating the therapist in this initial meeting. It is more than reasonable to ask questions about the way in which the therapist works, how often the therapist works with family-centered problems, as well as whatever else seems germane. This is an important choice requiring commitment of emotion, time, and money. We should approach it that way and not just throw ourselves into the hands of whomever we see first just on the basis of the cathartic effect that often has on us. "Whew, now that's done, now we're on the right track, this person's going to take it all from here" characterizes how some of us come to the process. Unfortunately, that often sets everyone up for failure or disappointment. Once again, it is good to remind ourselves that this person is a facilitator, not a surgeon. We are going to be partners, to a certain extent, working together to discover our patterns of behavior and their roots, and perhaps some ways of doing things differently within the family so that it will be a better place to be. So we need to be deliberate and fair in our assessment—we are not marrying this person. Does the therapist listen well? Is the therapist good at getting people comfortable and talking? Is the therapist too directing or not directing enough? Does the therapist focus on causes to the exclusion of helping to foment change that might create positive momentum? We need to be straightforward with ourselves as well as with the therapist about what our needs and expectations are. We have everything to gain from being careful and deliberate in this essential choice, but if you find there is no one you could successfully work with, then that might define another problem that you could talk about with a therapist.

A friend of ours often remarks, when the world is particularly chaotic, that the view of the earth from an aircraft at sixteen thousand feet on a clear day suggests such a high degree of order that it seems a most lovely and habitable place. It is, of course, the distance, the perspective, that allows us to look down and see the patterns below. That is what we sometimes think of when we think of therapy, a process in which, through the engagement of a good therapist, with us equally engaged, we search out the patterns of our lives, our problems, our conflicts, and look for ways to change the way we are as a family. The result may be well worth the effort, just like the agony of asking for the first date, the commitment made when that first tiny bit of matter started to grow from our love for each other and became a child, the tears shed on the loss of the firstborn to the world on that first day of school.

The therapeutic process is no miracle. As a result of having engaged fruitfully in it, conflict will not disappear. It *should* not go away, for it is the basis of change and progress. But with our own good efforts and care we will learn better how to deal with it in our lives so that what we may have seen as destructive becomes a force for creative and life-affirming change.

APPENDIX A:
First Aid for Fights

There are often times when a "quick fix" or temporary solution to a conflict is what we most want. With that in mind, we offer this collection of common problems together with common responses, adding what we think might be a better solution or way of thinking about the problem. We have only included those developmental periods in which we think the first-aid approach makes good sense.

Do you stop with the first aid? Sometimes, yes, because there isn't any more to the problem than the surface. In other instances, you will obviously want to take further and fuller action at a more suitable time. But in the meantime, you will have taken the pressure off when it is necessary.

BIRTH TO TWO YEARS*

Problem (conflict)	Common Response	Better Response
kid won't eat what or when parents want	parents feel anxious; leads to force feeding, parent(s) insisting	parents try to relax, feed kid more or less when and what

*Note that many of the problems/conflicts here revolve around the issue of *control*: Who's in charge, the parent or the kid?

Problem (conflict)	Common Response	Better Response
	on own schedule; table as battlefield; parent makes kid eat	kid wants; aim for a gradual adjustment of feeding schedule (remember that puppies, kids, and kittens rarely starve to death); kid eats when ready
kid won't sleep	parents see kid as tyrant; get angry at child, get angry at spouse; anger at child may lead the child to feel anxious and insecure, which may lead child to sleep less well, to cling—which makes parent feel trapped	try to think ''Eastern'': this too shall pass; try to keep kid up during the day, find ways to handle being up; accept chronic fatigue as a (short-term) fact of life
kid throws stuff on floor	parents see behavior as prophetic of lifelong piggishness, a behavior that has to be stamped out *now*	remember, this is developmental *good* news; child is learning about objects, space, own initiative, and motor control; enjoy—all that bending is good for your waistline
Mom feels overwhelmed, abandoned, dissatisfied; Dad feels excluded,	spouses experience greater distance in relationship; get angry, nurse grudges, seek	try to respect each other's ''autonomy'' as individuals; consider taking

Problem (conflict)	Common Response	Better Response
unappreciated, pressure to support a family; unfair "redistribution" of family chores	support elsewhere (Mom's friends, Dad's work, etc.), accuse each other of lack of interest, caring, understanding; self-fueled hostility and disappointment; possibility of lasting patterns of distancing	turns with family chores/ responsibilities; look for some special time together (change context for a while), look for new activities to share (teach Dad to cook, learn to love TV meals); *Dad*, know that pressure is normal; look at friends with older children (they make it somehow); tell your wife how you feel; the more you give to her, the more she'll be able to support you; *Mom*, recognize your spouse has an adjustment to make; support him by listening, telling him he is important
interfering parents, in-laws, friends	parents feel inadequate, bossed around; this leads to conflict with the "intruders"	listen to advice, but be firm with relatives; let them know that you're in charge; freely use the phrase "our pediatrician says . . ."

Problem (conflict)	Common Response	Better Response
kid is not what parents wanted or expected—too loud, quiet, wrong sex; etc.	try to change the child ("do this . . ." "why can't you . . .")	*accept* the child; get to know your kid; let him or her teach *you* who and what the child wants, who he/she is
baby is sick— *you'll* have to stay home from work (ongoing conflict over whose work obligations take priority)	lurch from crisis to crisis; play hardball, a game of win-lose in which the question is who will knuckle under first	anticipate crises; have hard talks about objective criteria; try for a longer-term plan; have backups in place, if possible

AGES 2-5 (TODDLER AND PRESCHOOL YEARS)*

Problem	Common Response	Better Response
kid wants to sleep in bed with parents	absolutely *no* (concern about setting precedent) *or* absolutely *yes* (whenever kid asks, since kid's the boss)	make kid's room more attractive; be flexible ("Okay, you've got five minutes, then you go back to your own bed"); put in room with story on tape cassette; be consistent ("Kids sleep in their own beds . . .")

*Note that (in Karen Horney's parlance) much of the Common Response by parents falls either into the category of "moving against" or "moving away" from the child (confrontation vs. conflict avoidance); much of the Better Response consists of finding ways of "moving with" the child.

Problem	Common Response	Better Response
noise (kid talks too loud, too much, inappropriately)	confrontation (''be quiet or else . . .'') tuning out by parents (ignoring the kid, walking away . . .); excluding the child (sending to room)	teach kid about turn-taking in conversation by engaging in dialogue; try modeling (speak respectfully to the child yourself); try introducing the idea of ''quiet time'' (give yourself a chance for privacy, while child plays alone)
kid gets into everything	parents label kid ''destructive''; yell at kid, ''Don't touch.''	remove valuables (decrease temptation); ''child-proof'' some areas; abandon hope of ''house beautiful''
toilet-training slowness	parents worry; yell at kid; scold; make bathroom into a battlefield	try to accept the idea that the child controls her/his own body; praise mature behavior in other areas (talking, running, self-care, etc.); avoid humiliation; respect the child's timetable; protect the child from other people's criticism

Problem	Common Response	Better Response
fights with sibs	going after the louder, bigger sib; calling the foul on the *second* offender; punishing both kids	try not to get angry; clarify feelings ("You are both really angry with each other"); introduce a "time out"; avoid comparisons
trouble leaving home for preschool	extremes: either capitulation (bring kid home) or going "cold turkey"; issue is one of control (if kid's in control, I give in; if I'm in control, the kid does what *I* say)	try involving teachers, who can help a child become part of a group or activity, allowing parent to leave quietly; let Dad take child to school (kids don't protest as much when Dad says bye)
oppositional behavior ("NO, NO, NO")	face-offs; threats and punishments; labeling and humiliation	let the child say no as much as it wants; gradually move toward the desired goal (children often keep saying no, even as they do exactly as required); what is required is a way for kids to avoid face-loss of capitulation
kid fights with friends	blaming by parents; shame	try diverting attention by

Problem	Common Response	Better Response
	(parent feels embarrassed, humiliated by kid's behavior— kid as animal); punishing *your* child	moving to a new activity involving the friends; keep activities structured until peace reigns; praise cooperation and peaceful behavior
kid dawdles (slow to dress, get moving in the morning, etc.)	parents yell, nag	help child to pick out clothes in advance; get up earlier, start sooner; reward quickness ("If you're down by seven-thirty, you can eat your cereal with Mighty Mouse")
kid won't go to bed	spanking, yelling *or* letting the child stay up as long as it wants (conflict avoidance)	look for reasons child may be anxious, not want to go to bed; consider telling kid to stay in his or her room but not having to sleep at a designated time; be firm and patient
parental disagreement about limits	ongoing fights; mixed messages to the child; child may be confused or may learn to	try to resolve most disagreements privately, when possible; look for

Problem	Common Response	Better Response
	manipulate parents and play one off against the other	objective bases to set limits; if necessary, compromise

SCHOOL DAYS (AGES 6-12)

Problem	Common Response	Better Response
fights in school	either blaming your kid, etc; or blaming school, other kid, parents, teachers, etc.	try to understand the *context* in which fight occurs; work *with* teachers to sort out what's happened
kid doesn't do homework	grounding; other forms of punishment (e.g., no TV); criticism	try to make homework more fun—less of a chore and more of a joint task; praise kid for interest and work well done; consider daily involvement in homework, as needed; express interest, no worry or concern
kid doesn't clean room	"Clean your room, or else!"; "Slob" (embarrassment)	make cleaning a joint activity ("I'll help you clean your room and you'll help me clean mine"); let child make decisions about

Problem	Common Response	Better Response
		his/her own room; express pride and enjoyment in pleasant environment; work toward helping child to feel sense of "ownership" of room
fights with sibs	same as before (2-5); *but* now kids are bigger, parents expect more, therefore parents get more involved, escalate conflict (expectations are greater, therefore stakes are greater)	help kids talk to each other, put feelings into words (serve as mediator); keep your own anger under control (kids learn what they see; if Mom and Dad yell and argue, kids will do the same)
kid doesn't help in house (dishes, garbage, dog, cat, gerbils . . .)	parental nagging; getting mad; criticizing; humiliating kid in front of friends—*or* ignoring problem (conflict avoidance), hoping it will go away	create ongoing discussion about interdependence, family chores, need to divide up responsibilities; let kids choose own chores and make a schedule for carrying them out; be patient, clear about expectations and fact that this is long-term issue

Problem	Common Response	Better Response
		(don't give up or give in to temptation to do it yourself); create small tasks that are doable quickly, even fun!
kid doesn't practice (piano, soccer, art, etc.)	parents get angry, nag; feel the child is letting them down personally, as if the child's lack of accomplishment is an affront to parents	remember that child is *not* an extension of you; work to create a reasonable schedule that child feels he or she can manage; help child keep to schedule on a daily basis; if still not working, it may be time to reevaluate (maybe Johnny doesn't have to replace Yaz in left field or make it to Carnegie Hall)
irresponsible about possessions	nag, blame, induce guilt, threaten to take possessions away; make invidious comparisons ("Look how neat and responsible your sister is . . .")	try gentle reminders; help child develop a reminder checklist, then post this list daily; lower your expectations; set expectations at level of child's

Problem	Common Response	Better Response
		capability and reward success; involve child in purchase of new clothes and toys
fresh/talks back	punish; scold, lose temper	set an example by speaking respectfully to and about others; separate content from style; let child know criticism is okay, as long as each respects the other's opinions
doesn't eat right	dinner table becomes a battleground	never argue about food; serve nourishing food— in the long run, the child will eat what is available
child acts "lazy" (doesn't meet responsibilities; slow to respond)	criticism; accusations by parents and worries about character flaws	children are rarely "lazy"; if your child seems lethargic, lacking in energy, he or she may be preoccupied or depressed; look for source of problem; if necessary, seek professional advice

Problem	Common Response	Better Response
too much TV watching	"you're watching too much TV" accusations; TV bans; *or* giving in (easier to let them watch than argue over it)	evaluate TV in context; remove TV as a general scapegoat; if child is not doing homework, it doesn't make sense to blame TV; you have to get involved to increase child's motivation, interest, and responsibility for homework; keep child busy; develop interests, friends, get involved

TEENAGE YEARS (13-19)*

Problem	Common Response	Better Response
the car (and other possessions)	limit, forbid use of car; if you've got enough money, get a second car (conflict avoidance)	discuss underlying interests/needs: if *transportation*, maybe there are other ways of getting to destination; if *autonomy*, maybe there are other ways of

---

*A couple of common themes here: (vain) parental struggle to retain control versus the child's struggle for individuality, identity, separation from parents. A second general theme: parental need to be flexible versus importance of setting limits on tolerable, safe behavior.

Problem	Common Response	Better Response
		exercising it; establish objective criteria (rules) about priorities, responsibility for maintenance (who pays for gas, repairs, insurance), time limits on use of car
messy room	scolding ("clean up your room, you porker!"); punishing ("Since you didn't clean your room, you can't go to the movies.")	many kids need to assert their autonomy somewhere; if your kid is doing pretty well elsewhere, maybe you should shut the door and try to forget about it; if the messy room is part of an overall pattern of disorganization or depression, consider seeking professional opinion
clothing (wrong, dirty, bizarre)	forbidding certain things to be worn ("at least as long as you're living in *my* house"); yelling and screaming (parents feel that *they* will be judged by their	accept that he or she owns and ultimately controls his or her own body; ask your child to inform you about the subtleties of meaning of

Problem	Common Response	Better Response
	kid's appearance on the street; therefore, this is a particularly emotional, volatile issue)	peculiar garbs and costumes; don't pretend you approve if you don't, but try to understand; be an anthropologist
wrong, bad, bizarre friends	"banning" certain friends, criticizing them; using these "odd" choices of friends to be more generally critical of kid's behavior ("So-and-so is a bad influence on you.")	try to get to know your child's friends as people (talk to them); you don't have to like them, but at least get to know them; really bad news friends (e.g., drug users) probably *should* be banned; be flexible *but* make it clear that there are *limits*
staying out late	punishment (grounding, limiting access to friends on phone, after school, etc.); guilt tripping ("Your mother and I could not sleep a wink until you got home.")	discuss curfews and reasons for them; discuss concerns about child's welfare; having done this, don't give in; be clear about limits but don't get too upset about transgressions; be prepared for confrontations when necessary
verbal tirades at parents	parental yelling back; shouting	criticism of parents (by kid) is

Problem	Common Response	Better Response
	matches; grounding and other forms of punishment	developmentally *normal*, so try not to get too angry; think "Eastern"; try to cultivate a sense of humor; try not to escalate; discuss really serious issues if possible, at a time when both you and the kid are relatively calm; use these times to try to understand what the underlying issues may be
drug use	yell at kids about the *law*, preach the stories of dead athletes (fear appeals); *or* denial ("not *my* little Benji")	educate yourself about drugs; be alert to indications your child may be using drugs; have an ongoing dialogue with kids about drugs; if you suspect drug use, get advice from school counselor or other professionals; if you use drugs yourself, know that your child is at increased risk for a drug problem

Problem	Common Response	Better Response
drinking alcohol	yell, scream, grounding *or* denying or ignoring the problem *or* praising drinking (''He loves his beer just like his father'')	be informed and educated, as above; share this information with your child, re: the dangers of alcohol, *social* pressures to drink; be *firm* about requests to serve beer to your child's underage friends; try talking to your child's friends' parents, and develop a ''united front''
a sexually active son or daughter who's ''doing it''	anger, accusations, disgust *or* failure to deal with the issue (denial); *or* overcontrol of child's behavior, suspicion (efforts to keep the prince/princess in the castle)	initiate ongoing discussions about sexuality, contraception, and what you consider to be responsible sexual behavior; be clear with your child about what your own beliefs are, but say that you know that he or she must ultimately make his/her own decisions; young adolescents who are sexually

Problem	Common Response	Better Response
		active (fourteen or fifteen) often have other worries or problems; consider professional advice
isolation from the family ("We never see you. How come you won't go on vacation with us? Why are you never home?")	guilt-tripping ("You won't have us parents to kick around much longer))'; *or* efforts to exclude the isolate from future family activities	know that teenagers at times need autonomy, privacy, and space from the family; give the child "space" without communicating that "anything goes" (when they go out, insist on knowing where they are going, and with whom); be open when they are ready to communicate; don't retaliate by withdrawing yourself

LEAVING HOME

Problem	Common Response	Better Response
child leaves before parents are ready (insists on moving out)	asserting parental authority ("Come home or else"); wait for child to fail and come "crawling back" ashamed; angry accusations: "How can you do this to us?"	realize that an abrupt departure may mean your child is really worried about making it on his/her own and about how dependent he/she feels; try to help: support your children's efforts to take care of themselves emotionally and/or financially; let them know the door is open; they can be on their own and retain ties to home and family
child stays too long (refuses or is unable to leave home, even though parents are ready)	home becomes a battleground; parents and young adult live together in conditions of prolonged mutual antagonism	try to help your child with moves toward autonomy, e.g., getting a job; encourage, and do not judge job, friends, and other choices; do not permit continued financial dependence (do not give cars, money, etc); if the situation

Problem	Common Response	Better Response
		becomes one of protracted conflict, get professional help (family doctor, etc.)
a seventeen-year-old twelfth grader is—by definition—a "monster"	antagonism; parental hopelessness and despair	realize that your son or daughter's obnoxious behavior serves to create temporary distance so that separation is possible; remember that however difficult and stressful the situation is for you, it is even more difficult for your child, who faces an uncertain future
child can't make it on his/her own—comes home making demands	"I told you so . . . I knew that (job, school, etc.) was no good and that you wouldn't make it," *or* "You poor thing—let Mummy or Daddy take care of you"	help child understand what went right and what went wrong in previous venture; renegotiate rules and policies for young adult at home; be explicit about financial arrangements; offer encouragement and be optimistic

Problem	Common Response	Better Response
increased fighting among remaining family members (after departure of the oldest child)	pick on *one* person, blame him/her for deterioration	remember that family is a *system*: departure of one family member makes a difference, needs to be acknowledged and grieved over; the destabilizing effects of the loss need to be understood; more specifically, plan a regular family meeting to exchange feelings about the departure and its effects

APPENDIX B:

National Organizations that Provide Information, Refferals, and Assistance

1. Substance Abuse (Alcoholism, Drug Addiction)

National Clearing House for Alcohol Information	(301) 468-2600
National Institute on Drug Abuse (Hotline)	(800) 662-HELP
National Cocaine Hotline	(800) COC-AINE
National Federation of Parents for Drug-Free Youth	(800) 554-KIDS

II. Family Violence and Abuse

Parents Anonymous Hotline	(800) 421-0353
National Child Abuse Hotline	(800) 422-4453
Crisis Intervention for Adolescents	(800 621-3860
National Coalition Against Domestic Violence	(800) 333-7233

III. Divorce and Separation

Parents Without Partners	(800) 638-8078
Academy of Family Mediators (this organization may be able to supply you with the name of a mediator in your region)	(503) 345-1205
Massachusetts Council on Family Mediation	(800) 537-6665

For more information at a local level, contact one or more of the following:

> the local Family or Probate Court (ask for their Family Clinic)

> a local or regional university with a law school (ask for their professor of family law)

> the local branch of the American Bar Association (ask for the lawyer referral service)

IV. Agencies Making Referrals for Psychotherapy or Family Counseling

Ask the Operator for the telephone number of your state or local psychological association, social work association, or medical association.

As an alternative, consult your:

> family physician or pediatrician
> priest, minister, or rabbi
> school principal, guidance counselor, or school psychologist

Index

ABOUT THE AUTHORS

An expert on negotiation, Dr. Jeffrey Rubin is a professor of psychology at Tufts University. He also serves as executive director of the Program on Negotiation at Harvard Law School. Dr. Carol Rubin is a clinical instructor at Harvard Medical School. They live with their three children, Noah, Sally, and David, in Newton, Massachusetts. All five Rubins enjoy nothing more than a good fight.